Elements of Banking 1 & 2

Elements of Banking 1 & 2

Desmond Fitzgerald BA(Hons), AIB

Financial Training

First published in Great Britain 1983 by Financial Training Publications Limited,
Avenue House, 131 Holland Park Avenue, London W11 4UT

ISBN: 0 906322 33 2

Typeset by Kerrypress Ltd, Luton
Printed in Great Britain by Livesey Limited, Shrewsbury

Contents

Table of Cases

Table of Statutes

Preface

Elements of Banking 1 and 2 is designed mainly for banking students in the second and third year of their careers. The book is suitable for use either as background reading and a reference book for a two-year course, or as a study guide for an intensive one-year course. It will also be helpful to other students who are working in different fields and who wish to extend their knowledge of the financial system. Because no prior knowledge has been assumed, the book can be read as a guide for non-bankers and the contents should deepen the reader's understanding of banking operations. However, as its title suggests, it has been written mainly to help students to pass either 'Elements of Banking' in the Stage 1 Conversion Course of the Institute of Bankers or 'Elements of Banking 1 and 2' in the BEC examinations. It should provide a good foundation for progression to Stage 2, particularly in the subjects of monetary economics and the law relating to banking.

In the new option module specifications for the BEC Elements of Banking papers, greater emphasis has been placed on monetary economics, the law relating to banking and the interpretation of accounts. This book deals with all the topics required for this new syllabus.

The contents cover the whole range of banking services and special attention has been given to recent developments in British banking. It is hoped that its topicality will prove invaluable to teachers of the subject who are either non-bankers or who left the banking industry some years ago. It is not essential that students or teachers should read straight through the book from beginning to end. Teachers may feel that the last one or two chapters in some parts could be left to the latter part of the course, especially if their students are studying a one-year conversion course.

Acknowledgements

I would like to thank the following people for the assistance they gave me during the preparation of this book. Don Fiddes and Brian Rawle of the Institute of Bankers gave good advice and encouragement during the course of my writing. Thanks are also due to Mr. B. O'Donnell of National Westminster Bank, Public Affairs Department and Mr. M.T. Siddons of Midland Bank, Marketing Department for the information they gave me. I am also grateful to Miss T.A. Burke and Miss S. Ridpath of the Bank of England's Information Division for answering my questions.

I should also like to thank the following organisations for permission to reproduce material which they supplied:

(*a*) Bank of England for a copy of their weekly return.
(*b*) Barclays Bank International for specimen bills of exchange from their 'Services to Exporters' book.
(*c*) Midland Bank for a specimen of a Gold MasterCard and the diagram of operations in the London International Financial Futures Exchange, which first appeared in the Midland Bank Review.
(*d*) National Westminster Bank for a specimen of a crossed cheque, an Access card and a Diners Club card.

While I am grateful to all these people and organisations for the help they gave me, the views expressed in this book and any errors of omission and commission are my responsibility.

Finally, I would like to express my appreciation to my past students at the City of London Polytechnic and Uxbridge Technical College for providing me with the stimulus to start writing this book. Their determination to master this subject gave me the necessary impetus to provide the best possible textbook for their successors.

Part 1: The Banking Environment

1 *The Nature of Money and its History*

In an earlier period of history, men lived in nomadic tribal groups, hunting for food. There were no surplus goods to form the basis of even the most simple market economy. In the course of time, the tribes changed over to subsistence farming, but people were always on the borderline of starvation, seldom having surplus goods to exchange with those of their neighbours. As farming skills improved and specialisation of labour took place, producers found that they had a surplus of one particular commodity. They then sought out others who were short of this particular commodity and who, in turn, had a surplus of another.

For example, one farmer might have too many goats but he might need another horse. A second farmer might have too many horses but might need another goat. If there is a 'double coincidence of wants', barter will take place. This means that the first farmer will exchange a surplus goat for a surplus horse owned by the second farmer.

In practice, it is very unlikely that this exact matching of needs will take place. The position may be as shown in Table 1.1:

Table 1.1

Farmer	Present stock	Future needs
A	30 goats	1 horse
B	15 horses	1 cow
C	20 cows	2 goats

Only if C agrees to give a cow to B, B agrees to give a horse to A and A agrees to give two goats to C will these barter transactions work, provided the exchange takes place simultaneously.

Because of the difficulties encountered in a barter system in agreeing an exact match of needs, intermediate steps, using bullion, were introduced. Returning to Table 1.1, the problem could have been solved by A paying some silver to B for B's horse, B paying some silver to C for C's cow and C paying some silver to A for two of A's goats. By using silver, simultaneous transfers of the animals did not need to take place. The silver acted as a medium of exchange in assisting the farmers to complete the desired transactions.

If the chain of transactions was begun by A, his silver (or most of it) would be returned to him when he sold his two goats to C. The silver could be used again in a further series of trading deals. In this way the silver is acting as a store of value.

Different weights of silver would have been used in these transactions because the actual value of each animal varied. By using different weights of silver to complete these transactions the farmers would be trading with an agreed weight of silver acting as a unit of account.

It might have been inconvenient for A to deliver his two goats to C at the same time as C delivered his cow to B. An agreement could have been reached for the goats to be delivered by A in two months time in return for a fixed weight of silver from C. In this case, the original holding of bullion would be said to be acting as a standard of deferred value.

If anything has the following functions:

(a) medium of exchange;
(b) store of value;
(c) unit of account;
(d) standard of deferred value

it is said to be acting as money. These are the qualities we ask of our money although, in an inflationary era, it is sometimes difficult to regard money as a store of value and a standard of deferred value, except over short periods. The essential quality or attribute that a money material must have is to be 'acceptable in exchange for goods and services' or to be 'acceptable in settlement of debts'. Money does not have to have a value in its own right so long as it is acceptable in these two ways.

Money which is legal tender is that currency which the state has directed must be used in payment of debts. Some forms of money are not legal tender but are acceptable to the public in exchange for goods and services.

In an industrial community, money consists of either cash or bank deposits. Table 1.2 below shows the sub-divisions in these two main forms of money.

Table 1.2

Cash (mainly legal tender)	Coins	face value
		token
	Bank notes	convertible
		inconvertible
Bank deposits (not legal tender)	Sight deposits	non-interest bearing
		interest bearing
	Time deposits	interest bearing

Bank notes are now the largest part of the public's cash but in the United Kingdom both forms of cash are dwarfed by the total of bank deposits.

1 COINS

In a civilised community, during a stable period of peace, the state mint will be responsible for, and must maintain, an adequate supply of small change for the trading community. The Royal Mint alone is now responsible for providing sufficient coins to meet the needs of the British public. Distribution of these coins takes place through the large commercial banks. They pay for the coins by transfers from their accounts at the Bank of England to the account kept there by the British government. Limited quantities of local coins are issued in the Isle of Man and the Channel Islands but these coins can only be used on those islands.

The origin of coinage in a settled community was that the government undertook to issue pieces of metal of a standard degree of fineness and a standard weight. Prior to this time, metal had to be exchanged in bullion form. The bullion was weighed and tested at each transaction to check its quality and fineness. To avoid the necessity for this slow process, the government of the day undertook the minting and issue of a properly regulated currency with a guaranteed fineness. The weight and quality of the pieces of silver were attested by having the king's head stamped upon them.

My father-in-law worked many years ago in the jewellery industry. He told me that jewellers used to be so confident of the weight and the purity of the English sovereign that when they needed a certain quantity of 22 carat gold, they would often melt down the required number of sovereigns rather than buy a quantity of gold wire or gold bars.

In almost every country of the world today, the government has a state monopoly of the issue of coinage. The business community finds this more convenient, provided that there is sufficient small change for trading purposes. If the output of coins was below the demand for them, traders would often provide their own supply.

During the English Civil War, in the middle of the seventeenth century, there were often acute shortages of small change. These shortages were partly overcome by town corporations and merchants issuing their own supply. A similar situation arose at the end of the Napoleonic wars. The shortfall in the supply of coins in Britain at the end of the eighteenth and beginning of the nineteenth century was potentially serious for the business community. Demand for coins was met by local tradesmen issuing their own copper tokens. Small silver tokens were also issued during the early nineteenth century.

Although these tokens were not legal tender they circulated freely because of the insufficient supply of legal tender currency to satisfy the public's requirements. In 1817 the tokens were made illegal and large quantities of copper and silver coins were issued to replace them. Even so, some tokens were circulating freely in country towns as late as 1823. This is a further demonstration of the principle that money need not be legal tender currency to be acceptable in settlement of debts.

The Bank of England also tried to overcome the shortage of silver coins around this time by overstamping dollars issued in Spain and the Spanish colonies of Central and Southern America. A value of four shillings and ninepence was given to these overstamped coins and, seeing the countermarking of the head of George III on the head of the Spanish king, wits would say 'Two kings' heads not worth a crown'. Another comment made was 'The Bank of England, to make their dollars pass, stamped the head of a fool on the head of an ass'. At the same time the shortage of silver coins was so acute in Ireland that private banks in the Irish provinces issued their own notes with denominations of from three to six shillings.

A coin such as the English sovereign, where the value of the metal in the coin was equivalent to the value of the coin as legal tender, is known as a 'face value coin'. Virtually every coin minted in the world today, however, is a token coin, which means that the value of the metal in the coin is well below the value of the coin as a means of settling debts.

Although the present price of silver has made pre-1921 English silver coins worth more than their face value, all these coins were token coins when they were issued. The English silver coinage has been a token coinage since 1816, while the copper coins have been token coins since 1860. The level of metal prices in the 1960s created a difficult problem for the Royal Mint in continuing to issue copper coins. This problem was solved in 1971 with the introduction of new lightweight decimal coins which required much smaller quantities of metal.

The committee of enquiry on decimal currency, which reported to the British government in 1963, suggested, as a point in favour of decimalisation, the replacement of the seven pre-decimal coins by six new decimal types. Alas, the impact of inflation is such that with the new 20p and £1 coins, introduced in 1982 and 1983 respectively, we now have eight coins in general circulation compared with the seven we used in 1970.

The present issue of coins has been described as 'notes printed on metal'. This is because their value as metal is very much less than their face value. It is of no consequence or importance in the case of legal tender currency, used in the final discharge of a debt or in payment of goods and services. The important qualities which a coin must have are these:

(a) difficult to counterfeit;
(b) easily recognised;
(c) universally accepted in payment of debt.

2 BANK NOTES

The origin of the use of bank notes was to some extent an accident. During the reigns of James I and Charles I it was usual for the City of London merchants to store their gold and silver bullion in the Tower of London. In 1640 a large consignment arrived from overseas and was deposited in the Tower so that it could be held in safe keeping with the rest of the bullion belonging to the merchants. Charles I was in desperate need of money and he ordered that this consignment should be seized. Because there was a public outcry, the King climbed down and removed only £40,000 out of a total of £200,000. The public's confidence had been shattered, however, and the merchants began to avoid depositing bullion in the Tower and began to leave it with goldsmiths instead. The goldsmiths had secure safes and a reputation for honesty which gave the merchants confidence that their bullion was in safe keeping. Receipts were issued by the goldsmiths and the practice grew of passing these receipts from hand to hand as a primitive form of bank note. The receipt could be presented to the goldsmith for exchange, and gold coins would be given in settlement. Because the holder was always entitled to receive the face value of his note in the form of coins or bullion, the notes were said to be convertible.

In 1694 the Bank of England was established and, apart from lending money to the British government and carrying on a normal banking business, it issued notes. These became very popular in London as a means of settling debts and during the course of the eighteenth century became the only notes which were generally acceptable. At this time they were convertible into gold coins.

The passing of the Bank Restriction Act in 1797 by the British Parliament, during the French revolutionary wars, allowed the Bank of England to issue bank notes without the obligation to change the notes into gold coins on demand. In other words, the notes were made inconvertible. From 1797 to 1821, the Bank of England note was not legal tender but it was accepted everywhere in England and Wales as a means of settling debts, even though the note was only a document of title or a claim to a debt owed by the Bank of England.

The final removal in 1821 of the ban on converting Bank of England notes into gold and the withdrawal of their £1 and £2 notes led to considerable difficulties. It was several years before the bank was able to build up a sufficient reserve of gold to meet everyday demands upon it, but for a period of just over a century the gold sovereign was in its heyday as a universally accepted medium of exchange.

During the eighteenth century, after the foundation of the Bank of England, many small private banking partnerships issued their own notes in various provincial centres. Because of the considerable shortage of gold and silver coins during the French revolutionary and Napoleonic wars, the numbers, both of the country banks and their bank notes, increased considerably in the early part of the nineteenth century. The over-issue of notes, backed by inadequate resources, led to a number of failures in the first forty years of the 1800s. The recurring crises led to demands for reform and the Bank Charter Act 1844 was passed to give the Bank of England an eventual monopoly of the note issue in England and Wales. The Scottish and Northern Irish banks still have limited powers to issue their own notes and they find it administratively convenient to continue to exercise these powers. Local notes also circulate in the Isle of Man and the Channel Islands.

The Bank of England does not attempt to influence the economy of Great Britain by controlling the supply of bank notes. As was stated by their representatives who gave evidence to the Radcliffe Committee as long ago as 1959, the Bank of England regard their function in issuing notes as the passive one of ensuring that sufficient notes are available for the practical convenience of the public. Their evidence went on to state that this was the principle which had long governed the issue of coins and its application to the note issue was recognition that bank notes were, in effect, the small change of the monetary system. The Royal Mint and the Bank of England regard it as their duty to supply adequate quantities of coins and notes to meet the reasonable needs of the trading community. Both these organisations carry out their tasks very efficiently.

In contrast to this happy state of affairs, Italy suffered from a chronic shortage of change during the 1970s. Sweets, postage stamps and even bus tickets were often used in place of the coins which seemed to have disappeared from circulation. Eventually these substitutes for cash were replaced by the small 'circular cheques' which Italian banks issued to their own customers who were desperate for change. These cheques had a value of no more than a few pence each, being in denominations of between lire 50 and lire 200. They were not legal tender and could not be exchanged outside Italy.

There was a similar acute shortage of currency in France during the closing stages of the First World War. This was overcome by French chambers of commerce and municipalities issuing their own notes. A link was kept with the legal tender currency by printing an undertaking on these special notes that they would be exchanged for Bank of France notes on a future date, usually three or five years after the date of printing.

The occupied Channel Islands suffered from grave shortages of currency during the Second World War. Almost all the silver and bronze coinage was exported by the Germans, while Bank of England notes were hoarded by the local population and almost disappeared from circulation. Although the Germans introduced their own notes and coins as legal tender, the supply proved inadequate. In Jersey, local notes for sixpence, one shilling and two shillings were issued in place of coins and the hoarded Bank of England notes. In Guernsey, 'States' notes with denominations of sixpence, one shilling, one shilling and three pence, two shillings and sixpence and five shillings were issued to relieve the shortage.

These extreme examples show the importance of an adequate supply of small units of currency. From these historical examples one can conclude that it is essential for the note issuing authorities not to fix the value of their notes at too high a figure unless there is a plentiful supply of acceptable small change. An illustration of the distortions caused by using the wrong unit of account arose during the British Eighth Army's advance into Tripolitania at the end of 1942. During the occupation of Cyrenaica, Egyptian currency had circulated and had been freely accepted by the local population. When the Eighth Army moved forward into Tripolitania the Army's advisers decided to go over to a new system of currency. British military authority notes of one shilling, ten shillings and one pound were issued to the troops. At the same time the local population was told that Italian lire coins would continue to be used for small transactions. The choice of one shilling as the lowest value note proved to be a mistake. The local population was reluctant to hold Italian coins when small denomination British notes were available. British troops found, therefore, that all small transactions were priced at one shilling. Whether the purchase was a razor blade, a shoeshine, a haircut, or a handful of dates, the price was quoted as one shilling.

This mistake was not repeated in Italy, where Allied military currency notes of one lira upwards were issued to the Allied Troops. As well as acting as money these notes were an invaluable propaganda weapon. On the back of the notes was printed President Roosevelt's four freedoms 'Freedom of Speech: Freedom of Religion: Freedom from Want: Freedom from Fear'. These notes were following a well-established tradition — nearly all bank notes have a message of some sort. Most countries give prominence on their bank notes to nationally famous people. The Bank of England £5 note carries a portrait of the Duke of Wellington; the £10 note has a portrait of Florence Nightingale; William Shakespeare appears on the £20 note and Sir Christopher Wren is shown on the back of the £50 note.

3 OTHER MEANS OF EXCHANGE

Anything which is acceptable in exchange for goods and services is money. The important condition it should fulfil is that the public must have confidence in its negotiability. Cigarettes acted as currency in post-war Germany because they were accepted in exchange for goods. Those who took the cigarettes knew that they could be freely traded for other goods or services at a recognised rate of exchange (i.e., a cigarettes/goods – prices ratio). The cigarettes had the essential quality which money must have of being taken without question in exchange for goods and services. It is not enough for money just to be legal tender currency, that is money which the government directs can be legally offered in settlement of debts. A legal tender currency can sometimes be rejected by the public as a means of buying goods and services.

In Germany in 1945, the reichsmark, which was the legal tender currency of the day, became unacceptable to the Germans because of the instability of value brought about by defeat and inflation. Cigarettes, soap, and bars of chocolate were used instead to settle debts or pay for goods and services. Not until the 1948 currency reforms, when 10 reichsmarks were exchanged for 1 deutschmark, did the legal tender currency become generally acceptable.

Another illustration of this principle arose in Indonesia at the end of the Second World War. The Netherlands guilder was the legal tender currency but it was unacceptable to the Indonesians who insisted on continuing to use the Japanese occupation money. British and Indian troops serving there received their pay in guilders, the official currency of the

Dutch. They were also given a special allowance of rupiahs (the occupation currency) as spending money. The local population had no confidence that the Dutch would stay permanently and, in consequence, the Indonesians would not accept the Netherlands guilder, which was the legal tender currency. Instead they preferred the rupiahs issued by the departed Japanese.

In contrast, the money issued by the Japanese during their occupations of Burma and Malaysia became unacceptable as soon as the British retook control of these countries. The notes became wastepaper overnight and the words on them represented a promise that could never be kept. No attempt was made either by the British or Japanese governments to redeem them. In the Channel Islands, on the other hand, the occupation notes issued by the Germans were redeemed by the British government at their face value.

4 SUBSTITUTES FOR MONEY

It is commonplace to see coupons in newspapers which state that purchasers will be allowed a discount on the price of a named article, if the coupon is presented to the retailer. Book tokens, record tokens or other gift tokens are given and received as presents. The post office provide stamps towards the purchase of television licences, and electricity showrooms will sell stamps which can be used towards the payment of electricity bills. In many companies luncheon vouchers are issued to employees when no canteen facilities are provided.

All these items might be thought of as a form of money. They provide some of the functions of a medium of exchange, store of value, unit of account and standard of deferred value which we ask of our money. There are severe restrictions in their use, however. They can only be used in a limited number of retail shops for a limited number of commodities. A book of Coop dividend stamps can only be cashed at a Cooperative store, paid into a Cooperative share account or exchanged for goods in a Cooperative shop. Dividend stamps, record tokens, television stamps and similar items are unlike real money which is unconditionally accepted everywhere in exchange for goods and services.

Bank deposits are not legal tender but they are the most efficient means of settling debts because they are not only repayable on demand, in the case of sight deposits, but the public are confident that they can settle any transaction by means of transfers of bank funds. Because of their immediate acceptability, bank deposits are the most important part of the money supply in a financially sophisticated economy. Bank deposits do not limit expenditure to a particular group of goods or in a particular way. In a market economy, the person with a bank deposit has command over goods and services up to the value of his deposit. Possession of unlimited money gives unlimited freedom of choice in a market economy.

In a socialist country, a managed society, or a country at war the priorities of consumer choice are influenced by government decisions. The most extreme examples are rationing of scarce commodities during periods of shortages. A system of rationing is felt to be fairer than goods being sold to the highest bidder and one of the demands made in Poland during 1980 and 1981 by the Solidarity movement was for the introduction of meat rationing.

Under a rationing scheme distribution is based upon the government's assessment of need and coupons or 'points' are allocated to the customer. The coupons can only be used to acquire a limited range of goods. During the oil crisis of 1973, Britain introduced a system of petrol rationing. Every motorist received a basic supply of coupons and those who could prove a special need, such as doctors and health visitors, were given an extra allocation of coupons. The exchange of coupons for petrol had to be accompanied by payment of money and the coupons on their own were no substitute for money.

It would be possible, theoretically, to introduce a system of rationing which would dispense altogether with the use of money and the market economy which goes with it. When the communists took over the government of Kampuchea, at the end of the 1970s, they blew up the Central Bank building and abolished money. Rationing of food and clothing was introduced, jobs and houses were allocated by government or communist party committees and the central government decided on the levels of imports, exports and capital investment. The amount of industrial and agricultural production was decreed by local party officials, in accordance with a central government plan. Internal distribution of output was rigidly enforced by means of ration books. In the sphere of international trade, bilateral barter arrangements were made with other countries.

This experiment in the complete abolition of money proved a ghastly failure and, within two years of the communist seizure of power, nearly a third of the population of Kampuchea had died of starvation.

A better way of allocating resources is through the market mechanism combined with a sophisticated banking system. An advanced financial system can run smoothly with a relatively small amount of cash in the form of notes and coins. The bulk of the money supply in a developed country consists of bank deposits and, in economic functions, there is no difference between a bank note and a bank deposit. Money in the last quarter of the twentieth century is not a physical commodity but a claim against a financial institution. A Bank of England £5 note is signed by the chief cashier and bears the words 'I promise to pay the bearer on demand the sum of five pounds'. This indicates that it is a claim against, or a debt of, the Bank of England. At the same time, it is an asset in the hands of the holder. In effect, the bank note is an interest-free loan made by the holder to the Bank of England.

A current account at a commercial bank is a similar claim which the customer has against the bank. In other words, it is a debt of the bank, repayable on demand, and is an asset of the customer. Just as a bank note can be transferred to someone else so can a bank deposit be transferred in settlement of debt. Their acceptability in exchange for goods and services, combined with their transferability from a debtor to a creditor, are the features which enable us to classify bank deposits as money.

2 *Bank Deposits*

To the average person it may sound strange to talk about a £50 note as 'small change'. However, this is the way the Bank of England, commercial banks and the government look at it. The total sterling deposits with the commercial banks (or High Street banks, as they are sometimes called) is approaching £70,000 million. This is around six times as much as the amount of the Bank of England notes in circulation. Bank deposits are regarded as money by customers of the banks because these customers know that the balances of their accounts can always be used to pay for goods and services, without having to be turned into cash first. Settlements of debts are arranged by a speedy transfer of funds between bank accounts. This is much more efficient and convenient than moving bank notes and coins from one commercial premises to another, which is the only practical alternative at the present time.

1 SIGHT DEPOSITS

This term refers to funds left with a bank, which are repayable on demand. When these are non-interest bearing demand deposits, they are referred to as current accounts. These current accounts are the most common form of bank account. As the credit balances held are repayable without notice, they are widely used for the instant transfer of funds by means of cheque payments. A cheque is simply a printed form, signed by the bank's customer, asking the bank to pay a sum of money to a named person, on that person's demand. A very simple cheque form would look something like Figure 2.1.

Figure 2.1

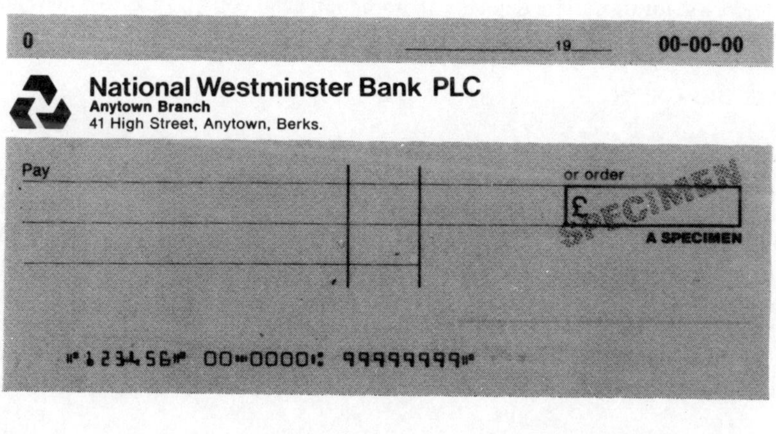

Customers can also make arrangements to withdraw cash at any branch of any bank, provided prior notice is given. At the discretion of branch managers, some customers are issued with a cheque card. This enables a customer to draw up to £50 a day at all offices of major British and Irish banks. The cheque card also guarantees cheques issued in payment of purchases, not exceeding £50 in any one transaction. Visa cards are issued to customers by Barclays and some other banks and perform a similar role to the cheque card as well as acting as a credit card.

Many employers now arrange for salaries and wages to be paid directly into the current accounts of their employees, thus reducing the risk of cash handling. Companies can also arrange for pensions and dividends to be credited to bank accounts. Provided written authorities are given by the customer, whether on a private or business account, the bank will also make regular payments for such items as insurance premiums, local rates, mortgage repayments, or club subscriptions.

Statements showing the entries on the account are sent to the customer at pre-arranged intervals. At one time paid cheque slips were also sent out with bank statements, but this practice is now largely confined to a few large commercial accounts.

The banks publish personal account tariffs of bank charges for private accounts. These show the minimum cleared credit balances required to avoid paying charges. If these balances are not kept, a laid down scale of charges is applied, offset by an allowance for cleared credit balances. In the case of the National Girobank and Cooperative Bank, free personal account banking is on offer, provided the customers' accounts remain in credit.

2 INTEREST BEARING SIGHT DEPOSITS

These deposits are known as 'money at call'. When building societies, pension funds, insurance companies or industrial companies have substantial money for investment but they cannot find a suitable outlet for these funds, they open an interest bearing sight deposit. The money is left with the bank 'at call', meaning that it is repayable on demand, pending a favourable investment opportunity. The minimum deposit is usually £50,000. Interest is paid at rates which vary according to market conditions. Provided notice of withdrawal is given before noon, the deposit can be repaid the same day. While any investor with sufficient funds can approach a branch bank for this type of deposit, the terms are negotiated by a central department at head office. In some instances, large depositors have arrangements to approach the bank's treasurer direct, but this privilege is usually reserved for those with deposits of more than £250,000 who are extremely active in the money market.

3 TIME DEPOSITS

The most common form of time deposit is the deposit account kept at a branch bank. These incur no charges and interest is allowed at rates which are varied from time to time. A press statement is always made when deposit rates change and a notice is displayed in the public space of each branch bank. The interest is paid without deduction of tax but, under current legislation, the bank must advise the Inland Revenue when large amounts of interest are paid.

Because withdrawals from deposit accounts are subject to seven days' notice, cheque books are not issued to depositors. Similarly, standing order payments cannot be transferred from deposit accounts nor can direct debits be accepted. There is no limit on the amounts which can be withdrawn at any time, provided seven days' notice of withdrawal is given. In case of an emergency, cash withdrawals are allowed the same day, subject to loss of seven days' interest. Unlike building society share accounts there is no limit to the amounts which can be credited to a bank deposit account. Statements of the accounts are sent out in the same way as for current accounts.

The rates of interest paid on bank deposit accounts have sometimes reached very high figures. In 1973 the Chancellor of the Exchequer told the banks not to pay more than 9½ per cent per annum interest on deposit account balances below £10,000. Building societies were paying less than 9½ per cent per annum interest on share accounts at the time and it was felt that funds would flow from the building societies into the banks. It was also arranged for the societies to borrow large sums of money from the government, at subsidised rates of interest. The restriction on the banks was lifted in 1975 but the government lending scheme for the building societies remained in force for some time after that.

4 OTHER TIME DEPOSITS

In 1973 the above restriction did not apply to investments of over £10,000 and the rates of interest and periods of notice were matters of negotiation between the customer and the bank.

The present position is that deposits of £2,500 and upwards will attract higher rates of interest, provided that the depositor agrees to a long period of notice. With deposits of £10,000 or more, these can be left for periods of notice agreed between the bank and its customer or can be left for a fixed term. If the period of the deposit is fixed, the interest is fixed also. With a deposit which is subject to notice, the interest varies according to market conditions. Higher rates of interest are usually paid on deposits of more than £25,000.

Negotiable sterling certificates of deposit are issued by banks for minimum amounts of £50,000. The periods for which they are issued are between three months and five years. Interest rates are agreed when they are issued and remain fixed for the whole period. In the case of long-term certificates, interest is paid each year.

Similar arrangements are made for those who wish to deposit American dollars. Negotiable dollar certificates of deposit are issued for minimum amounts of US $25,000. The periods for which these dollar certificates of deposit are issued are between one month and two years.

The banks are now able to open deposit accounts in currencies other than sterling. Interest paid on these currency deposit accounts will be similar to the interest paid in the money market of the country in whose currency the deposit is made.

5 FINANCE HOUSE DEPOSITS

All the banks have finance house subsidiaries which are prepared to pay good interest for deposits. These deposits are either subject to a period of notice, which must be longer than seven days, or agreed for a fixed period of one month or more. The minimum deposit accepted is usually £500 and there is no maximum. Finance houses will often agree to partial repayment of a deposit on demand, in case of emergency, without loss of interest. Because of their longer period of notice, interest paid is always higher than that paid on the seven-day deposit accounts at the banks. Interest is paid gross, if the period of notice required is less than one year.

6 BUILDING SOCIETY SHARES AND NATIONAL SAVINGS BANK ACCOUNTS

Share accounts in building societies and the ordinary accounts in the National Savings Bank have few of the accepted features of money. Some building societies are experimenting with automated teller machines for cash withdrawals. One or two are feeling their way with the issue of cheque books, assisted by the Cooperative Bank. Generally speaking, however, the amount of cash you can withdraw on demand from a building society or the National Savings Bank is rather limited. You can withdraw large sums of money in cash if you give a few days' notice and most building societies will issue members with one of their society cheques up to a figure of £2,500 on the same day. These cheques are drawn on the building society's bank account and must be cleared through the member's own bank account.

A bank customer can instruct his bank to transfer funds to his own account at another bank or to another customer's account at another bank. This is not possible in the case of the building societies or the National Savings Bank, although there are facilities for payment of regular sums such as insurance premiums and mortgage instalments. If a member of Nationwide Building Society wishes to transfer £2,000 from his share account with that society to his share account in the Anglia Building Society, it could not be done on a society-to-society basis. The Nationwide would issue a cheque on one of their clearing bank accounts, the member would take this to the Anglia branch and hand it to them. The Anglia would credit their society's account at another clearing bank. That bank would be reimbursed by the first bank after the cheque has passed through the Bankers Clearing House.

Figure 2.2

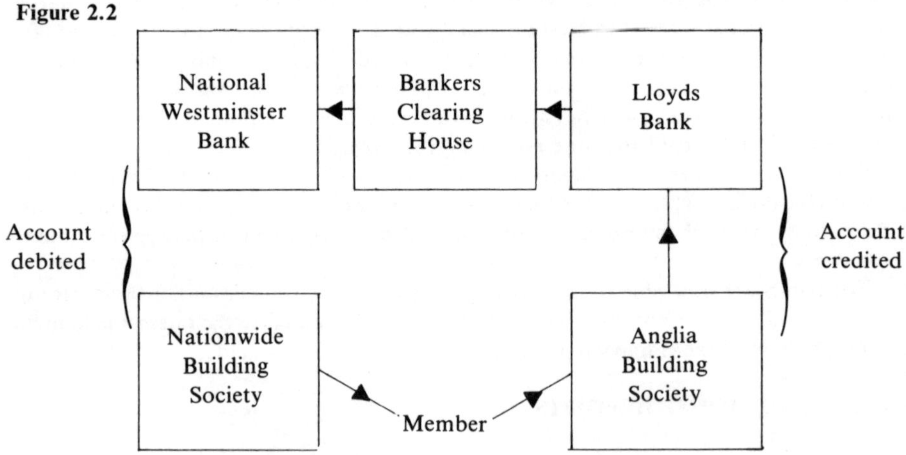

Figure 2.2 illustrates this procedure, and at the end of this series of transactions, th following events will have occurred:

(a) The member's balance with Nationwide has gone down £2,000.
(b) The member's balance with Anglia has increased by £2,000.
(c) Anglia's balance with Lloyds Bank has increased by £2,000.
(d) Nationwide's balance with National Westminster has gone down by £2,000.

(e) In settlement of these transactions, National Westminster has transferred £2,000 from its account with the Bank of England to the account which Lloyds has with the Bank of England.

There is no direct communication between Anglia and Nationwide and it is the movement of bank deposits which enables these transactions to take place in a speedy and efficient way.

Although the purists would argue that funds in the National Savings Bank and the building societies are not money, this is not the way the public look at it. They talk about 'money in the building society' or 'money in the National Savings Bank' because, to the public, these are amounts which can be turned into cash very quickly, without capital loss.

How does the British government regard them, especially since control of the money supply was put forward as one of the main objectives of the present government's economic policy? In the March 1982 budget, the Chancellor of the Exchequer proposed a target figure for PSL2. This is a measure of private sector liquidity which includes the totals of shares and deposits with building societies and balances with the National Savings Bank.

7 CREATION OF DEPOSITS

7.1 Old style

One of the reasons why the banking system is subject to such close scrutiny is that, unlike local authorities, finance houses, building societies, and other deposit takers, banks can be said to create money. A single bank, which is one of a group of competing banks in a country, cannot do this on its own. The bank system, as a whole, however, can be said to create claims against itself in two different ways:

(a) by accepting cash in exchange for deposits or the bank's own notes;
(b) by providing loans in the form of deposits or notes.

To see how this creation of credit works, let us go back to the seizure of the merchant's gold in the Tower of London by Charles I. From then on the merchants used the goldsmiths' vaults as safe deposits, and receipts were given in exchange for the bullion. These receipts passed from hand to hand as the early form of bank note. After the first issue of these notes, the goldsmith–banker's balance sheet would look rather like this:

Liabilities	£	**Assets**	£
Capital	500	Coins	200
Notes	1,500	Bullion	1,800
	2,000		2,000

The goldsmiths–bankers found that, although their notes were convertible, it was not essential to keep 100 per cent cover. They discovered that funds not needed in their own business could be used to make loans. The borrowers were prepared to take the goldsmith–banker's notes, knowing that they could be used as a medium of exchange. The resulting balance sheet was on similar lines to this:

Liabilities	£	**Assets**	£
Capital	500	Coins	300
Notes	2,500	Bullion	1,700
		Loans	1,000
	3,000		3,000

Because lending wisely was profitable, while bullion earned no interest, the early bankers found it possible to accept money from savers and to pay interest on these deposits. The next stage would be on these lines:

Liabilities	£	**Assets**	£
Capital	500	Coins	400
Notes	2,500	Bullion	1,600
Deposits	1,000	Loans	2,000
	4,000		4,000

Extra liabilities in the form of notes and deposits could continue to be created in this way so long as sufficient coins were kept to redeem notes on demand and to repay deposits on demand. Continued expansion could give us a balance sheet like this:

Liabilities	£	**Assets**	£
Capital	500	Coins	800
Notes	4,500	Bullion	1,600
Deposits	3,000	Loans	5,600
	8,000		8,000

With the issue of government securities at the beginning of the eighteenth century, the early bankers felt it was more profitable to invest in these interest-bearing government stocks than to hold non-income earning bullion. This led to the following position:

Liabilities	£	**Assets**	£
Capital	500	Coins	800
Notes	4,500	Investments	1,500
Deposits	3,000	Loans	5,700
	8,000		8,000

Expansion of the banker's business could take place not just by accepting bullion in exchange for notes, but also accepting coins in exchange for notes and by issuing notes in exchange for loans made to borrowers. The business of issuing notes was regarded as so profitable that the Bank of England Act 1709 gave the Bank of England a monopoly of joint stock banking by preventing other joint stock companies from issuing bank notes. The only people allowed to issue bank notes were partnerships, with a maximum of six partners. The early goldsmith–bankers and other small private banks in the London area gradually phased out the issue of their own notes during the eighteenth century and used Bank of England notes instead. The balance sheet of a London private bank at the end of the eighteenth century was a more complicated version of the following, although it was not until 1891 that the private banks first published their accounts:

Liabilities	£	**Assets**	£
Capital	5,000	Coins and Bank of England notes	9,500
Current accounts	60,000	Investments and bills	21,000
Deposit accounts	35,000	Loans	69,500
	100,000		100,000

How were the London bankers able to push up the total of their assets without issuing their own notes? As seen earlier, every loan can create a deposit. The London bankers popularised the holding of these deposits by providing an easy means of transfer in the form of cheques.

In the provinces, the pattern of development was different. By 1810 there were over 700 country banks who could issue their own notes and increase their assets by this method. An acute financial crisis in 1825 led to the failure of 90 private banks. In 1826 legislation was passed allowing the establishment of note-issuing joint stock banks provided that they did not operate within 65 miles of London. In 1833 joint stock banks were allowed to operate in London provided they did not issue their own notes. The banks which make up our present-day clearing banks were formed around this time. They followed the lead of the London private banks by encouraging the use of cheques as a means of transferring bank deposits.

During the nineteenth century the number of joint stock banks rose as the number of private banks fell. At the end of the nineteenth century there was a total of about 100 in each category. The financial crisis of 1890, in which Baring Brothers and some other banks faced acute difficulties because of over-generous lending to South American borrowers, led to public pressure for further amalgamations. Most of the private banks merged with larger organisations and by the time of the First World War the number of clearing banks had been reduced to 16. The last private bank to issue its own notes was taken over by Lloyds Bank in 1921.

Further mergers followed at the end of the First World War reducing the number of London clearing banks to 11. They were known as the 'Big Five' and the 'Little Six'. Other amalgamations took place in the 1950s and 1960s. There are now four London clearing banks, whose shares are owned by members of the public. There are two other London clearing banks, one of which is a wholly-owned subsidiary of the Royal Bank of Scotland and the other is a part of the National Westminster Bank group. Scotland now has only three banks, one of which is a subsidiary of Midland Bank. Banking in Northern Ireland is split between four banks: Ulster Bank and Northern Bank are wholly-owned subsidiaries of National Westminster and Midland respectively, while the other two are companies registered in the Republic of Ireland.

7.2 New style

The banks of England and Wales have lived quite happily for a considerable time without issuing their own notes and have prospered alongside their Scottish friends, who are able to issue their own notes up to a limited amount. Can these banks expand by lending money in the same way that their predecessors were able to expand when they exchanged notes for loans?

Let us assume that we are living in a country which has no commercial bank. There is a central bank which issues its own notes but has no wish to provide banking facilities for the public. A group of businessmen decide to start a commercial bank and invite the public to subscribe for shares. The public pay for these shares by means of notes issued by the central bank. The first balance sheet of this new commercial bank could be drawn up in this way:

Liabilities	£	**Assets**	£
Capital	100,000	Cash	100,000

While this bank has perfect liquidity 100 per cent cash cover for the share capital, it is making no profit to enable shareholders to receive their dividends and the bank staff to receive their salaries. They will, therefore, generate earnings by making loans to creditworthy borrowers. Instead of issuing notes, as in the earlier examples, the amount of the loan accounts will be credited to current accounts in the names of the borrowers. We then arrive at this position:

Liabilities	£	**Assets**	£
Capital	100,000	Cash	100,000
Deposits	90,000	Loans	90,000
	190,000		190,000

The deposits might be drawn out in cash in which case the balance sheet would look like this, after all the deposits were withdrawn:

Liabilities	£	**Assets**	£
Capital	100,000	Cash	10,000
		Loans	90,000
	100,000		100,000

It is much more likely, however, that the deposits will be transferred by means of cheques and any cheques issued will be paid into the bank. This will restore the total of deposits to the previous level.

Even if the borrowers had drawn out cash instead of writing cheques, the cash withdrawn will be surplus to their creditors' everyday requirements. The extra cash will be redeposited in the bank. The position would be restored to that immediately after the loan accounts were granted.

Liabilities	£	**Assets**	£
Capital	100,000	Cash	100,000
Deposits	90,000	Loans	90,000
	190,000		190,000

The bank will soon realise that such a large ratio of cash to deposits is unnecessary and extra loans will be made available, with the proceeds being credited to deposits. This process could go on almost indefinitely until a position such as this is reached:

Liabilities	£	**Assets**	£
Capital	100,000	Cash	100,000
Deposits	750,000	Loans	750,000
	850,000		850,000

There are other ways in which the bank could create its own deposits. Having reached this size, the bank may decide that they should acquire some premises of their own (up to now they have made do in rented accommodation!). They purchase freehold buildings and credit the accounts of the vendors. This would leave the balance sheet showing these figures:

Liabilities	£	**Assets**	£
Capital	100,000	Cash	100,000
Deposits	900,000	Loans	750,000
		Premises	150,000
	1,000,000		1,000,000

Purchase of a trade investment, i.e., a company in a related field such as consumer finance, could be paid for by crediting the accounts of the shareholders of the consumer finance company.

Liabilities	£	**Assets**	£
Capital	100,000	Cash	100,000
Deposits	960,000	Loans	750,000
		Trade investments	60,000
		Premises	150,000
	1,060,000		1,060,000

The bank may wish to diversify its assets still further by purchasing fixed interest government securities through the Stock Exchange. So long as they are sold by institutional or private investors, payment will take place by crediting the sellers' bank accounts. This leads to further creations of deposits on the following lines:

Liabilities	£	**Assets**	£
Capital	100,000	Cash	100,000
Deposits	1,000,000	Government securities	40,000
		Loans	750,000
		Trade investments	60,000
		Premises	150,000
	1,100,000		1,100,000

The principle that deposits can be created by the granting of loans or the purchase of other assets applies whether there is a single commercial bank or a number of competing banks in the financial system. So long as all the banks are lending at the same rate or acquiring other assets at the same rate, all their deposits will go up in the same proportion. The only problem will come if a large number of depositors wish to withdraw cash at the same time. As you can see from the last balance sheet shown, there will be insufficient cash to meet all demands and the bank will be compelled to sell investments and call in loans.

In a very volatile financial community, the prudent banker will need to keep a high ratio of cash to deposits. With a sophisticated financial system, the bank can hold large amounts of assets which can be easily changed into cash if the need arises.

7.3 Qualifications of 'creation of deposits' theory

So far it has been assumed that there can be an increase in bank deposits, on a substantial scale, without any increased demand for cash by the public. All the evidence we have concerning money suppy figures tends to point to the phenomenon that, with increased credit balances, the public will have a proportionate increased demand for cash in the form of notes and coins. This will lead to the withdrawal of cash from the banking system, thus preventing the banks keeping the previous ratio between cash and deposits.

Another instance where leakages may occur is through the sale of securities by the government to the commercial banks. The payment for these securities cannot take place by crediting deposits because the government will keep its account at the central bank. Settlement will take place by means of a transfer of money from the commercial banks to the central bank, thus limiting the commercial banker's ability to create extra deposits. In the United Kingdom, all but the smallest banks keep accounts at the Bank of England. If securities were to be sold to the banks in this way, it would lead to a reduction in the balances which the banks keep on their accounts at the Bank of England.

Until now we have considered the creation of deposits in a financial system consisting only of a central bank, which does not wish to transact private business, and one or more commercial banks. In real life, there are many other financial organisations competing for the public's savings. When the public find they have sufficient cash for their everyday requirements and adequate current account balances at their banks, they will consider a transfer of funds to other financial intermediaries. Building societies can offer competitive rates of interest and savings banks will be able to compete by providing a specialised service. When money is plentiful, the insurance companies will be able to sell more life assurance policies and funds will be transferred from customers' accounts at the banks to pay the premiums. Companies may make new issues of shares on the stock exchange which will be paid for by cheques drawn on bank accounts. The following three leakages qualify the theory of the creation of deposits:

(a) the public's increased demand to hold cash;
(b) sales of government securities to the banks;
(c) movements of funds to other financial institutions.

With these qualifications in mind, however, banks can create deposits so long as they keep enough cash (or cash substitutes) to meet foreseeable demands upon them. They are unlike other financial institutions in being able to do this and it is essential that bankers are prudent people to avoid misuse of this ability. If a cautious banker feels that a ratio between cash and deposits of 20 per cent is essential, then acquisition of £100,000 of new cash will enable loans to be granted to support an expansion of deposits up to another £500,000. Should experience have taught them that an 8 per cent cash ratio is sufficient, the £100,000 of new cash will enable an increase of £1,250,000 in the total of deposits. As well as cash, assets which can be turned into cash without delay and with no capital loss can be regarded as part of this ratio.

Central banks frequently intervene to instruct the commercial banks to keep a laid-down ratio of cash or cash substitutes to deposits. At the present time, the Bank of England insists that all recognised banks and some other deposit takers must keep ½ per cent of their deposits on a non-operational, non-interest bearing account at the Bank of England. This ruling only applies to institutions which have deposits of £10 million or more. Banks in Northern Ireland are only obliged to keep ¼ per cent of their deposits on these non-interest bearing, non-operational accounts at the Bank of England. The concession is a recognition of the special problems faced by Ulster at the present time. Certain major banks, known as 'eligible banks', must maintain 5 per cent of their deposits as money lent out on a secured basis to a limited number of specialised financial institutions in the London money market.

3 *The Bank of England*

At the centre of the British banking system stands the Bank of England. A Royal Charter was given to the Bank of England in 1694 when it was formed with an initial capital of £1,200,000. It was the only joint stock company allowed to operate as a bank at that time. The Bank of England was authorised to issue bank notes up to the amount of the loans made by them to the British government.

Its notes were convertible into gold coins until 1797 when the Restriction Act allowed the Bank of England to suspend gold payments and to issue £1 and £2 bank notes. This continued throughout the Napoleonic Wars and until 1821 when the £1 and £2 notes were withdrawn from circulation and the larger notes were made convertible again.

The Bank Charter Act 1844 was passed following one of the financial crises involving the over-issue of notes by small country bankers. The legislation introduced was designed to give the Bank of England an eventual monopoly of the note issue. No further issues of provincial notes were permitted. When a private bank amalgamated with a joint stock bank, the right of note issue was lost.

The Bank of England's accounts were divided into two for accounting purposes. The figures for notes in circulation were shown under the heading of Issue Department. This total is classified in the UK national accounts as being in the public sector. The figures for the other business conducted by the Bank of England were shown under the heading of Banking Department. Assets and liabilities shown in the Banking Department are included in the figures for 'other banks' in the UK National Accounts.

In 1914 the Bank of England went off the Gold Standard. Bank of England notes were no longer convertible and the British Treasury began issuing its own £1 and 10/– notes. In 1925 the Bank of England adopted the Gold Bullion Standard. This meant that for about £1,500 you could buy 400 ounces of fine gold. The Treasury notes first issued in 1914 began to be withdrawn in 1928 when the Bank of England reintroduced £1 notes and, for the first time, issued its own ten-shilling notes.

1931 was the year in which the Gold Bullion Standard was abandoned as a result of an acute foreign exchange crisis. Following that decision, Bank of England notes became inconvertible and have remained inconvertible ever since.

1 BANK OF ENGLAND ACT 1946

Between 1694 and 1946 the Bank of England was a joint stock company, incorporated by a Royal Charter. The Labour government which took office in 1945 decided to nationalise the Bank of England and the Bank of England Act received the Royal Assent in the following year. By this Act the British government acquired the whole capital of the Bank of England and with it the right to appoint the directors of the bank. In spite of this, the Bank of England still enjoys more freedom in its operations than other nationalised industries. Sir Stafford Cripps, Chancellor of the Exchequer between 1947 and 1949, once described the Bank of England as 'my creature'. He went on to add 'but like many creatures, it sometimes goes its own way'.

The first sub-section of Section 4 of the Bank of England Act 1946 authorised the Treasury to give directions to the Bank of England. To some extent this merely confirmed the existing state of affairs. A much more important change was made by the third sub-section of Section 4 of the 1946 Act. This gave the Bank of England power to give directions to any bank, subject to the prior authorisation of the Treasury. Provided that the direction did not relate to the business of a particular customer, the bank had to comply with the Bank of England's directive.

2 EXCHANGE CONTROL ACT 1947

While the Bank of England Act 1946 was intended to relate mainly to domestic operations, the Exchange Control Act 1947 dealt with foreign transactions. It was intended to help conserve Britain's reserves of foreign currencies by supervising both current and capital transactions. The Bank of England was authorised to give directions to the commercial banks concerning their foreign transactions. The Bank of England was particularly interested in capital movements and permission had to be given by the Bank of England before large sums could be moved abroad. The Exchange Control Act allowed the Bank of England to delegate certain powers to authorised banks. Provided the necessary documents were produced, authorised banks could give the necessary permission to make payments abroad for current transactions, without seeking prior approval from the Bank of England. This Act has not been repealed, although the Exchange Control Regulations, which were authorised under the Exchange Control Act, were abolished in October 1979.

Residents of the United Kingdom can now move funds anywhere in the world without needing permission. In the event of an acute foreign exchange crisis, the regulations covering exchange control could be reintroduced.

3 EXCHANGE EQUALISATION ACCOUNT

Since 1932 the Bank of England, acting as an agent of the Treasury, has operated the Exchange Equalisation Account. This account was set up to iron out the violent fluctuations in exchange rates which followed Britain's abandonment of the Gold Bullion Standard in 1931. The Bank of England is also responsible, through management of the Exchange Equalisation Account, for looking after Britain's reserves of foreign currencies. Their main aim is to iron out fluctuations in exchange rates and the Bank frequently intervenes in the City of London's foreign exchange market. In some transactions, the Bank of England will try to conceal the identity of the operator by asking another bank to act on its behalf. Sometimes the Bank of England operates abroad. In these transactions, it will ask other central banks to act as agents for the Bank of England.

If there is a deficit in Britain's balance of trade, the usual result is a depreciation in the rate for sterling because more people in Britain will be sending payments abroad and less people abroad will be sending payments to Britain. When the government wishes to stabilise the rate of exchange, it will ask the Bank of England to buy up sterling on the foreign exchange markets, using the foreign currency reserves of the Exchange Equalisation Account in payment. The demand for foreign exchange to pay for imports into Britain will equal the supply of foreign exchange, either from exports out of Britain or sales of foreign currencies by the Bank of England, and the sterling rate of exchange will stabilise.

When there is a surplus on Britain's balance of trade, there is normally an appreciation in the rate for sterling. This is because traders abroad have insufficient sterling to pay for British exports and, at the same time, there is a smaller demand for foreign currencies to pay for imports into Britain. In order to prevent too rapid a rise in the sterling exchange rate, the Bank of England will provide the traders abroad with the sterling they need. The proceeds of sales of sterling will be represented by purchases of foreign currencies both in London and abroad. The foreign currencies will be added to the holdings of the Exchange Equalisation Account, causing a rise in Britain's official reserves of foreign currencies.

4 BANK OF ENGLAND WEEKLY STATE

Since the Bank Charter Act 1844, the Bank of England has been obliged to strike a balance each Wednesday and publish the figures as a 'weekly state'. The example below is of a weekly return published by the Bank of England.

BANK OF ENGLAND

Wednesday the 9th day of March 1983

ISSUE DEPARTMENT

	£		£
Notes Issued:		Government Debt	11,015,100
In Circulation	11006,752,155	Other Govt. Securities	3431,645,375
In Banking		Other Securities	7582,339,525
Department	18,247,845		
	11025,000,000		11025,000,000

BANKING DEPARTMENT

	£		£
Capital	14,553,000	Govt. Securities	448,839,678
Public Deposits— including Exchequer, National Loans Fund, National Debt Commissioners and Dividend Accounts	1957,131,704	Advances and Other Accounts	1386,798,427
Special Deposits		Premises, Equipment and Other Securities	2891,657,910
Bankers Deposits	633,472,855	Notes	18,247,845
Reserves and Other Accounts	2140,529,895	Coin	143,594
	4745,687,454		4745,687,454

Dated the 10th day of March 1983

D.H.F. SOMERSET, Chief Cashier

Although the details given on the weekly state are far from full, most of the functions that the Bank of England performs can be identified by an examination of this return. This is not the case with the the Bank of England's operations in the foreign exchange market. The figures for the transactions carried out by the Bank on behalf of the Exchange Equalisation Account will not appear on the weekly state.

5 BANKER TO THE GOVERNMENT

There is a normal banker-customer relationship here with the government keeping its main account with the Bank of England. The working balances which the government leaves with the Bank of England are usually quite small and are shown under the heading 'Public Deposits'. Treasury officials aim to finish each day's business with a nil balance on the Exchequer account, which is the main government account. From time to time, the flow of money does not work out as anticipated. This leaves the government short of funds and the Bank of England must help it out with a short-term overdraft. This is known as a 'ways and means advance'. Any funds made available in this way are shown in the total for 'Advances and other accounts'.

As banker to the government the Bank of England has a duty to keep the Treasury informed of developments in the foreign exchange, stock market and money markets. It also has the responsibility for advising the government on a monetary policy. Even before nationalisation the government had ultimate responsibility for policy. As long ago as 1926 Montagu Norman, Governor of the Bank of England at that time, gave evidence to the Royal Commission on Indian Currency and Finance. He told the Royal Commission 'I look upon the Bank as having the unique right to offer advice and to press such advice even to the point of nagging, but always of course subject to the supreme authority of the government'.

The Bank of England is the government's agent for the sale of long-term securities, usually known as 'gilt-edged'. These are sometimes bought by the public direct as the result of advertisements in the financial press. As a general rule, however, the Bank of England acts through the government broker, who is a member of the London Stock Exchange. Because of the government's need for long-term finance, the Bank of England nearly always has a range of what are known as 'tap' stocks available for sale to the public, through the government broker.

The Bank of England also acts on its own behalf, by instructing the government broker to buy and sell securities, sometimes against market trends. This is to prevent interest rates fluctuating too wildly, caused by the too rapid movements in the prices of government stocks on the stock exchange. Any stocks purchased in this way, as well as any 'tap' stocks, are shown as part of 'other government securities' in the issue department section of the weekly return, or as part of 'government securities' in the banking department section.

Advice is always sought by the government from the Bank of England in operations such as the sale of British Petroleum shares, Cable and Wireless stock, Britoil shares and British Telecom stock. The government usually asks the Bank of England to act as its agent in the disposal of government assets of this nature.

The Bank of England is also responsible for the weekly tender of Treasury bills. Treasury bills are very short-dated government securities and the weekly tender describes the manner in which they are sold. Very short-term finance is frequently needed by the government to cover shortfalls of income compared with expenditure. It is the Bank of England's duty to ensure that these short-term requirements are always covered by the issue of Treasury bills.

Just as it operates in the stock market to influence long-term rates, the Bank of England buys and sells bills in the money market to influence short-term rates. It deals in Treasury bills or Bank bills for its money market transactions, with the object of creating an orderly market without violent changes in interest rates. Treasury bills are found in 'other government securities' (issue department) or 'government securities' (banking department).

When one trader is owed money by another trader he sends a request asking for the money to be paid on a certain date or after a fixed period of time. This is known as 'drawing a bill'. The creditworthiness of the person on whom the bill is drawn may not amount to very much. He will ask a bank to accept the bill, which means that the bank guarantees payment on maturity. The bill becomes known then as a bank bill and, when accepted by an eligible bank, will be bought by the Bank of England in the course of its money market operations. These bank bills are included in the figures for 'other securities' (issue department) and 'premises, equipment and other securities' (banking department).

If we go back to the weekly state and look under Public Deposits, we will see that this includes an item for 'dividend accounts'. This represents part of the role of the Bank of England as a registrar of government stocks. Maintaining the records of stockholders for the British government, some overseas governments, British nationalised industries, some British public boards, and local authorities is an important duty of the Bank of England. Any transfers of stocks are recorded by the Bank and they are responsible for the payment of interest and the redemption of stocks at maturity. Although a very high proportion of the Bank of England's staff are employed on these tasks, the transfer of stock records on to computer file has led to a more efficient and less time-consuming system of registration.

6 THE BANKERS' BANK

The Bank of England as the United Kingdom's central bank is banker to the commercial banks. 'Bankers deposits' are accounts kept at the Bank of England by the clearing banks, overseas banks operating in London, merchant banks and discount houses.

The most important of these are the accounts of the 'High Street' banks. These accounts are never overdrawn as the clearing banks keep part of their customers' deposits as working balances with the Bank of England. If the customers of a clearing bank keep £8,000 million on their accounts, that bank will retain around £100 million on its account with the Bank of England. The balances kept at the Bank of England are regarded as good as cash and no interest is paid on them.

When the clearing banks wish to settle for the cheques, bankgiro credits, salary payments, direct debits, standing order credits and other forms of movement of funds between banks, they will use their bankers deposits. A bank which has more cheques drawn upon it than it collects the same day will transfer funds from its balance with the Bank of England. The transfers will be made to those other banks which are collecting more cheques that day than those which have been drawn upon them.

Notes and coins are distributed throughout the United Kingdom by the commercial banks' branch networks. New bank notes are obtained from the Bank of England's London office or one of its eight branches. New coins are obtained from the Royal Mint by the commercial banks and distributed by their bullion departments. Old notes which are not fit for reissue are returned to the Bank of England. Let us analyse the effect of three different transactions on the Bank of England's weekly state.

(a) Bank G sends £2 million in old notes to Bank of England.
(b) Bank P draws £11 million in new notes from Bank of England.
(c) Bank T received £1 million of new 20p coins from Royal Mint.

The two weekly states shown here illustrate the position before and after these transactions.

Issue Department

	£ million		£ million
Notes issued		Government debt	11
In circulation	12,000	Other government securities	7,530
In banking department	50	Other securities	4,509
	12,050		12,050

Banking Department

	£ million		£ million
Capital	14	Government securities	600
Public deposits	36	Advances and other accounts	300
Bankers deposits	800	Premises, equipment and other securities	649
Reserves and other accounts	750	Notes	50
		Coin	1
	1,600		1,600

Following this series of transactions the weekly state would show these figures.

Issue Department

	£ million		£ million
Notes issued		Government debt	11
In circulation	12,009	Other government securities	7,530
In banking department	41	Other securities	4,509
	12,050		12,050

Banking Department

	£ million		£ million
Capital	14	Government securities	600
Public deposits	37	Advances and other accounts	300
Bankers deposits	790	Premises, equipment and other securities	649
Reserves and other accounts	750	Notes	41
		Coin	1
	1,591		1,591

The notes which Bank G sends back to the Bank of England are held in the Banking Department, pending reissue or destruction, and the amount (£2 million) is credited to bankers deposits. Notes in Banking Department increase by the same amount. If the Bank of England does not wish to reissue these notes, it replaces them with freshly printed ones.

The deposits in the name of Bank P fall by the amount of notes which it has drawn (£11 million) and the total of notes held by the Bank of England decreases by the same figure. The amalgamation of these two sets of transactions (£11 million minus £2 million) leads to an increase of £9 million in the notes in circulation. There is a fall of £9 million in the total of bankers deposits.

With the payment of £1 million for the new coins which Bank T has received direct from the Royal Mint in Cardiff, bankers deposits fall by a further £1 million, making a total fall of £10 million (£1m + £11m – £2m). Public deposits increase by £1 million in settlement for the issue of these coins. The Bank of England's own holdings of coins are unaffected.

Because of the active use made of these accounts for settling clearing transactions and as a cash reserve, the clearing banks keep working balances with the Bank of England. These credit balances form part of the assets used to offset the clearers' liabilities to the public in the form of deposits.

7 BANK OF ENGLAND AS BANKER TO OTHER CENTRAL BANKS

The Bank of England also acts as banker for overseas central banks, the International Monetary Fund and the International Bank for Reconstruction and Development (World Bank). As well as maintaining an account for the Bank for International Settlements

(BIS), the Bank of England cooperates very closely with other European central banks in the work of the Bank for International Settlements.

The communications between the Bank of England, World Bank, International Monetary Fund and BIS are not just part of the normal banker-customer relationship. The Bank of England's International Division and Territorial Division keep closely in touch with all these international organisations and other central banks. Representatives from the Bank of England attend meetings of the Bank for International Settlements as 'ex officio' directors. From time to time Bank of England officials attend meetings of the World Bank and the International Monetary Fund as alternate directors. Members of the Bank of England's staff are seconded to serve with these international financial institutions. The value of these close relations was shown in August 1982 when a 'rescue package' was speedily arranged for Mexico, after the country encountered acute financial problems. Similar international cooperation helped Yugoslavia overcome foreign debt difficulties in January 1983.

The balances kept by these other central banks and international organisations are included in the total for 'reserves and other accounts'. This is a rather misleading figure because 'other accounts' also includes the balances kept at the Bank of England by British local authorities, public corporations, public companies and a limited number of private customers.

8 LENDER OF LAST RESORT

While the Bank of England has the authority to give directions to banks and other financial institutions, it has a duty to reciprocate by helping them in times of trouble. This duty is that of behaving as 'lender of last resort', i.e. lending to them when there are no other sources of borrowing. Following the collapse of the property boom at the end of 1973, a crisis arose in the secondary banking market. Many of these 'fringe banks' had lent heavily to property companies and had financed these loans by means of short-term deposits, carrying high rates of interest. When repayment of the property loans became difficult the secondary bankers found themselves faced with massive withdrawals of deposits. Problems arose at London and County Securities in November 1973. This was quickly followed by difficulties at Cedar Holdings in December 1973. The situation for many of these secondary banks was now becoming critical. Assistance was sought from the Bank of England, supported by the English and Scottish clearing banks. On 21 December 1973 the 'lifeboat' was launched. Together the Bank of England and its associates provided nearly £1,300 million in support loans, in substitution of the deposits which had been withdrawn. Very few institutions were unscathed. Slater Walker Ltd, the darling of the press in the 1960s and early 1970s, had to be taken over by the Bank of England. Edward Bates and Sons, a bank in which Arab interests had a large stake, was acquired by Barclays Bank. Keyser Ullman, a respected merchant bank, received substantial help from the 'lifeboat' crew. The large finance house, United Dominions Trust, after being rescued in the 'lifeboat' operations, was taken over by the Trustee Savings Banks in 1981. Apart from those companies which went into liquidation, 25 institutions were assisted by the Bank of England and the 'High Street' banks in the years following the collapse of the property boom. The substantial amounts which were lent by the Bank of England and its associates were intended to prevent a crisis of confidence in the secondary banking market and to organise an orderly disposal of the property assets, mortgaged to the 'fringe bankers'.

In normal times, the Bank of England is not obliged to lend to other banks, however creditworthy. It confines its automatic 'lender of last resort' assistance to the discount houses. These discount houses borrow large sums from the clearing banks which they invest in Treasury bills, commercial bills, and other short-dated securities. If one or more of the clearing banks is asking for repayment of the sums borrowed, the discount houses will sell bills or securities in order to raise funds. These bills or securities are usually sold to the clearing banks. Should the banks be unwilling to absorb the sales and unable to lend more money at call, the discount houses may be involved in capital losses if they sell assets elsewhere. The discount houses in this difficulty can either sell their investments to the Bank of England or use them as security for loans from the Bank of England. Assistance is never refused to the discount houses, provided they have acceptable security, and the Bank of England's acting as 'lender of last resort' in this way enables the discount houses to borrow more freely from other banks. The rate of interest charged by the Bank of England on its loans is usually higher than the rates charged by the clearing banks. At the present time these loans from the Bank of England are less common than in previous years. If a discount house needs assistance now, the Bank of England is more likely to help by purchasing Treasury bills or bank bills than lending to the discount house at a penal rate.

The support loans made during the 'lifeboat' period as well as any secured loans made to discount houses are shown on the weekly state in the total for 'Advances and other accounts'.

9 OTHER SECURITIES

In addition to its holdings of Treasury bills, bank bills and British government securities, the Bank of England often buys local authority stocks and local authority bills. The main sellers are the discount houses and these purchases enable the Bank of England to monitor the investments made by the discount houses with the money at call they borrow.

In a similar way, the Bank of England will often ask discount houses to sell commercial bills. These are normal trade bills which have not been accepted by a bank. By this method of purchasing commercial bills, when the discount houses need funds, the Bank of England is able to test the quality of the finance provided in this way. In the clothing industry, bills are often used to purchase cloth which is then turned into clothes and sold to retail outlets. Another typical transaction financed by bills is the finance of exports during the period the goods are in transit to the foreign importer.

From time to time, there have been complaints that borrowers have been unable to obtain the right type of finance from the commercial banks. Following these criticisms, the Bank of England has taken the lead in establishing specialised institutions which can provide long-term finance. The Bank of England and the London and Scottish clearing banks are shareholders in the Agricultural Mortgage Corporation and Finance for Industry. The Bank of England's shares in these institutions are included in the 'Premises, equipment and other securities' item in the banking department totals. Industrial and Commercial Finance Corporation, Finance Corporation for Industry and Equity Capital for Industry are the best-known subsidiary companies of the Finance for Industry group.

10 CAPITAL AND GOVERNMENT DEBT

These items on the weekly return have remained unchanged for many years. Capital is the issued capital which was taken over by the British government when the Bank of England was nationalised in 1946. Shareholders received Treasury stock in exchange.

Government debt is an old legacy from the days when the Bank of England was a company incorporated by Royal Charter. In return for the granting and periodic renewal of the charter, the Bank of England provided loans for the British government. This figure no longer has any monetary or accounting significance.

11 BANK OF ENGLAND'S SUPERVISION OF THE FINANCIAL SYSTEM

The Bank of England has a special Financial Structure and Institutions Division. This division keeps a close check on the commodity markets and the stock markets. Close relations are maintained with the City Liaison Committee, the Council for the Securities Industry and the Council for the Stock Exchange. Progress in developing new techniques in the transfer and the clearing of funds, together with other banking innovations, are also monitored in this division.

There is also a Banking Supervision Division which is responsible for the supervision of the British banking system. While this had been based in the past on a close understanding between the Bank of England and the main commercial banks, the weakness of this control was shown not only by the 'fringe banking' crisis of 1973/74 but also by the difficulties of the Scottish Cooperative Wholesale Society's Banking Department earlier in 1973. The Scottish Cooperative's difficulties had arisen as a result of its money market dealings. A rescue operation had to be undertaken by the London and Scottish clearing banks.

The loss of confidence in the adequacy of the supervision of the financial system led to pressure for legislation. With Britain's joining the Common Market, opportunity was taken to bring our law into line with our Common Market partners as well as to extend the Bank of England's supervisory powers. The Banking Act 1979 was the result.

12 BANKING ACT 1979

This Act was drafted to control deposit taking and thus effectively restrict new entrants into the banking system. Only recognised banks or licensed deposit takers are authorised to accept deposits from the public. Professional people such as stockbrokers, solicitors, accountants and chartered surveyors are permitted to take deposits from their own clients, when transacting business on the clients' behalf. Local authorities, National Savings Bank, National Girobank, Trustee Savings banks, credit unions and building societies are at present exempt from the rules of the Banking Act. Friendly Societies are regarded as already satisfactorily governed by statutory regulations.

Section 2 Bills of Exchange Act 1882 defined a banker as 'including a body of persons, whether incorporated or not, who carry on the business of banking'. As a definition this was unhelpful because it did not tell us what the business of banking consists of. It is important to get this right because cheques, so widely used in payment of debts, can only be drawn on a banker. Section 73 Bills of Exchange Act stated that a cheque is 'a bill of exchange drawn on a banker payable on demand'.

Although the Cheques Act 1957 discussed the statutory protection of bankers paying cheques drawn on them, or collecting cheques for customers, it did not define a bank. It was left to the Banking Act 1979 to rectify this omission. The Act did not define a bank as such but said that a recognised bank would be an institution which was permitted by the Bank of England to use the word 'bank' in its name. To qualify as a bank, the institution must have a minimum of £5 million in shareholders' funds, enjoy a high reputation and be run by professional bankers. In addition, the bank was expected to provide a wide range of services. This range of services was set out in the Banking Act 1979 and consists of the following:

(a) acceptance of deposits;
(b) making loans;
(c) foreign exchange;
(d) provision of bill finance and handling the documentation for foreign trade;
(e) investment management and corporate finance.

As an alternative, an institution can be a recognised bank if it provides a highly specialised banking service and has a minimum of £250,000 in shareholders' funds. It must fulfil the other conditions concerning high reputation and being run by professional bankers. So far, only the discount houses have been admitted to this second group of recognised banks.

Although the Banking Act 1979 exempts the Trustee Savings Banks at the present time, it is their intention to apply for recognition in due course. There is no reason why they should not take their place alongside the clearing banks, accepting houses, discount houses, merchant banks and overseas banks who qualify as part of the British banking system by law and custom.

The institutions which are granted licensed deposit taker status will have to satisfy the Bank of England that their directors are prudent. In addition, they will need a minimum of £250,000 in shareholders' funds. If these conditions are fulfilled, licensed deposit takers will be able to advertise for deposits and take deposits from the public in the same way as recognised banks. A licensed deposit taker is not allowed to use the word 'bank' in its title unless most of its business is abroad and it is known by that title overseas. The fact that it is a licensed deposit taker must be indicated on its premises and stationery.

The decisions taken by the Bank of England were subjected to some adverse criticism. Bank of Cyprus and Bank of Credit and Commerce International were not granted 'recognised bank' status. Harrods had to be content with a licence as a licensed deposit taker. The Yorkshire-based finance group known as the People's Bank had its appeal against denial of status of a bank turned down by the Chancellor of the Exchequer. Commercial Bank of Wales was originally given licensed deposit taker status by the Bank of England. After an appeal to the Chancellor of the Exchequer, the Bank of England's decision was reversed.

The Banking Act has provided for the setting up of a 'deposit protection fund', managed by the Bank of England. Contributions have been taken from all recognised banks or licensed deposit takers. These contributions have been a small proportion of their sterling deposit bases and a fund of around £6 million has been set up. Further calls may be made up to a maximum of 0.3 per cent of the sterling deposits with less than five years to go before maturity of these deposits.

Where an institution is unable to meet its commitments, depositors, apart from other banks and licensed deposit takers, will be compensated up to 75 per cent of 'protected deposits'. The maximum amount of a protected deposit is £10,000 and the maximum compensation payable from the deposit protection fund will, therefore, be £7,500. Clearing bankers have criticised the establishment of this fund. The clearers are in the position of being the most secure institutions and yet being expected to pay the largest contributions. They feel that the recycling of deposits during the Scottish Cooperative

Wholesale Society's difficulties and the help given subsequently to the depositors of the 'fringe' banks showed that a fund was unnecessary. In spite of all the problems of the 1970s, no member of the depositing public lost a penny.

The bankers also felt it was unfair that the exempt deposit takers should not be asked to make any contributions to the fund, while the bank shareholders would be asked to support their competitors. As far as the building societies are concerned, the government felt that existing arrangements were adequate. The past failures of some building societies led to levies on member societies by the Building Societies Association. These levies enabled depositors in the defaulting societies to be paid, although there had been some delays.

4 *British Banking System*

1 CLEARING BANKS

The main commercial banks in England and Wales are known as the 'Big Four' (Barclays, Lloyds, Midland and National Westminster). They are called clearing banks or High Street banks to distinguish them from other banking institutions. These four banks together with Williams & Glyns (a wholly-owned subsidiary of the Royal Bank of Scotland) and Coutts and Co (a wholly-owned subsidiary of National Westminster) make up the six members of the Committee of London Clearing Bankers.

This committee owns the Bankers Clearing House which is responsible for the main system of settling debts in this country. Cheques and bank giro credits are speedily and efficiently moved from one account to another throughout the whole banking network.

The Bank of England has been an 'ex officio' member of the Bankers Clearing House since 1864. In 1974 the Cooperative Bank was given direct access to the Bankers Clearing House for the purpose of clearing facilities. The members of the Committee of London Clearing Bankers extended invitations to other institutions at the same time. The Central Trustee Savings Bank joined the clearing system as a functional member in 1975 and was followed by the National Girobank in 1981. Yorkshire Bank and the three Scottish banks were invited to join as functional members of the Bankers Clearing House but these invitations were not accepted.

Because the clearing banks have nearly 12,000 branches covering the whole country, they handle the great majority of commercial banking transactions and almost all personal banking business in England and Wales.

During the past fifteen years, the clearing banks have expanded abroad at a steady pace. Many branch offices have been opened overseas as well as investments made in foreign banking companies. They also have substantial shareholdings in banks operating in Ireland and Scotland.

2 OTHER DEPOSIT BANKS

There are four banks which are 'retail' banks in the same way as the clearing banks but which are not members of the Bankers Clearing House. These banks are as follows:

(a) C Hoare & Co (a privately owned company).
(b) Isle of Man Bank (wholly owned subsidiary of National Westminster Bank).
(c) Lewis's Bank (wholly owned subsidiary of Lloyds Bank).
(d) Yorkshire Bank — 40% of shares owned by National Westminster
32% of shares owned by Barclays
20% of shares owned by Lloyds
8% of shares owned by Williams & Glyns.

3 NORTHERN IRELAND BANKS

Four banks operate in the province and have the same role in the transmission of funds as the English clearing banks. Two of this number, Allied Irish and the Bank of Ireland, are publicly quoted companies, with head offices in the Republic of Ireland. The other two banks, Northern and Ulster banks, are wholly owned subsidiaries of Midland and National Westminster respectively. All four of the Northern Ireland banks have large branch networks throughout the whole of Ireland. Guidance concerning their branches in the Republic of Ireland is left to the Irish authorities, but the operations of their branches in Northern Ireland are subject to the supervision of the Bank of England. Because of the special circumstances of ownership and operations, control over the banks incorporated in the Republic of Ireland tends to be slightly more flexible than controls over their English and Scottish counterparts.

4 SCOTTISH BANKS

While there are a very few branches of English banks which have been opened in Scotland in recent years, Scottish banking is dominated by the three Scottish clearing banks. Scotland has a very sophisticated financial system and the Scottish banks provide a very efficient payments mechanism for their own country's financial community.

Although the Bank of Scotland is a public company, 34.6 per cent of its shares are owned by Barclays Bank. Clydesdale Bank is a wholly owned subsidiary of Midland Bank. Royal Bank of Scotland is an independent public limited company in which Lloyds Bank has a minority shareholding interest.

There was considerable public controversy during 1981 and the beginning of 1982 when Royal Bank of Scotland was the subject of a take-over battle between Hong Kong and Shanghai Bank and the Standard and Chartered Bank. The Hong Kong bid was opposed by the Royal Bank's directors who favoured the bid from Standard. The Bank of England indicated that the Standard Bank would be more acceptable than the proposed merger with Hong Kong and Shanghai. Public feeling on the subject, combined with the nationalistic sentiments expressed by some groups of Scots, led to a government reference to the Monopolies Commission.

In its wide-ranging report, the Monopolies Commission turned down the claims of both bidders. The government accepted the Commission's report and the Royal Bank of Scotland remains independent. While it is possible to accept the arguments that ownership of a major British bank is a matter of public concern, it seems very hard on the shareholders to prevent them realising the best price for their investments. The inability of foreign groups to acquire British banks at a fair price may have a debilitating effect on performance and could lead to a diminution of incentive to innovate.

5 OTHER BANKING FACILITIES

Apart from providing the payments system for the United Kingdom and Northern Ireland, accepting term and demand deposits and making overdrafts and term loans available, all the deposit banks have extended into related financial fields. Investments have been made in hire purchase companies and merchant banks in order to widen the clearing banks' traditional range of services. In addition, English, Scottish and Northern Irish banks act as unit trust managers, insurance brokers, corporate trustees and credit factors as well as providing computer services for commercial users.

Because some borrowers require more varied finance than the traditional overdrafts and loans which the banks make available, the English and Scottish clearing banks, together with the Bank of England, have subscribed capital for institutions which provide long-term finance. They are major shareholders in Finance for Industry which arranges long-term loans or equity investments, mainly for manufacturing companies. All the English and Scottish clearing banks also have major shareholdings in Agricultural Mortgage Corporation, which arranges finance for long-term development of farms.

6 ACCEPTING HOUSES

A bill of exchange is an unconditional order in writing, instructing the drawee to pay a fixed sum of money to the drawer or to the order of the drawer. The bill can be drawn to be payable on demand, at a fixed date, or at a determinable future date. Although a few bills of exchange are used in the finance of internal trade, most of them are used in foreign trade. Bills of exchange enable credit to be given to the foreign buyer and, at the same time, the exporter receives an acknowledgement of the debt. The acceptance of the bill by the drawee is the agreement to the drawer's instructions. After acceptance, the bill can be discounted, which is a sale at less than face value. The bill when drawn could look like this:

	Leeds
£1200	11 February 1983
Three months after sight pay to me or my order One thousand two hundred pounds sterling for value received	
To Matthew Williams & Co Lagos, Nigeria	Peter Pickering

While it is possible for a bill to be accepted on the back, it is customary for the drawee to signify assent by writing across the front of the bill in the following manner:

'Accepted 19 February 1983
Matthew Williams & Co'

If the traders involved are not well-known to each other, the foreign importer may be asked to instruct his bank to open an acceptance credit with a London bank. The London bank concerned is usually an accepting house but clearing banks will also act in this way for their correspondent banks abroad. The exporter in Britain sends the shipping documents to the London bank and, if the accepting bank is satisfied, they will accept the exporter's bill of exchange and forward the documents to the importer's bank. A small commission charge will be paid to the accepting house by the importer or the importer's bankers. The exporter will be able to get the bill discounted more quickly and at a finer rate of discount because of the standing of the accepting bank compared with the standing of the importer. Because of this, the exporter may reduce his price to compensate the importer for the commission payable.

The bill of exchange drawn on the London bank would be on the lines of this example:

SPECIMEN

£4,108

London
11th August 19..

AT 90 DAYS AFTER DATE OF THIS FIRST OF EXCHANGE (SECOND OF THE SAME TENOR AND DATE BEING UNPAID) PLEASE PAY TO OUR ORDER THE SUM OF STERLING POUNDS FOUR THOUSAND ONE HUNDRED AND EIGHT ONLY FOR VALUE RECEIVED

Drawn under Irrevocable Credit of Barclays Bank International Ltd.,

168 Fenchurch Street, London No. FDC/2/6789 dated 20th July 19..

To: Barclays Bank International Ltd
168 Fenchurch Street
London EC3

For and on behalf of
SPEIRS AND WADLEY LTD
W. H. Speirs
Director

The leading accepting houses are organised in the Accepting Houses Committee. Members of the Accepting Houses Committee include some of the most famous names in the merchant banking world. N M Rothschild and Sons, Morgan Grenfell & Co, Hambros Bank, Lazard Brothers & Co, Charterhouse Japhet, and Rea Brothers are among the better-known merchant banks.

7 MERCHANT BANKS

The traditional acceptance business of the accepting houses has become much less important in recent years. In addition, they have been faced with increased competition from the clearing banks and the London branches of foreign banks. Both these groups have been seeking to increase their share of the market for acceptance of bills.

Merchant banks have responded by diversification. They have opened up branches in other financial centres such as Birmingham, Edinburgh, Glasgow, Leeds and Manchester. As well as providing acceptance credits, the merchant banks are active in the fields of investment management, corporate finance, capital issues and financial advisory services. They have also branched out into broking, factoring and leasing. Although many merchant banks offer current account services for customers, greatest emphasis is placed on their function as issuing houses. This involves their arranging the underwriting of capital issues both for the domestic market and for organisations overseas. About sixty banks, including all the members of the Accepting Houses Committee, are organised in the Issuing Houses Association.

Merchant banks are best known to the public as advisers on company acquisitions and mergers. In any 'take-over' battle, the participants usually engage a merchant bank to consider the terms and to prepare a defence, if this is thought to be necessary.

With the expansion of services undertaken by the merchant banks and their increased geographical spread, merchant banks are becoming more like other commercial banks. The clearing banks have reciprocated by expanding their own merchant banking facilities. Barclays Merchant Bank is a wholly-owned subsidiary of Barclays, while County Bank is a wholly-owned subsidiary of National Westminster. Samuel Montague & Co is a member of the Accepting Houses Committee even though 60 per cent of its shares are owned by the Midland Bank.

8 DISCOUNT HOUSES

The London money market is principally involved in the borrowing and lending of very short-term money. The major operators in this market are the public limited companies who are members of the London Discount Market Association. There are a handful of private companies who are also members of the London Discount Market Association and a few bill brokers who carry out similar functions to the discount houses, although they are not members of the Association. The discount houses act as financial intermediaries between the Bank of England and the rest of the banking system. Discount houses traditionally used to borrow up to 30 times their issued capital. The Bank of England introduced new rules on 3 June 1982 for the prudential supervision of the discount houses. The discount houses are now able to hold assets up to 40 times their capital base. The Bank of England, in return for this increased limit, stated that their investment policies would be more strictly controlled than they had been in the past. Restrictions have been imposed on the quantity of longer-term securities which the discount houses are now allowed to buy.

The main lenders to the discount houses are the clearing banks who provide them with money at call or short notice against acceptable security. Discount houses also accept seven-day deposits, mainly in large amounts from corporate bodies. In addition, they borrow on an unsecured basis from the inter-bank market.

The main operations of the discount houses are the trading of and investment in short-dated securities. At one time these securities were mainly Treasury bills and government stocks coming up to redemption. More recently, most of the funds taken by the discount houses have been invested in commercial bills of exchange. Large amounts have also been invested in bills and stocks of local authorities as well as short-term loans to local authorities. The discount houses have also been active traders in negotiable certificates of deposit issued by banks.

In its capacity as 'lender of last resort', the Bank of England will lend only to discount houses, except in extraordinary circumstances. Because of this, the clearing banks use the funds lent by them to the discount houses as a liquidity buffer. At certain times, such as when customers have subscribed for a large issue of government stock or during the tax-gathering season at the beginning of the year, clearing banks will lose cash to the Bank of England. This cash can be replaced either by calling in loans made to the discount houses or by the banks selling securities to the discount houses. Either method may lead to the discount market being tight for funds and may have undesirable side effects on the rate of interest.

In these circumstances, the Bank of England may provide loans against approved security, purchase Treasury bills from the discount houses or discount bank bills for them. At the present time, the major part of the help given by the Bank of England is in the form of buying bills rather than making loans.

Until 1981 the Bank of England would only discount bills which had been accepted by a limited number of banks. These banks were the members of the Committee of London Clearing Bankers, Scottish Clearing banks, members of the Accepting Houses Committee and a few British overseas banks. Since August 1981, the number of banks whose bills can now be discounted at the Bank of England has greatly increased. These banks are known as 'eligible banks'. The new list of banks whose bills are eligible for discount at the Bank of England includes some merchant banks who are not members of the Accepting Houses Committee, Cooperative Bank and a large number of Commonwealth and foreign banks. Not all recognised banks are classified as eligible banks.

The different status accorded to the eligible banks also carries additional responsibilities. In order to ensure that there is always an adequate supply of bills available in the London money market for both purchase and sale, the Bank of England laid down the following conditions for eligibility:

(a) Where Commonwealth and foreign banks are concerned, British banks must have reciprocal opportunities for business in the other banks' domestic markets.

(b) The eligible banks acceptance must command the finest rate in the bill market.

(c) The eligible bank must have a large and widely spread acceptance business in Great Britain.

(d) An eligible bank must keep a ratio of 2½ per cent between the bank's secured loans to members of the London Discount Market Association and the bank's eligible liabilities (roughly, deposits placed with the bank by the public).

(e) An additional 2½ per cent of eligible liabilities must be lent against security to:

(i) some approved money brokers
(ii) some approved gilt-edged stock jobbers
(iii) members of London Discount Market Association.

Eligible banks are at liberty to choose between these three groups for the investment of the residuary loans to the money market. Loans to the brokers and jobbers will tend to command a higher rate of interest than loans to discount houses because only the discount houses have automatic 'Lender of last resort' facilities at the Bank of England.

On 19 July 1983, following representations from the Committee of London Clearing Bankers, the Bank of England reduced the ratios which eligible banks needed to keep between secured loans to the money market and the banks' own eligible liabilities. From 18 August 1983, there was a reduction from 6 per cent to 5 per cent of these banks' eligible liabilities for the amount kept by them with discount houses, approved stockjobbers and approved money brokers. As far as the daily minimum of funds to be kept with members of the London Discount Market Association was concerned, this was reduced from 4 per cent to 2½ per cent of eligible liabilities.

5 *A Clearing Bank's Balance Sheet*

Bank customers are often given to making comments on bank balance sheets when they are talking to bank staff. Some of these comments are made without a great deal of understanding and, regrettably, this lack of understanding is shared with many of the staff. It gives the customers confidence in the staff of their own bank if the staff can discuss the accounts with an air of confidence. All the banks have slight variations in the way these accounts are presented. The general principles are the same, however, and it is advisable to have a copy of a clearing bank's most recent audited accounts with you when you study this section. A simplified version of a bank balance sheet would look something like this:

Liabilities	£M	**Assets**	£M
Shareholders' funds		Coin, bank notes and balances with the Bank of England	600
Ordinary share capital	300	Cheques in the course of collection	800
Reserves	1,500	Money at call and short notice	1,500
		Bills discounted	600
Other liabilities		Certificates of Deposit	700
		Investments other than trade investments	600
Loan capital	300	Advances and other accounts	17,500
Deferred taxation	100	Amounts due from subsidiary companies	3,400
Current and deposit accounts	25,000	Investments in subsidiary companies	600
Creditors	100	Trade investments	100
Current taxation	25	Premises and equipment	1,000
Dividends	75		
	27,400		27,400

The liabilities of the bank are other people's assets. Shareholders' funds consist of money paid to the bank for its shares and also past profits taken into reserve funds. When the bank needs more money for expansion it must set aside part of its profit or ask the shareholders to subscribe for new shares.

The shareholders are investors who receive dividends on their share capital in return for which they take the risk of losing their money if the bank trades unprofitably. Banking is an unusual business in that the security of the shareholders' money is not regarded as being as important as the security of the depositors' money. The safety of the depositors' funds, in the form of current and deposit accounts, is always given priority.

1 LOAN CAPITAL

Where investors wish to be certain of an income and guaranteed repayment of their capital, one option will be to purchase loan stock issued by a bank. The rate of interest payable is usually fixed which means that on a 9 per cent loan stock, $4\frac{1}{2}$ per cent interest would be paid every half-year.

In some cases the interest is a floating rate. Interest on these stocks varies according to the changes in a previously arranged indicator. This indicator can be any variable rate such as Treasury bill average rate for the previous three months, London Inter-Bank rate for the previous six months or increases in the retail price index.

Repayment of the loan can be either at a fixed date or between a spread of dates. A fixed date loan stock would be one repayable on, for example, 2 February 1989. A spread of dates such as 1989/1995 shows the stock to be repayable at any time between 1989 and 1995, at the borrower's option.

In recent years the banks have raised substantial sums of money by issuing loan capital, denominated in foreign currencies. This has enabled expansion abroad to take place, with assets and liabilities in the same currency being matched. British banks have also been able to take advantage of the lower interest rates prevailing in some foreign financial centres.

2 DEFERRED TAXATION

When capital assets are purchased, capital allowances of 100 per cent of purchase price are usually given against the corporation tax assessment in the year in which the assets are purchased. If the assets are sold before the end of their useful life, some of these capital allowances are repayable to the Inland Revenue. It is unlikely that the assets will not be replaced and fresh capital allowances given against the replacement assets. No tax would, therefore, be paid and a deferred taxation account helps to smooth out timing differences when depreciation of fixed assets is being charged to the profit and loss account.

With clearing bank balance sheets the figure for deferred taxation also includes capital allowances on equipment purchased by the banks and subsequently leased to customers. The deferred taxation total could also include any liability for capital gains tax which might arise in the future. This could occur when assets such as investments in subsidiary companies or bank properties are revalued at more than cost price. If these assets were subsequently sold, an assessment for capital gains tax could arise unless the bank claims 'roll-over' relief.

3 CURRENT AND DEPOSIT ACCOUNTS

Most of the money which a bank uses in its business is lent to the bank either on demand or at very short notice. There are some medium-term deposit accounts and certificates of deposit on the liabilities side of a bank's balance sheet. Most of the bank's funds, however, are likely to be current accounts, repayable on demand. The greater part of the rest will be deposit accounts, repayable at seven days' notice.

While the nationalised industries have accounts with the main clearing banks and local authorities also have accounts with these banks, the treasurers of these organisations try to keep very small balances on their bank accounts. Any surplus funds are usually invested in the short-term money market. In a similar fashion, financial directors of industrial companies and building societies tend to keep relatively small balances with their banks.

This means that most of the funds required for use in a bank's business are obtained by taking deposits from private customers. Because of the necessity of maintaining these deposits in order to continue in business, the clearing banks are more 'personal service orientated' than other financial institutions. During the middle of the 1970s, American and Canadian banks in London actively encouraged their private customers to transfer their accounts to British clearing banks.

When the banks need additional funds for lending purposes and they are unable to raise money by selling bills or investments, they will borrow money in the wholesale money markets. These funds are taken in the form of short-term and medium-term deposits. If this situation arises, the item 'Current and Deposit accounts' on the balance sheet will become 'Current, Deposit and other accounts'.

4 CREDITORS, CURRENT TAXATION, DIVIDENDS

These three items should be self-explanatory. Any business will have expenses and not all these expenses will be paid as soon as they are due. The figure for creditors shows liabilities for local rates, electricity, gas, transport costs and purchases of stationery.

Current taxation is the figure for tax assessed by the Inland Revenue and now payable. It must not be confused with the figure of deferred taxation which may never be paid if the business continues to invest in capital assets.

Dividends shows the amount which the directors propose should be declared as a dividend in the current year. Theoretically, an annual general meeting of shareholders can declare a lower dividend but they cannot pay themselves a higher amount.

5 INVESTMENT OF A BANK'S FUNDS

A bank is always conscious of the need to safeguard the depositors' money. They could obtain 100 per cent security by holding all their assets in the form of cash. Unfortunately, cash not only produces no income, but heavy transport costs are involved in moving it around between branches and also insuring this cash in transit. Heavy expenses are also incurred through insuring the cash while it is in the bank vaults. If all the bank's funds were held in the form of cash, the bank would obtain no income to pay interest to depositors, salaries to staff or dividends to shareholders.

It would be perfectly possible for a bank to obtain maximum profitability by making long-term loans at high rates of interest. Good dividends could be paid to shareholders, high salaries paid to staff and deposits could be attracted by paying high rates of interest on deposit accounts. Unfortunately, with all its assets tied up in long-term loans, the bank would always be vulnerable in the event of a sudden withdrawal of deposits. Heavy repayments of deposits could force the bank to borrow in the wholesale money market, paying very high rates of interest for the funds borrowed. If the financial community lost confidence in the bank's ability to repay current liabilities on demand, the bank might be unable to borrow money on any terms and be forced out of business as a result. This situation arose at the end of 1973. During the secondary banking crisis many of the 'fringe' banks were unable to pay out money to repay their depositors and had to seek support from the Bank of England and the clearing banks.

It is always essential for a bank to retain the public's confidence in the bank's ability to repay deposits on demand. In seeking to retain this confidence, the bank is faced with the continuing problem of reconciling conflicting objectives. The profitability of the bank has to be balanced against the security of the depositors' money.

The banks try to overcome this problem by arranging their assets in order of liquidity. If we look at the assets side of the bank's balance sheet we see that the assets are arranged in descending order of liquidity. The most easily realisable assets appear at the top with 'premises', as the least easily realisable asset, at the bottom. Profitability tends to rise as you go down the assets side from 'coin, etc' to 'trade investments'. Premises are the exception to this rule. A bank's branches are very costly to maintain and the only income they produce is from those parts of the premises which are let-off to tenants.

6 COIN, BANK NOTES AND BALANCES WITH THE BANK OF ENGLAND

None of these items earn any interest. Because of this, banks always try to keep their cash holdings as low as possible. A prudent bank will always retain a comfortable margin of safety, however, bearing in mind that current accounts are repayable on demand. If the public has confidence that all demands on a bank will be repayable in full and without delay, the bank is never likely to be faced with the exceptional withdrawals that have forced some financial institutions to close their doors.

Seasonal variations in demand for coins and notes occur from time to time. Heavy cash withdrawals take place just before Christmas and also during the summer holiday season. There are corresponding inflows of cash in February and November of each year. As a general rule, the average ratio between cash kept in branches plus cash kept in head offices and the bank's liabilities in the form of deposits varies between 1 and 2 per cent.

Since 20 August 1981 it has been mandatory for institutions in the new monetary sector to keep ½ per cent of their eligible liabilities (roughly deposits minus one or two items on the asset side) in the form of non-operational, non-interest bearing accounts at the Bank of England. These funds will provide the Bank of England with roughly the same income as that which used to be provided by the 1½ per cent of their funds which the clearing banks alone had to lodge in the past with the Bank of England.

Apart from these compulsorily lodged accounts with the Bank of England, the clearing banks have additional operational accounts at the Bank. These accounts which are voluntarily retained at the Bank of England are used primarily to settle clearing house transactions by means of transfers from one Bank of England account to another. When clearing banks need to replenish their cash holdings they will run down their balances with the Bank of England and obtain bank notes instead.

7 CHEQUES IN THE COURSE OF COLLECTION

Cheques paid into the accounts of customers of British banks are credited straight away unless they are drawn on banks outside the United Kingdom. Cheques drawn abroad have to be negotiated (sold to the bank at the current rate of exchange) or sent for collection. Those cheques which are drawn on the same branch as they are paid in will be debited to the drawer's account that day. Most cheques, however, are drawn on banks or branches elsewhere. The bank which is collecting the cheque through the clearing house does not receive payment until the drawer's account is debited. It receives payment on the clearing settlement, but payment may have to be returned if the cheque is dishonoured. This means that at any time there will be items for which customers have been given credit and for which the bank has not yet received payment. Although these items are credited to customers' accounts straight away, the bank does reserve the right to refuse to allow drawings against uncleared cheques.

8 MONEY AT CALL AND SHORT NOTICE

The next most liquid asset, after cash, is money at call. When exceptional withdrawals run down a bank's holding of cash, the bank's reserves will be replenished by asking for the return of money lent out at call. The majority of this money is lent by the banks to the discount houses but there are some loans made to other financial institutions. Low rates of interest are paid out on money lent out at call in view of the bank's ability to demand immediate payment. If all the banks ask for repayment of money at call together, the discount houses will be forced to approach the Bank of England for temporary help. When the Bank of England acts in this way it is called 'Lender of last resort'.

Money at short notice consists of loans to the money market which are repayable at a fixed date up to 14 days ahead or after a fixed period of notice which is usually between 2 and 14 days. Whether lent at call or short notice, these loans to discount houses are agreed on a secured basis. The discount houses have to lodge acceptable security and a margin of cover has to be maintained. If a bank agreed to make a secured loan of up to 90 per cent of the value of the security lodged by the discount house, security valued at £1,111,111 would need to be lodged if a loan of £1,000,000 was granted. Should the value of the security fall because of rising interest rates, the loan would either have to be repaid or additional security lodged to restore the agreed margin of cover.

The total shown under the heading 'Money at call and short notice' represents the loans made to members of the London Discount Market Association and those money brokers and gilt-edged stock jobbers who are authorised by the Bank of England to borrow money at call from banks. Only money lent to these approved institutions may be included in the figure for 'Money at call and short notice'. Any money at call lent out to other financial companies is included in the figure for 'Advances and other accounts'.

Since August 1981 any bank whose acceptances are eligible for discounting with the Bank of England must keep minimum ratios between money at call with the discount market and the liabilities the bank has to the public. It follows from this that money at call can no longer be looked upon as a true liquid asset because it cannot be turned into cash, unless substantially more than the minimum ratio is kept.

The total amounts lent out to members of the London Discount Market Association, on a secured basis, and secured loans to recognised money brokers and authorised gilt-edged stock jobbers must average at least 5 per cent of an eligible bank's eligible liabilities. A minimum ratio of 2½ per cent must be kept at all times with discount houses who are members of the London District Market Association. Eligible liabilities are defined as:

> Deposits from the public **MINUS** (funds lent by one institution in the financial sector to another, i.e. call money and 'inter bank' funds) and also **MINUS** (money at call lodged with recognised money brokers and gilt-edged stock jobbers against acceptable security).

9 BILLS DISCOUNTED

These fall into two main categories. The first category is Treasury bills and the second group is commercial bills. Treasury bills are short-dated government securities. The minimum amount for which a Treasury bill is issued is £5,000. Bills for larger sums are also available. The Treasury bill is merely an IOU of the British government and, unlike a commercial bill, is not presented for acceptance. When a purchaser acquires a Treasury bill it is bought for less than its face value. For example, a £5,000 bill might be sold for £4,875 with the difference of £125 representing the discount.

Treasury bills are usually issued to mature in 91 days' time. At certain times of the fiscal year, when the government expects substantial tax receipts within two months, they will also issue 63-day bills. These Treasury bills are an attractive security for the banks because they are relatively short term and can always be turned into cash by the banks discounting them in the London money market. The interest received on these Treasury bills is usually lower than interest available on other securities. This is to compensate for their undoubted security and their high liquidity.

Commercial bills are used where the parties to a trading transaction agree to the postponement of payment of a debt. Drawing a bill enables the drawer to give credit, the drawee to obtain credit and, when the bill is accepted, creates a security for the future payment of the trade debt. The accepted bill can be converted into cash at less than its face value. Discount houses or banks buying bills in this way will calculate the discount by assessing the following factors:

(a) general level of interest rates;
(b) credit-worthiness of the parties to the bill;
(c) whether any similar bills held.

If interest rates are expected to go down in the future, a better price will be paid for the bill. When interest rates are expected to rise, the discount will be larger.

Although banks will discount bills for their own customers, where the parties to the bills are small private companies, they set stricter standards when purchasing commercial bills from the discount houses. They usually insist that at least two parties to the bill, whether drawer, drawee, acceptor or endorser, must be British public companies. These bills will command a finer rate of discount than the normal trade bills which banks discount for their private limited company customers. The highest standing of all is given to a bank bill. This is a bill which has been accepted by a bank that has been given recognition by the Bank of England as a bank whose acceptances are eligible for re-discounting at the Bank of England. Because these eligible bank bills can be turned into cash quickly they command the finest rates and are regarded as first class bank securities.

The volume of commercial bills in a bank's bill portfolio has increased in recent years. The value of the commercial bills held is nearly three times as large as the holdings of Treasury bills. For this reason, considerable care must be taken to achieve a 'good spread' of bills. Limits should be set on the total amount of bills which can be discounted for one company. The bill finance used by one particular industry should not be too large a proportion of the bills held. In the same way, a careful check should be made periodically to see that there is not too high a proportion of the bills being used to finance the trade of a particular country. The banks must be satisfied, in addition, that all the bills are normal trade bills with an underlying commercial transaction, where it is usual to settle by means of a bill of exchange.

While there is no need to make enquiries in the case of Treasury bills or eligible bank bills, the bank must be satisfied that the parties are credit-worthy, in the case of normal trade bills. A banker's enquiry will be made requesting the banker of the drawer, acceptor, or endorser to express an opinion as to whether the respective party is good for their liability.

10 CERTIFICATES OF DEPOSIT

While the calling in of loans made to the discount market and the sale of bills are the traditional ways to relieve a shortage of cash, dealings in certificates of deposit are now a common way of providing banks with a buffer of liquidity.

These certificates are denominated either in sterling or in other currencies. When sterling certificates of deposit were first issued in October 1968 their purpose was to attract funds from industrial and commercial customers which would otherwise be lost to the banking system. The minimum deposit is for £50,000. The maximum deposit is usually £500,000 and other certificates are issued for between £50,000 and £500,000, in multiples of £10,000. A receipt is given by the bank for a deposit at a fixed rate of interest for a fixed term. The certificates are issued at par and are repaid at an agreed date, which is usually between three months and five years after the date of issue.

The certificates are shown to be repayable to 'bearer' and are thus a fully negotiable security. Should the holders of the certificates of deposit require funds before maturity, they are able to sell them through the certificate of deposit market, where discount houses and banks are active both as purchasers and as sellers. This secondary market provides a very useful outlet for a bank's surplus funds. Certificates of deposit can be purchased as investments which can be quickly and easily sold if the need arises to raise additional cash.

Currency certificates of deposit were first issued in London in 1966. They are negotiable in the same way as sterling certificates and are bought and sold in the same secondary money market. Although the usual amount of the certificate issued is US$1,000,000 some certificates are issued for amounts as low as US$25,000. The agreed periods of maturity vary between 30 days and two years. Nearly all the currency certificates of deposit are denominated in US dollars but a few other currencies are also used. The most interesting variation is the issue of certificates denominated in special drawing rights. These SDRs as they are called are the units of account used by the International Monetary Fund. In January 1981 seven banks in London issued SDRs certificates of deposit and have made a market for these certificates ever since. The beginning of 1981 was chosen because that was the date chosen by the International Monetary Fund to value SDRs against a basket of five major currencies instead of the sixteen used before. The weight given to the currencies was:

US Dollar	42%
Deutsche Mark	19%
£ Sterling	13%
French Franc	13%
Japanese Yen	13%

11 INVESTMENTS — OTHER THAN TRADE INVESTMENTS

Most of these investments are securities issued by, or guaranteed by, the British government. The government stocks are all dated stocks, quoted on the Stock Exchange. About half of them are due for redemption within five years, while most of the remainder are repayable in between five and ten years' time. By arranging its investments carefully, a bank can always have a proportion of its investments turning into cash in the near future. This helps to avoid capital losses caused if banks are forced to sell investments prematurely during periods of very high interest rates.

Although settlement for the sale of short-dated government stocks can be arranged through the Stock Exchange on a 'cash settlement' basis, it could still be three or four days after the sale before the bank will receive the proceeds of the sale of stock. As these stocks are less liquid than bills, the interest on them is usually higher than the yields from Treasury bills or bank bills.

Banks will sell these short-dated government securities when their liquid assets (cash, money at call and bills) are running down and need to be replenished. It is now mandatory for a ½ per cent ratio to be maintained between a bank's non-operational account at the Bank of England and the bank's eligible liabilities. The banks are also obliged to keep a 5 per cent ratio between their money at call and the total of their eligible liabilities. Although investments are less liquid than bills or money at call, they form an additional liquidity buffer which can be used in case of need.

Other investments held by the banks consist almost entirely of stocks and bonds issued by British local authorities, stocks issued by British nationalised corporations, stocks or bonds of Commonwealth governments and stock of the Republic of Ireland. Even where banks hold shares in other institutions and these shares are quoted on stock exchanges, they are not included under the total of investments. Instead they are shown under 'Trade investments' because these shares in other financial institutions are long-term investments, not available for re-sale in the markets.

12 ADVANCES AND OTHER ACCOUNTS

By tradition, the bulk of a banker's assets have been in the form of loans or advances to customers. Until the later 1960s, the ratio between a bank's advances and deposits was about 50 per cent. The introduction of 'Competition and Credit Control' in 1971, combined with the speculative property boom in 1971/3, led to a large increase in this ratio. Although the ratios have fallen back from these peak figures, the banks are still lending between 60 and 70 per cent of their deposits. Most of the lending is in the form of overdrafts. These are said to be repayable on demand, although it would be difficult to obtain prompt repayment for all but a few overdrafts. The reason for lending on a day-to-day basis with interest calculated in the same way is because most of a bank's funds are obtained from current accounts, also repayable on demand.

The term 'Other accounts' is used to describe loans which are not made directly to bank customers. Nearly all this type of lending is arranged in the inter-bank market. Main participants in this market are the clearing banks as principal lenders and other banks, mainly as borrowers but also as lenders to some extent. Most deals are arranged on a direct bank-to-bank basis but some are negotiated through deposit brokers. A great deal of money is lent overnight or for very short periods although there are some long-term loans. The lending is normally unsecured. The rates are higher than on money at call to the London Discount Market because of the lack of security and also because, unlike the discount houses, the borrowers do not have the Bank of England supporting them as 'lender of last resort'. The minimum loan is for £250,000. Although these 'market loans', as they are known, are included in the figures for 'Advances and other accounts', a separate note must be made in the annual report showing the figures due from customers, the placings of money with banks and loans to other non-customers.

In recent years the banks have increased the proportion of their medium-term structured lending. Personal loans, business development loans and farm development loans are examples of lending made at fixed rates of interest and for a fixed period of time. Banks have also lent for the purchase of professional practices over a period of years. Home mortgage loans to private customers for the purchase of residential property are seen as a logical extension to banking services. Home loans can be given for a period of twenty years, although the interest rate charged will vary in line with market conditions.

Figures published by Barclays Bank show that in 1981 Barclays Bank UK Ltd had 68 per cent of its loans repayable within one year, 19 per cent of its loans maturing in between one and five years, while 13 per cent of its loans were not due for repayment until after five years.

The interest charges on advances are higher than the income from investments. This is to allow for the illiquid nature of many of the advances made by a bank. The higher income to be obtained by lending money should never encourage the bank to sacrifice security for profitability. A risky lending can never be justified by charging higher than normal rates of interest. In all his dealings with borrowing customers a banker will remember that the security of the depositors' money is his first concern. If he does this the bank is unlikely to suffer the substantial losses made by institutions such as Crown Agents and First National Finance Corporation during the collapse of the property market in 1974. Similar concern for the safety of the depositors' money would have avoided the embarrassment caused to some banks by the well-publicised 're-scheduling' in 1982 and 1983 of debts owed by countries such as Argentine, Brazil, Mexico and Poland.

Although collateral security is often taken by a bank, the deposit of security does not turn a risky lending into a safe one. A bank never expects to realise its security and only takes security to safeguard the lending, in the event of unforeseen circumstances arising. In judging the merits of a loan, the bank looks firstly at the method by which the borrower will repay and, secondly, at the likelihood of this happening. A personal customer is judged on his creditworthiness and integrity. A company is assessed on the quality of its management. Both personal and business customers will be judged by their past borrowing records and their future prospects.

13 SUBSIDIARY COMPANIES

13.1 Amounts due from subsidiary companies

In addition to lending to its own customers and to discount houses and other financial institutions through the London money market, a bank will lend to its own subsidiary companies. A company is described as a subsidiary when more than 50 per cent of the share capital is owned by the parent company. Examples of subsidiary companies are Isle of Man Bank and Ulster Bank which are subsidiaries of National Westminster Bank. Bank of Scotland and Union Bank of Nigeria are associated companies of Barclays Bank because Barclays own less than 50 per cent of the shareholding in these two banks.

13.2 Investments in subsidiary companies

These investments are purchases by the bank of controlling interests in other financial groups. Lewis's Bank is a subsidiary of Lloyds Bank, Thomas Cook is a subsidiary of Midland, while Coutts and Co is a part of the National Westminster group. Valuation of these shares is extremely hard. There is no Stock Exchange quotation and each bank values its subsidiaries in a slightly different way. In some cases the shares are shown at cost, less amounts written off. In other balance sheets, the book value of the net tangible assets of the subsidiaries is shown. It is also permissible for a valuation of these unlisted investments to be at the discretion of the directors on the board of the parent company. With all three sorts of valuation there is likely to be a substantial hidden reserve because these trading subsidiaries could be sold at a high price, if disposed of as 'going concerns'.

14 TRADE INVESTMENTS

The banks have a number of joint undertakings in which they hold shares. National Westminster, Barclays, Lloyds and Williams and Glyn's own all the capital of Yorkshire Bank between them. Lloyds, Midland and National Westminster own equal parts of all the ordinary share capital of the Joint Credit Card Company, which runs the Access credit card. The Bankers Clearing House and Bankers Automated Clearing Services (BACS) are two of the jointly-owned investments of the London clearing bankers. In January 1982 the clearing banks made a joint purchase of International Commodities Clearing House, which acted as a clearing house for commodity futures and traded options. This company was a subsidiary of United Dominions Trust, whose hire purchase business was bought by the Trustee Savings Banks at the same time.

Finance for Industry and Agricultural Mortgage Corporation are two public companies where the majority of the shares are owned by the London clearing banks but some shares are also owned by the Bank of England and the Scottish clearing banks.

In addition to these holdings in British companies, the banks all have minority shareholdings in other banks abroad, apart from their own wholly-owned subsidiaries. Some of these investments, whether in the United Kingdom or overseas, would be very difficult to sell quickly and they are treated by the banks as long-term investments. Dividends are paid on all these trade investments, providing the banks with a return on the capital employed in this way. Because of the fixed nature of these investments it would be very unwise for the banks to use any of the customers' short-term deposits for the financing of these holdings. As a rough rule of thumb, the figure for fixed assets (in the form of investments in subsidiary companies, trade investments and premises and equipment) should not exceed the figure for shareholders' funds (ordinary capital and reserves).

15 PREMISES AND EQUIPMENT

The premises and equipment owned by the banks are usually shown in the balance sheets at fairly conservative figures. The basis of valuation is that of 'existing use' and no allowance is given for any potential development value. Banks aim to retain almost all their properties on a long-term basis but revaluations are carried out from time to time. Any surplus over book value shown on revaluation is always credited to reserves and never used to pay dividends to shareholders.

Occupying, as they do, prime sites in the high street of most towns, it could be argued that the banks would make a fortune by selling off their branches and moving to less accessible locations. However, it could also be claimed that if all the banks sold off all their high street branches at the same time, their offices would fetch very little because it would be difficult to put the premises to any other use.

Part 2: Payment and Collection of Cheques and Bills

6 *Bills of Exchange*

This document is an unconditional order in writing. It is signed by the drawer of the bill instructing the drawee to pay a fixed sum of money. The amount payable may be either on demand or at a fixed or determinable future time.

There need only be two parties, drawer and drawee, to a single bill of exchange which could look like this:

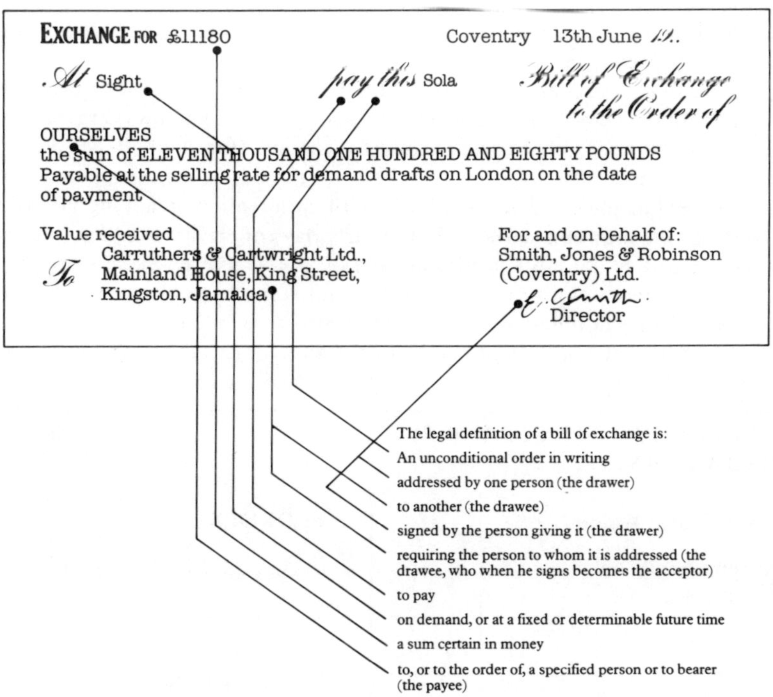

Smith, Jones & Robinson (Coventry) Ltd is the drawer of this bill while Carruthers & Cartwright Ltd is the drawee.

If instead of being drawn 'at sight', the bill had read 'Three months after date pay . . .', Carruthers & Cartwright would have been expected to write 'Accepted' across the bill followed by the firm's signature. The bill is then returned to Smith, Jones & Robinson for them to present, usually through their bankers or their bankers' agents, in three months' time. There are still only two parties to the bill, although the drawee has now become the acceptor. In some circumstances a bank can be asked to accept a bill on behalf of the drawee, in which case the accepting bank will be the acceptor.

With an accepted bill, payable three months after date, the drawer may need funds before the bill becomes due for payment. The drawer discounts the bill by selling it to his bank at less than face value. Before negotiation, the drawer is asked to endorse the bill by signing on the back. This endorsement transfers the legal title to the bank who then becomes the holder of the bill.

1 CHEQUES

Section 73 of the Bills of Exchange Act 1882 defined a cheque as a 'Bill of Exchange drawn on a banker payable on demand'. Neither the Bills of Exchange Act 1882 nor the Cheques Act 1957 define a banker in a satisfactory manner. The Banking Act 1979 defined a 'recognised bank' but exempted building societies, local authorities and credit unions from the provisions of the Banking Act 1979. It is not altogether clear if, for example, building societies are covered by the statutory protection given to bankers by the Cheques Act and the Bills of Exchange Act, now that some societies provide share account members with their own cheque books.

Unlike other bills of exchange, cheques cannot be payable at a fixed or determinable time in the future. They must be drawn in such a way that they are payable on presentation. There need only be two parties to a cheque. One would be the drawer, the other the drawee bank. Usually, however, there are three with the third party being the payee. This is because most cheques are drawn with the intention of making a transfer of a bank deposit to the drawer's creditor. In the early days of private banking, the issue of notes was regarded as the most profitable part of a bank's business and cheques were seldom used. The restrictions imposed on the joint stock banks prevented them from issuing notes and they popularised the use of the cheque as an efficient means of settling debts. By the 1840s, the majority of commercial transactions were settled in this way.

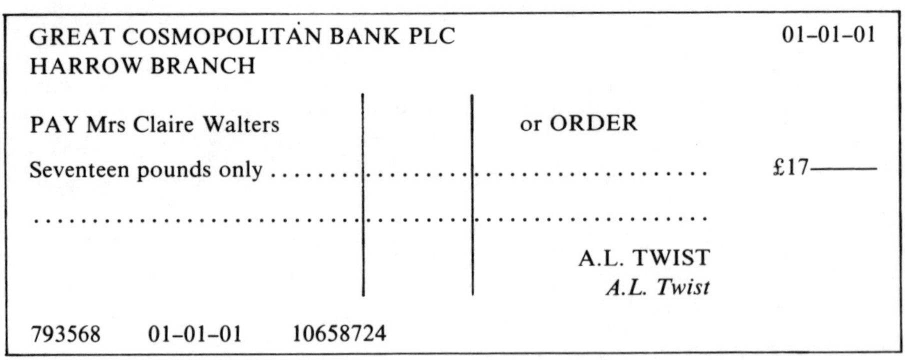

Figure 6.1

Figure 6.1 is an example of a crossed order cheque. The Great Cosmopolitan Bank is the paying bank because it is the bank on whom the cheque is drawn. Mrs Walters is the payee and the collecting bank would be the bank who received payment on her behalf. If instead of paying the cheque into her bank account, Mrs Walters wished to credit her account with the Nationwide Building Society, she would be asked to endorse the cheque on the back and the society could then pay it into their own bank account. This means the cheque has been negotiated by the payee.

2 METHODS OF PRESENTATION

The two lines across the cheque are known as a general crossing. The effect of this crossing on the cheque is that payment can only be made to a bank. Cheques crossed in this way have to be credited to a bank account, although not necessarily the account of the payee. While endorsement is required if the payee negotiates the cheque to a third party, no endorsement is needed if the cheque is credited to the payee's own bank account.

Crossed cheques cannot be cashed except in the following circumstances:

(a) They are presented by the drawer and accompanied by a cheque card.

(b) They are presented by the drawer or the drawer's known agent at the branch on which they are drawn.

(c) They are presented by the drawer or the drawer's known agent at a bank where a credit open arrangement has been made for the drawer.

An open cheque is one which does not have the two parallel lines which form a crossing. Contrary to popular belief, an open cheque cannot be cashed to anybody. If it is presented by the payee at the counter of the branch on which it is drawn, it can be cashed. In other circumstances, it is collected through normal channels by the collecting banker.

There are other forms of presentation which are known as special collections. These occur when a customer wishes to know the fate of a cheque very quickly. If it is a special presentation by hand it will be presented over the counter of the paying branch by a member of the collecting bank's staff. A more usual form of special collection is presentation by post. The cheque is sent direct by first class post from the collecting bank to the paying bank.

3 CHEQUE CLEARING

When the recipient of a cheque pays it into his own bank, it will be sent through the bankers clearing house to the bank on which it is drawn. A very simple drawing (Figure 6.2) will illustrate this. You should also refer back to Chapter 2 paragraph 6.

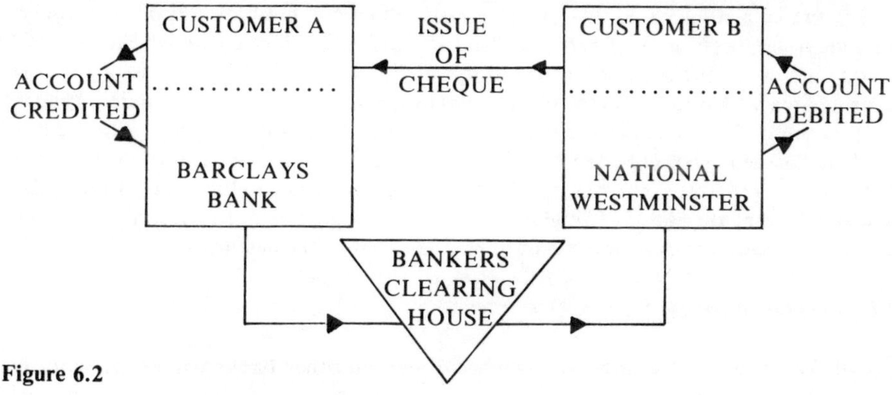

Figure 6.2

The most usual method of transmitting money is by issuing cheques in this way. Settlement between the banks takes place when customer B's account is debited. A transfer between the two banks will take place by adjusting the account which they have with the Bank of England. Barclays will be better off and National Westminster will be worse off after this cycle of transactions is completed.

Uncleared funds are very difficult for many private customers to understand. This arises when the bank gives immediate credit for a cheque paid into a customer's account. After the cheque is remitted by the collecting bank to the clearing house in London, it is sent to the drawee bank, who will not pay over the funds until it has been debited to their customer's account. This means that it may be between three and five days before a bank can be certain of payment for cheques they are collecting for customers. An even longer period elapses over a Bank Holiday, New Year, or Christmas period. When a bank allows a customer to draw cash against cheques for which the bank has not yet received payment, they are in the position of providing 'cash now' against 'cash in the future'. The provision of this instant credit is charged at normal rates of interest for overdrafts.

3.1 Town clearing

This special type of cheque clearing is restricted to branches within walking distance of the clearing house in Lombard Street. Only large cheques drawn on a town clearing branch and paid into another town clearing branch are cleared in this way.

During the course of the day the town clearing branches will extract the big cheques paid in which are drawn for collection on other town clearing branches. These cheques are machined and taken to the clearing house by 3.50 pm. At that time, the branch representative will collect any town clearing cheques drawn on them and bring them back to the branch for payment. Any cheques which the branch is unable to pay must be sent back to the clearing house by 4.45 pm.

The Stock Exchange, Lloyds and other main financial and commodity markets are situated in the 'town clearing' area. It follows from this that although the town clearing cheques are only a small fraction of the number of cheques drawn each day, their value is much greater than the cheques drawn in the remainder of Britain. The town clearing is based upon same day payment of large cheques and special presentations are not permitted in the town clearing area. Some banks, however, have special arrangements where branches outside the area can send cheques, drawn on a town clearing branch, for presentation through the collecting bank's head office.

It is the collecting banker's duty to send cheques for presentation by the quickest possible route. In the case of *Forman* v *Bank of England* (1902) a customer paid in a £500 cheque at Law Courts branch of the Bank of England. This branch was in the town clearing area at that time and the cheque was drawn by Norwich Union on their clearing bank account. It was payable either in Norwich or in Lombard Street. The Bank of England passed this cheque through what was then the 'country clearing' and dishonoured a cheque of their customer's which was presented to them the following day. It was held that the Bank of England had been negligent in not collecting the cheque through the town clearing and it had to pay damages to the customer.

3.2 General clearing

All cheques paid in at branches which are drawn on other banks will be sent through 'general clearing' section at the bankers clearing house. The only exception to this rule is the clearance of large town clearing cheques paid in at other town clearing branches.

Cheques which are drawn on the paying bank and paid in at branches of the same bank are not sent to the bankers clearing house. Instead of this, they are sent to the clearing department of their own bank where the cheques are sorted into batches for forwarding to the drawee bank. Some banks have systems whereby cheques cashed over the counter are not sent to their Clearing Department at all but are 'truncated'. This means that the cashed cheque is retained at the branch which paid out the money but details of the transaction are sent over the computer terminal to the bank's computer centre.

All cheques, apart from truncated cheques, are collected from the branches in the evening. This business day is known as 'day 1'. Security vans are used for this purpose and the cheques are delivered to the bank's own clearing department where cheques drawn on that bank are removed. Cheques drawn on other banks are then delivered to the bankers clearing house between 9 am and 11.15 am on day 2. These cheques are automatically sorted and computer figures are agreed between the banks. Outward delivery of the cheques takes place in the evening and security vans are used for this purpose. These same vans also pick up (from the bank's clearing department) cheques drawn on their own bank which have been credited at other branches of the same bank.

The security vans travel during the night so that all the incoming clearing is ready for the branch's staff on the morning of day 3. These cheques are then paid, if in order, and debited to the customers' accounts. Any unpaid cheques have to be returned the same day by first class post to the collecting bank. If, through inadvertence, a cheque is missed which should have been returned, the paying bank can telephone the details of this 'late return' to the collecting bank before noon on day 4.

3.3 Bank giro credit clearing

This is similar to the general clearing. It is concerned with the transfer of credits paid in at bank offices other than the account-holding branch. Through the bank giro system, which started in 1960, it is possible to pay in at any branch for the credit of an account at any other bank or branch. In some circumstances, a charge may be made to non-customers who tender third party credits.

The sorting of bank giro credits is organised by the banks on the same lines as the cheque clearing. They are collected by security van at the same time as the outward cheque clearing. On arrival at the bank's clearing department, credits for the bank's own branches are extracted and sorted separately, while the credits for other banks are delivered to the banker's clearing house.

Inward bank giro credits from other banks are picked up from the banker's clearing house in the afternoon and, together with credits from the bank's own branches, delivered by security van to the recipient branches for processing on the following day.

A number of banks now have arrangements whereby details of bank giro credits are sent over their computer networks. This saves the expense and inconvenience of despatching paper all over the country.

3.4 Bankers Automated Clearing Services Limited

The banks have become concerned at the possibility of being overwhelmed by mountains of paper involved in the transfers of bank deposits. In April 1968 they set up the Inter-

Bank Computer Bureau to handle electronic transfers. This has since been reorganised as Bankers Automated Clearing Services Limited (BACS) with the 'Big Four' each owning 24 per cent of the share capital and Williams & Glyn's owning 3 per cent. Other banks such as the Co-operative Bank and the Bank of England are associate banks.

BACS is primarily used for standing order payments, direct debits and salary payments. BACS uses magnetic tapes, cassettes and floppy discs in place of the details which were formerly shown on vouchers. The banks prepare the magnetic tapes for processing on the BACS computer while some non-bank customers who have direct access to BACS use magnetic tapes, discs or cassettes.

A new system of settling trade bills was introduced a few years ago with the establishment of the purchase ledger settlement procedure. Companies can prepare tapes well in advance, send them to BACS, together with instructions for the purchaser's account and the suppliers' accounts to be debited and credited on the same day. The date of settlement is laid down in advance by the purchaser.

3.5 Settlement of clearing transactions

Settlement of all clearing house transactions takes place at 4.45 pm each afternoon of a full working day. The transactions include:

(a) Town clearing totals for that day.
(b) General clearing totals for cheques exchanged on previous day.
(c) Bank giro credit clearing totals for credits exchanged on previous day.
(d) BACS totals for electronic items processed on the previous day.

The payments due to all other banks are set-off against payments receivable from all other banks. The net figures are agreed by inspectors in the clearing house and the net figures are transferred to or from the accounts which the clearing banks have at the Bank of England under 'bankers deposits'.

4 PAYMENT OF CHEQUES

In order to debit a customer's account with a cheque drawn by the customer, the bank must pay 'in due course'. Section 59 Bills of Exchange Act 1882 defines payment in due course as payment to the holder in good faith and without notice that the holder's title is defective. When cheques are paid over by the customer to third parties, especially when they are passed on to someone else after endorsement by the payee, this section could present paying banks with a problem.

Fortunately statutory protection is given to the paying bank by Section 60 Bills of Exchange Act 1882 if the cheque is paid over the counter and by Section 80 of the same Act if the cheque is presented through the clearing or by special presentation. In order to get the protection of Section 60 the banker must act:

(a) in good faith;
(b) in the ordinary course of business.

To act in good faith means to behave honestly. There have been no actions against paying bankers where bad faith has been alleged.

'In the ordinary course of business' is a more difficult phrase to describe. The bank would obtain statutory protection if a cheque was paid over the bank's counter during normal business hours. Protection might be lost if a member of the bank staff cashed a cheque off bank premises.

What constitutes normal business hours was discussed in the case of *Baines* v *National Provincial Bank Ltd* (1927). In that case a bookmaker issued a cheque just before 3 pm, which was the normal closing time in 1927. The payee entered the bank a few seconds before 3 pm. There were a number of people on the public space being attended to and the payee could not cash the cheque until five minutes after closing time.

The following morning the customer's son arrived at opening time with an authority to stop payment of the cheque. When the customer was told that the cheque had already been paid he sued the bank, claiming that as the cheque had been paid after its advertised closing time it had no right to debit his account. The judge held that the bank was entitled to a reasonable margin of time after closing to complete the transactions of those present in the branch.

The majority of cheques cashed over the bank counters will be one of three types:

(a) Open cheques (those which have no crossing).
(b) Uncrossed cheques. These are cheques which were previously crossed but which have been opened by the drawer writing 'Pay cash' inside the crossing and signing below these two words.
(c) Crossed cheques presented by the drawer.

Open cheques may be presented by strangers but uncrossed cheques should only be presented by the drawer's known agent or someone authorised to cash the drawer's cheque. The banker is not called upon to identify people who present open cheques. Provided the circumstances are not suspicious and the payee's endorsement appears to be in order, the bank will be protected by Section 60 against any claim that the person who was paid was not the holder in due course.

4.1 Section 80 Bills of Exchange Act 1882

This is the statutory protection given to a banker who pays a crossed cheque sent through the clearings or by special presentation. A cheque which comes to the paying bank through either of these routes must be paid

(a) in good faith;
(b) without negligence;

for the paying bank to get statutory protection.

Section 1 Cheques Act 1957 gives protection to bankers paying unendorsed or irregularly endorsed cheques. Although it appears to supersede Sections 60 and 80 of the Bills of Exchange Act 1882 these two sections were not repealed and paying banks still rely on them for statutory protection.

How does a paying bank have to behave in order to avoid the charge of acting 'without negligence'? These are the procedures that must be followed if a charge of negligence is to be avoided.

The paying cashier must make the following checks:

(a) Is the signature that of the customer?
(b) Do the words and figures agree?
(c) Has the drawer countermanded payment?
(d) Is the cheque post-dated?
(e) Is the cheque more than six months old?
(f) Has the cheque been drawn on the branch?
(g) Is there only one banker's crossing on the cheque?
(h) Has the cheque been mutilated?
(i) Is the name of the payee clear? Any material alterations?
(j) Where a receipt or endorsement is required, is the endorsement in order?

Let us examine these checks in turn. A cheque is a special form of bill of exchange. For any bill of exchange to be complete it must be signed by the drawer. It follows from this that if the signature on the cheque is not that of the customer, or someone authorised to sign for the customer, the bank has no right to debit the customer's account.

4.1.1 Paying banker

Section 9 (sub-section 2) Bills of Exchange Act 1882 states that where the sum payable is expressed in words and also in figures, and there is a discrepancy between the two, the sum denoted by the words is the amount payable. Bankers tend not to rely on this section in practice. The paying cashier will examine the cheque and, if there is a discrepancy, will pay the smaller sum, provided that the difference is small. If the difference is large, it is customary to return the cheque with the answer 'words and figures differ'. Sometimes the collecting bank will attach a slip stating the amount claimed by them and, provided this is the smaller sum, the paying bank will honour the cheque as a courtesy to the collecting bank.

Whether the cheque is presented through the clearing, by means of a special collection, or over the counter, the alert cashier should know if there is a 'stop' recorded on that customer's account. If the drawer countermands payment of a cheque, the details are recorded on computer file. Should this cheque be presented through the clearing, the computer print-out details will show a possible 'stop'. Although this is helpful, it does not take away the initial responsibility from the paying cashier. The stop card must be examined especially when cheques are presented by post or over the counter. When instructions to countermand payment are received from the customer, the day's clearing must be examined for a possible stop. Even when details are passed over the computer link to the computer centre, the data may be rejected or incorrect details passed over the computer terminal. The paying cashier must be aware of all the most recent stops and not rely on the computer to decide which cheques are to be paid. The courts are very hard on banks where countermanded cheques are paid as the case of *Burnett* v *Westminster Bank Ltd* (1965) shows. The customer had accounts at Bromley and Borough branches of the bank. He issued a cheque from his Borough cheque book but altered the name of the branch to Bromley. Shortly afterwards he telephoned Bromley to countermand payment and confirmed the stop in writing to Bromley branch. The magnetic ink characters on the cheque were read by the computer in the bank's clearing department and the cheque was sent to Borough branch as part of their in-clearing. Borough branch paid the cheque and the bank were held liable because they had not complied with instructions to stop the cheque.

4.1.2 Post-dated and stale cheques

A cheque is a bill of exchange, drawn on a banker, payable on demand. Because an instruction to pay a sum of money in the future is not payable on demand, a cheque form which is completed with a future date is not strictly speaking a cheque at all. Under no circumstances can a post-dated cheque be honoured. The customer may well have completed it in this fashion deliberately to allow time to meet his commitments. If he is not satisfied with the goods supplied, he may place a stop on the cheque after the post-dated cheque is issued.

Cheques do not become overdue because they are not presented to the paying bank, or handed to a collecting bank, on the day they are issued. While the holder of a cheque is expected to present it within a reasonable time, in practice, bankers return cheques which are six months or more old. The answer given is 'out of date' and the payee is expected to ask the drawer to alter the cheque or issue a fresh one .

Problems are often caused at the beginning of a new year. Many customers continue to use the old calendar year when completing cheques for some time after the start of the new year. In practice, bankers honour small cheques which are dated for the previous January provided they are otherwise in order. This concession only applies in the first month and is confined to trustworthy customers. If there is an element of doubt as to when the cheque was issued, reference can always be made to the cheque book register. Examination of this register will show when the cheque book was issued.

Additional complications arise where cheques are issued backed by a cheque card. As the bank has guaranteed payment of cheques backed by a cheque card, which are drawn before the expiry date of the card, it is difficult to return post-dated or out-of-date cheques backed by a cheque card. In a similar way customers must be advised that when they issue a cheque and present a cheque card to the shopkeeper as a guarantee of payment, the cheque must be paid. The instructions contained in the cheque cannot be countermanded.

4.1.3 Cheques to be drawn on the branch

In these days of computerised banking, it may seem superfluous to stress that the drawee bank's address must be scrutinised. After all, if the drawer has no account, who is the bank to debit? As the unfortunate case of *Burnett* v *Westminster Bank* (1965) showed, automatic sorting of cheques does not necessarily get the cheques to the right branch.

A cheque can be drawn on any material and, provided the instructions are in writing, the cheque is legally admissible. Customers are not obliged to draw cheques on the standard forms issued by the bank and many shops, clubs or casinos keep blank cheque forms for customers to complete.

These 'club' forms as they are known, together with cheques which are mutilated, altered in any way, or wrongly encoded, will be separated from the remainder of the in-clearing and sent to the paying branch in a special bundle. Computer rejections of various sorts may account for up to 7 per cent of the total of cheques presented. It is especially vital that these computer rejections should be scrutinised with the same degree of care as the scrutiny given to cheques specially presented by post or over the counter.

A customer who is in the habit of drawing non-standard cheques should be asked politely to use the normal cheque forms. If he persists in the practice of using cheques which are not printed by the bank, it is worth considering passing a special charge to the customer's account.

4.1.4 Banker's crossing

As has been pointed out previously, a crossed cheque will be transversed by two parallel lines. Sometimes the words 'and company' or a form of abbreviation of these two words is placed between the two lines. This is a very old practice and relates to the days when the holder of the cheque would add the name of his own bank. By doing so the holder crossed the cheque specially. The words 'and company' no longer have any real significance as the practice of writing the banker's name on the front of the cheque has long since fallen into disuse.

Bankers still follow the practice of crossing cheques specially to themselves. Whether the cheque is an open one (a cheque without a crossing) or a crossed cheque (one with two parallel transverse lines on the front), a bank which has a cheque drawn on another bank or branch handed to it for collection will cross the cheque specially. This is done by marking the front of the cheque with the bank's crossing stamp.

Section 79 (sub-section 1) of the Bills of Exchange Act, 1882 states that where a cheque is crossed specially to more than one banker, except when crossed to an agent for collection being a banker, the banker on whom it is drawn shall refuse payment. Cheques which are crossed by a non-clearing bank, before being handed to a clearing bank for collection, are always accepted by the paying banker. If a cheque has to be returned because of lack of funds or through a technical irregularity, it is customary to post the cheque direct to the non-clearing bank shown on the crossing but to send a claim for unpaid debit, via the outward remittances, to the clearing agent.

An example of a cheque which could be crossed by two clearing banks is that of a cheque which has been previously unpaid. If a shop manager pays in a cheque for his company's account he might well use the bank giro credit clearing. As a chain store manager, he might prefer the greater convenience and security of using a nearby bank branch, even if it is one of the branches of a bank where his company has no account. The collecting bank will stamp their own special crossing on the front of the cheque. On the cheque being returned unpaid the manager might be instructed to forward it to his head office, who will represent the cheque by paying it into the bank where the company's account is domiciled. This bank will stamp their own crossing on the cheque and when it reaches the paying banker for the second time, it should be returned with the answer 'crossed by two bankers'. Sometimes the account holding bank will provide an indemnity to the paying banker. It is customary to rely on this indemnity, as a matter of banking courtesy, and the cheque will be paid provided funds are available and there are no technical irregularities.

When cheques are paid into building societies or post offices, they will be specially crossed by these organisations before they are paid into their local clearing bank branches for collection. The collecting bank will also place their special crossing on the front of the cheque. The drawee bank will not be liable for negligence if they ignore the crossing of the non-bank deposit taker. For the purposes of Section 79 of the Bills of Exchange Act 1882, building societies and post offices are not regarded as bankers. In the event of a paying bank wishing to return a cheque crossed in this way, both the unpaid cheque and the debit claim will be sent direct to the clearing agent.

4.1.5 Mutilated cheques

In the absence of evidence to the contrary, the paying banker must assume that a cheque which has been torn, cut or otherwise defaced has been cancelled by the drawer. The cheque must be returned to the collecting bank with the answer 'mutilated cheque'.

While there may be a reasonable explanation for the mutilation, it is also possible that the cheque was torn by the drawer, or even the payee, before being thrown in the waste paper basket. It could be extracted later by a thief who could try to pass the cheque as his own.

Accidents do happen. Even in banks it has been known for cheques to be torn when opening the morning's post. In those circumstances, an authorised officer of the bank will write on the back of the cheque 'accidentally torn by us' and then append his 'per procuration' signature on behalf of the bank.

Should the payee of the cheque mutilate it in a similar fashion, this customer will be asked to sign a statement of the circumstances on the back of the cheque. The authorised official of the bank will then write 'statement of mutilation confirmed' followed by his own 'per procuration' signature.

In both those circumstances, it is customary for the paying bank to follow normal practice and pay the cheque. The 'per procuration' signature is an indication that the official is acting as an agent of the collecting bank who will indemnify the paying banker against any possible claim.

4.1.6 Payee's name

Except in very rare circumstances, it is no longer necessary for paying cashiers to concern themselves with endorsements to cheques. Since the passing of the Cheques Act 1957 only a small percentage of cheques are endorsed before being paid into an account. Those which require endorsement are those paid into an account other than that of the payee, but this is of no concern to the paying banker.

The paying cashier is expected, however, to notice any material alteration to cheques. If these are confirmed by the drawer's signature, they can be paid. Otherwise, they must be returned with the answer 'alteration requires confirmation'.

The drawer of the cheque is expected to take precautions to prevent fraud. In the *Joachimson* v *Swiss Bank Corporation* (1921) case, the judge laid down that the customer undertakes to exercise reasonable care, so as not to mislead the bank or to facilitate forgery. While the date, the amount in words and the amount in figures should be checked for obvious alterations, great care should be taken in examining the payee's name.

In the case of *Slingsby and others* v *The District Bank Ltd* (1931) a cheque was drawn in favour of John Prust and Co, a firm of stockbrokers. It was given to the drawer's solicitor to forward to the stockbrokers in order to purchase securities. The solicitor added the name of his firm in different handwriting, so that the payee's name now read 'John Prust & Co per Cumberbirch and Potts'. The solicitor then endorsed the cheque and paid it into the account of a finance company to whom he owed money. When the fraud was discovered, the drawer sued the paying bank for negligence and won the case.

4.1.7 Receipt or endorsement required

There are very few instances where the payee's endorsement to a cheque is required. One example of this type of cheque is one issued by an insurance company to a policy holder receiving the proceeds of a maturing endowment policy. If the payee is intended to endorse the cheque by way of receipt, a bold outline letter 'R' must be printed on the front of the cheque. It must be placed as close to the £ sign as it is possible to print it. A receipt form will be printed on the back for the payee to sign and this will bear a note to the effect that the payee's signature will be both a receipt and endorsement.

When a cheque of this type is passed to the paying banker, the cashier or other official responsible for examining the in-clearing will check to see if the receipt form has been signed. If the payee's signature has been omitted, the cheque is returned 'payee's discharge required'. Most payees will complete the receipt form. It is necessary with these cheques to examine the endorsement. Examples of regular and irregular endorsements are shown in the Institute of Bankers *Questions on Banking Practice*. When a banker is not satisfied that the payee's endorsement is in accordance with normal practice, it is usual to return the cheque with the answer 'endorsement requires confirmation'.

There are two other examples of instruments where the paying cashier must be satisfied with the endorsements. When normal commercial bills of exchange are presented for payment, either in the town clearing, general clearing or by special presentation, the payee's endorsement is required and the paying cashier must be satisfied that it is in the correct form. While Section 1 of the Cheques Act 1957 protects bankers paying unendorsed or irregularly endorsed cheques, this statutory protection only applies to cheques. Trade bills, which are drawn on commercial concerns other than banks, still require endorsement.

In a similar way, it is the responsibility of the paying cashier, who is asked to cash a travellers cheque, to ensure that the endorsement is signed in his presence and that this endorsement is similar to the original signature.

4.2 Check for funds

The experienced cashier will have a good knowledge of those accounts which are less than creditworthy. This will be reinforced by a 'black list' of customers whose cheques should be referred. The composition of this list will change from time to time. Some customers will improve, while others will transfer their accounts elsewhere. The usefulness of the 'black list' as a visual aid is that the names can be seen at a glance and careful pruning should take place from time to time.

While the majority of the clearing will be accepted on the computer, there will be a residue which is rejected. The rejected items should be carefully examined and any doubtful cheques put on one side for reference to one of the bank's lending officers. The same procedure should be followed with special presentations and cheques cashed over the counter. If there is any element of doubt, put through an enquiry on the computer link and ask for the cleared balance. In many banks there is a system of 'floor limits'. This refers to the practice of automatically asking for balances when a customer asks to cash a cheque over a stipulated figure. The cheque and balance is then shown to a lending officer. The same process takes place with the in-clearing. Any cheques over a laid-down limit, which is larger than for cashed cheques, are referred to a lending officer for examination. Even for cheques below these two limits, the prudent cashier will refer items where there is any element of doubt.

7 *Collecting Banker*

Statutory protection is now given to the collecting bank by Section 4 Cheques Act 1957. Unlike Section 1 Cheques Act 1957, which did not repeal Sections 60 and 80 Bills of Exchange Act 1882, Section 4 replaced a great deal of previous legislation.

It is necessary to give the collecting banker protection against claims that the banker's customer has a defective title or no title. If this was not available, banks could be liable to the true owners of cheques which had been wrongfully credited to another account. In the great majority of transactions the bank will collect cheques on its own behalf because they will have already credited the customer's account before clearance. Section 4 Cheques Act 1957 still provides protection and the bank is not obliged to concern itself with the absence of an endorsement or the irregularity of any endorsement.

This section applies not only to cheques but also to bankers drafts and paymaster general warrants. The protection given is not only against absence of or irregular endorsement but also against absence of a good title.

In order to get protection the bank must comply with three conditions. Collection must be:

(a) for a customer;
(b) in good faith;
(c) without negligence.

Who is a customer? Is a person who cashes cheques for a third party a customer? Would changing notes for coins constitute a person a customer? The answer to these questions is that a customer is a person from whom a bank will accept funds for the purpose of allowing cheques to be drawn against them. In the case of *Commissioners of Taxation* v *English, Scottish and Australian Bank* (1920) it was laid down that a person, whose money was accepted by a bank on the footing that they would honour cheques to the extent of his credit, was a customer, irrespective of whether the connection was of long or short standing. While this clearly indicates that a person who has a current account is a customer, what of a person who opens a deposit account with a bank? The conclusion seems to be that the prudent banker will not accept cheques for a deposit account unless the same precautions, such as asking for references, are taken when the deposit account is opened as would be taken when a current account is opened.

A banker's good faith is taken for granted and there have been no cases involving the collection of cheques where bad faith has been alleged.

1 NEGLIGENCE

Conversion refers to the transfer of property to someone who is not the rightful owner. If a bank collects a cheque for someone who is not the true owner, this is innocent conversion which is neither premeditated nor fraudulent. Section 4, Cheques Act 1957 will protect the bank against claims provided they do not act negligently. Most successful claims for conversion are based on negligence by the banker. It is vital, therefore, that all cheques presented for collection, whether paid in over the counter or received by post, are examined to see if further enquiries concerning ownership need to be made.

A limited company is a separate legal entity apart from its directors. The correct place for limited company cheques is the company's bank account, so that the company's assets are available to pay its creditors. In the case of *A L Underwood Ltd* v *Bank of Liverpool and Martins Ltd* (1924) the bank was found guilty of conversion. They had allowed the sole director of a limited company to credit his private account with cheques in favour of the company. The bank would have obtained statutory protection but lost it through its negligence in failing to make enquiries. Normal banking practice is to accept limited company cheques for the credit of the account of that limited company only. The bank would only vary this procedure in exceptional circumstances and only then after careful enquiries had been made.

The same principle should be adopted when collecting cheques which are signed by a customer in his capacity as an agent. The case of *Midland Bank Ltd* v *Reckitt and others* (1933) shows the degree of care required. In this case Sir Harold Reckitt, a customer of Barclays Bank, gave his solicitor, a customer of Midland Bank, a power of attorney to use during Sir Harold's absence abroad. By virtue of the authority contained in this document, the solicitor drew fifteen cheques, for a total of nearly £18,000, and credited them to his private account at the Midland Bank, who had been pressing for a reduction in his personal overdraft. These cheques were signed 'Harold G Reckitt by Terrington his attorney'.

The bank were regarded as negligent in not making enquiries concerning their customer's power to pay his principal's funds into the customer's private account. It was felt that the bank should have asked to see the power of attorney before crediting the cheques to the solicitor's account and damages were awarded against Midland Bank.

Cheques payable to customers as agents should have careful scrutiny. If cheques are made out to a customer as agent, they should not be credited to the customer's private account without extensive enquiries being made. The bank was held to be negligent in *Marquess of Bute* v *Barclays Bank Ltd* (1954) and lost the statutory protection which it was otherwise entitled to as a collecting bank. A manager of three sheep farms, owned by the Marquess of Bute, applied for the government's hill farming subsidy. Three months later he left his job and moved from Scotland to Lancashire. Six months after this, the warrants for the subsidy were redirected by the Post Office to his Lancashire address. They were made out D McGaw (for the Marquess of Bute). With these government warrants, McGaw opened an account at Barclays Bank, Barnsley.

Although the bank claimed statutory protection against conversion, Barclays were regarded as negligent in crediting Scottish Department of Agriculture warrants for hill-sheep subsidies, made out to McGaw as agent, to McGaw's private account. The judge in this case felt that it was an elementary banking practice not to credit a personal account in such circumstances without any enquiry.

2 COLLECTING THIRD PARTY CHEQUES

In the majority of cases, the bank is in no danger in collecting a third party cheque, provided it appears to have been properly endorsed by the payee. A third party cheque is one where there is another party involved apart from the drawer and payee. If Tom Jones draws a cheque in favour of Joseph Andrews and the cheque is endorsed by Joseph Andrews, the bank can accept it for the credit of Henry Fielding. Even if Henry Fielding has obtained it dishonestly, the bank is not negligent.

Different principles apply when collecting cheques in favour of business firms and placing them to the credit of other accounts. Enquiries must be made if an individual wishes to credit his private account with cheques payable to trading concerns. The case of *A L Underwood Ltd* v *Bank of Liverpool and Martins Ltd* (1924) established this principle in connection with limited companies. The same rules apply with partnerships or even sole traders.

Motor Traders Guarantee Corporation Ltd v *Midland Bank Ltd* (1937) was a case where the bank was regarded as negligent. The company was persuaded by a car dealer to issue a cheque in favour of a firm called Welsh and Co for the purpose of completing a hire-purchase deal. The car trader forged the endorsement of Welsh and Co and paid the cheque into his private account. Although the cashier asked about the underlying transaction, the judge in this case said that insufficient enquiry had been made. The bank had to refund the money to Motor Traders Guarantee Corporation Ltd.

Baker v *Barclays Bank Ltd* (1955) was another case where the bank was found guilty of conversion because insufficient enquiries had been made. Baker was a partner in a confectionery business which owned two shops. The partnership account was with Midland Bank. Nine cheques, in favour of the confectionery business, were endorsed by Baker's partner and paid into the account of a third person at Barclays Bank. When the manager of Barclays asked his customer for an explanation he was told that there was only one partner, the one who had endorsed the business cheques. He was also told that his customer was owed money by that partner and that the customer was helping as a financial adviser prior to going into partnership in the business.

The bank was found to be negligent in not making further enquiries. The claim for damages for conversion of the cheques was successful but as the partnership cheques had been appropriated by the fraudulent partner and paid into his accomplice's account, damages were reduced to half the amount claimed. Although Baker's partner was in no position to sue the bank, this did not prevent Baker suing in respect of his own interest.

Another interesting case is that of *Guardians of St John's Hampstead* v *Barclays Bank Ltd* (1923): a private account was opened with a deposit of cash by a man who called himself 'Stewart'. The reference taken up by the bank subsequently proved to be a forgery. In the meantime, two payment orders for £416, in favour of D Stewart and Company, were endorsed by 'Stewart' and paid into the private account. The address of D Stewart and Company, given in the telephone directory, was different from the address given when the account was opened at Barclays. The funds were drawn out shortly afterwards and the customer disappeared. It was subsequently found that the payment orders had been stolen by a temporary employee of the Guardians of St John's. Although the bank was found guilty of wrongful and negligent conversion on the grounds that they had made insufficient enquiry to establish 'Stewart's' identity, acceptance of large business cheques for a private account was also stated to be out of the ordinary course of business.

The rule illustrated by these cases is that business cheques should not be credited to private accounts unless very careful enquiries are made first. A cashier who has any doubts on the matter should always refer the transaction to a lending officer of his bank so that further investigation can be made.

3 ENDORSEMENT OF CHEQUES

It might be thought that these cases concerning negligence would involve careful checking of endorsement of cheques handed in for collection. This is not the conclusion to draw. Section 2 Cheques Act 1957 states that where a bank is handed a cheque for collection by the holder, the bank does not lose any rights because the holder has not endorsed the cheque. The holder does not need to be a customer of the bank. Provided that the drawer's signature has not been forged or the payee's endorsement forged, the holder has a good title which can be passed on to the bank. Collecting banks' cashiers should still look at the payees' names of cheques paid in but it is no longer necessary to ask for endorsement of cheques credited in the following ways:

(a) Paid in for the account of the payee.

(b) Cheques in favour of a sole payee credited to a joint or partnership account on which the sole payee can sign cheques, either solely or jointly.

(c) Cheques collected on behalf of non-clearing banks, licensed deposit takers, post offices, or building societies. It is assumed that the bank would have recourse against the other institution in the event of a cheque being returned unpaid.

It is necessary to ask for endorsement in the following circumstances:

(a) Cheques in favour of joint payees credited to a sole account.

(b) Cheques cashed over the counter. In the majority of cases banks will waive this requirement when they are cashing the customer's own cheques or paying out to the customer's known agent. Travellers cheques must still be endorsed before encashment, however, and third party cheques exchanged at the counter must still be endorsed by the customer before cash is handed over.

(c) Where some form of receipt is printed on the front or back of the cheque or warrant, this should be completed before being credited to the account.

(d) Any cheques payable overseas must be endorsed before acceptance for collection. The Cheques Act 1957 only applies to Great Britain and Northern Ireland although the Republic of Ireland has very similar legislation.

(e) Bills of exchange, other than cheques, require endorsement before being taken for collection or discounting.

(f) Cheques which have been negotiated. In these instances the endorsement of the payee and any subsequent endorsee is required. It is not essential to insist on the endorsement of the customer whose account is being credited although this is preferable.

At one time it was believed that the statutory protection given by Section 2 Cheques Act 1957 only applied if the cheque was credited to the account of the payee. The judges in the case of *Westminster Bank Ltd* v *Zang* (1966) said that, if a bank is collecting for a holder, they have the same rights under Section 2 in respect of an unendorsed cheque as they have with an endorsed one. It follows from this, that if a negotiated cheque is endorsed by the payee, further endorsement is not obligatory. The prudent cashier, however, will write the customer's name or account number on the back of the cheque before passing it forward.

4 ACCOUNT PAYEE

Cheques are sometimes issued with the words 'Account payee' or 'A/c payee' written or printed between the two lines of the crossing. These words have no legal significance because they are not mentioned anywhere in either the Bills of Exchange Act 1882 or the Cheques Act 1957. Addition of these words does not affect the negotiability of the cheque. The payee is not prevented by the addition of these words from transferring the cheque to a third party. Are there any problems, therefore, in collecting cheques crossed in this way?

The difficulty in collecting this type of cheque is that the crossing is an instruction given not to the paying bank but to the collecting bank. Care should therefore be exercised in accepting cheques crossed 'Account payee'. If the collecting banker credits the account of the named payee, he will be protected by Section 4 Cheques Act 1957. While there is no legal bar to a bank collecting a cheque, crossed in this way, for someone other than the named payee, there is a possibility of the bank losing the protection of Section 4 Cheques Act 1957 on the grounds of negligence. With customers of undoubted integrity and creditworthiness, the risk is very small and the bank would almost certainly oblige the customers, after enquiries had been made.

In the two law cases of *Bevan* v *National Bank* (1906) and *House Property Co of London Ltd* v *The London County and Westminster Bank Ltd* (1915), the respective banks were found to be negligent in accepting 'account payee' cheques for third parties without enquiry. Damages for conversion were awarded against the banks in both cases. In the House Property Co of London Ltd case, even the fact that the cheque was credited by the bank to the account of a solicitor customer did not enable them to escape liability.

5 'NOT NEGOTIABLE' CROSSING

When any instrument such as a bank note, bill of exchange or bearer bond is said to be negotiable it means that it is transferable with a minimum of formality and the transferee obtains the full legal title. Provided value has been given, the transferee's title is not affected by any defect in the title of the transferor. By custom cheques have always been negotiable, allowing the holder to sue in his own name. This principle of negotiability was preserved by the Bills of Exchange Act 1882, which went to great lengths to give any person who took a cheque honestly the right to claim against the drawer of the cheque.

What then is the significance of the words 'not negotiable' written between the two lines of the crossing on a cheque? Unlike 'Account payee' the words 'not negotiable' are recognised in the Bills of Exchange Act 1882. Section 81 of that act states:

> Where a person takes a crossed cheque which bears on it the words 'not negotiable', he shall not have and shall not be capable of giving a better title to the cheque than that which the person from whom he took it had.

This does not prevent a bank collecting a 'not negotiable' cheque even if the bank's customer is not the payee. A collecting banker is protected by Section 4 Cheques Act 1957 when collecting a cheque for a customer even when crediting a cheque crossed 'not negotiable' to an account other than the payee. It is necessary to ask for an endorsement in the circumstances outlined earlier.

Statutory protection is only given to a banker collecting a 'not negotiable' cheque for a customer. Different rules apply where a cheque crossed 'not negotiable' is cashed. The bank cannot obtain a better title than the person for whom they cash the cheque and, if the person who cashes it has obtained the cheque by fraud, the bank could be liable for conversion to the true owner.

In the *Great Western Railway* v *London and County Bank* (1901) case, a poor law overseer fraudulently obtained a cheque from the railway in payment of their poor rate. This overseer did not have a bank account but had been in the habit of cashing rates cheques at the bank for several years. The railway cheque was crossed 'not negotiable'. The bank was forced to refund the money to the Great Western Railway. They could not claim to be a holder for value because the 'not negotiable' crossing prevented the bank obtaining a better title than the person for whom they cashed it. The overseer had not given value for the cheque and so was unable to pass any title to the bank.

6 CHEQUES CROSSED BY ANOTHER BANK

The effect of Section 79 of the Bills of Exchange Act 1882 has already been mentioned in the section on bankers' crossings. This section prevents a cheque which is crossed by two different bankers being honoured by the paying banker, although it is customary for payment to be made if the back of the cheque is stamped with a banker's indemnity. If a customer of another bank asks you to collect a cheque for them, which has already been crossed by the other bank, it is preferable to ask them to pay it into or post it to their own bank. Should one of your own customers present a cheque for the credit of their account which has already been crossed by another bank, the customary indemnity should be signed by an official of your bank before it is sent off to the clearing house. This frequently occurs when a chain of shops banks with you. The local shop managers will pay in their shop takings at the nearest bank branch, which will often be an office of your competitors. The other banks will collect cheques for your customer's account but any cheques returned because of technical irregularities will bear the other bank's crossing. After the shop managers have forwarded the returned cheques to their head office for rectification, they will be paid into your bank and, at that time, an indemnity will be given by you to the paying banker.

In a few cases the drawer of the cheque will write the name of the bank across the face of the cheque as a special crossing. This is an instruction which the collecting bank ignores at its peril. A cheque which the drawer has crossed 'Royal Bank of Scotland' should only be paid into a branch of the Royal Bank of Scotland. If the payee is a customer of another bank, he should be advised to request the drawer to cancel or amend the crossing.

8 Bank as Holder in Due Course

Section 29 of the Bills of Exchange Act 1882 defines a holder in due course as a holder who has taken a bill (e.g. a cheque) in good faith and for value and, when the bill was negotiated, had no notice of any defect in title. This is an extremely valuable section for any banker or any other holder of a negotiable instrument. A bank can be said to have given value in the undermentioned circumstances:

(a) The customer has been allowed to draw against uncleared cheques.

(b) The bank has cashed a cheque for a customer (caution — remember 'not negotiable' crossing in *Great Western Railway* v *London and County Bank* (1901) case).

(c) A cheque has been returned unpaid after it has been credited to a customer's account. If the cheque was now debited to the customer's account an overdraft would be created.

(d) It has been agreed that the cheque will reduce an existing loan or overdraft.

(e) The bank has discounted a bill of exchange for the customer and credited the proceeds to the customer's account.

An example of a case in which a bank was regarded as a holder in due course of an unendorsed cheque was *Barclays Bank Ltd* v *Harding* (1962). The drawer of the cheque was a Mr Harding who was persuaded to issue a cheque for £4,500 by a Mr Walker in favour of 'Geoffrey Roberts'. This was a name under which a limited company traded. Barclays Bank honoured cheques up to £4,500 on the limited company's account in anticipation of receiving payment of Harding's cheque which was paid, unendorsed, into the limited company's account. The drawer countermanded payment and was sued by Barclays Bank who were able to prove that the bank was a holder in due course. Section 2 Cheques Act, 1957 gave protection in that, as the bank had given value for the cheque, the bank had the same rights as the holder of a cheque which had been endorsed in blank.

A variation on this theme was seen in the *re Keever, ex parte Cork* v *Midland Bank Ltd* (1966) case. Mrs Keever had both an overdraft and a loan with Midland Bank. A cheque was paid into her current account and sent off for special clearance. Payment was received the following day. At the same time a receiving order was made against Mrs Keever. The bank was unaware of any bankruptcy proceedings. Although the receiver claimed the proceeds of the specially cleared cheque, it was held that the bank had a lien in respect of their customer's overdraft and loan.

Barclays Bank Ltd v *Astley Industrial Trust* (1970) is another illustration of the principle of negotiability. A garage company was allowed to overdraw in anticipation of the receipt of finance company cheques. Astley Industrial Trust stopped payment of five cheques which had been credited to the account of the garage company and, within a very short space of time, the garage company went into liquidation. The directors of the garage company were subsequently convicted of fraud. Barclays Bank sued Astley Industrial

Trust on the grounds that Barclays were holders in due course, having given value for the cheques which had been paid in. The bank was successful in its claim and the judge said that there was nothing in Section 2 Cheques Act 1957 to prevent a bank being both an agent for collection and a holder for value.

1 LOSS OF PROTECTION AS HOLDER IN DUE COURSE

A bank which collects cheques negligently does not collect the proceeds as a holder in due course. Because of this, a bank which is negligent has an obligation to account for the value of the cheques. This principle was upheld in *Bank of Montreal* v *Tourangeau and Royal Bank of Canada* (1980).

In normal circumstances an action for conversion of a cheque can only be brought by a party to the cheque i.e. drawer, endorsee or payee. The Bank of Montreal had taken an assignment over a company's book debts. The Royal Bank of Canada collected three cheques payable to this trading company but, unfortunately, credited these to a personal account opened with them by á signing official of the company. No enquiries were made when the cheques were accepted.

Although the Bank of Montreal was not a party to these cheques and could not claim conversion, they won the case because it was held that, as the Royal Bank of Canada had acted negligently, the Royal Bank had a fiduciary duty to account for the value of these cheques.

2 HOLDER FOR VALUE

While the payee of a cheque or bill of exchange is always the original holder, any subsequent possessor can also be a holder. Section 27 of the Bills of Exchange Act 1882 states that a holder for value is a holder of a bill or cheque where value has at any time been given for the bill or cheque. It is not necessary that a holder for value should have given value himself. Someone to whom a cheque has been given as a gift by the payee, after endorsement by the payee, is a holder for value.

The circumstances in which a bank can be a holder for value are where the bank is acting as an agent for collection. If a customer is engaged in foreign trade and has delivered a bill to the bank for the bank to collect on the customer's behalf, the bank will have a lien on it if the customer's account is overdrawn. The bank will have the same rights as a holder for value even though they have neither discounted the bill nor credited the proceeds to the customer's account. Similar rights will arise when the customer hands a banker a foreign cheque for collection. If the account is overdrawn, the bank has a lien and will have the same right as a holder for value.

It is normal practice for cheques drawn on banks in the United Kingdom to be credited at once to the accounts of customers of British banks. Customers very often draw against these uncleared effects before the bank has received payment. When this happens, the bank will be a holder for value even if there has been no arrangement for drawings to be allowed against uncleared effects. In the event of a cheque or bill being returned unpaid the bank can choose one of the following courses of action:

(a) Debit customer's account and inform him of the non-payment.

(b) If the unpaid debt would overdraw the customer's account and the bank is reluctant to see this, the amount should be debited to a suspense account. The customer should be informed and all other parties advised of the dishonour. A branch banker should not take this action, especially with unpaid foreign bills or cheques, without consulting with his head office.

3 PRESENTATION OF BILLS OF EXCHANGE

A cheque is a bill of exchange payable on demand. While Section 45 Bills of Exchange Act 1882 states that a bill, payable on demand, must be presented for payment within a reasonable time of issue, in practice, bankers allow six months after the date of a cheque before returning it with the answer 'out of date'.

Where trade bills are concerned the procedure is slightly different. The banker must be guided by the custom in that particular trade, the nature and size of the bill, together with the circumstances of the case. With a trade bill, payable on demand, it would be normal to seek confirmation from the drawee before payment. Even if the paying banker has received prior advice of this bill, authority of the drawee is necessary if there is a delay of more than a few days in presenting the bill.

A trade bill is often payable at some time in the future, e.g. 90 days after sight, six months after sight, 180 days after sight. It is first of all presented for acceptance. The drawee will write across the front of the bill to accept it and then hand it back to the presentor. Sometimes an authorised agent such as a bank or accepting house will accept the bill in place of the drawee. An accepted bill of this nature, which is not payable on demand, must be presented on the due date. If the bill is accepted at a bank or accepting house, it is customary for the collecting banker to send it by post to the paying banker two or three days before the due date, so that payment can be made on the due date. Should a bill be accepted by a bank in the town clearing area, the accepted bill is presented through the town clearing on the due date.

Sometimes a drawee will accept a bill and write across the front 'Accepted payable at STU Bank Ltd'. This type of bill is called a domiciled bill. It is the duty of the collecting bank to present the bill to the bank where it is said to be payable. As is the case with all accepted bills, presentation should be arranged so that the bill arrives on or just before the due date.

A bill which is neither accepted by an authorised agent nor domiciled at a bank, must be presented for payment at the acceptor's business premises. One presentation is sufficient and if the bill is not paid on presentation, the drawer is advised and asked for instructions. In practice, banks use their own branches or other banks to present bills. The nearest bank office is used and the presenting banker acts as an agent for the drawer's bank, who is the collecting banker. The same degree of care is required and, if any documents are attached, these must not be handed over until the bill is paid.

It is customary in some trades for some banks to be used as agents when bills are presented for acceptance. While it is possible to allow the drawee to have the bill until acceptance, because they are not liable on it until after acceptance, the presenting bank must never release an accepted bill except against payment.

4 THE EFFECTS OF FORGERY

A banker can only debit his customer's account on the customer's written authority. It follows from this that if a bank pays a cheque on which the drawer's signature has been forged, the customer cannot be held liable. Similarly, if an acceptance of a bill of exchange has been forged, the bill cannot be charged to the acceptor's account.

There are times, however, when a customer may be estopped from denying that his signature is genuine. In *Greenwood* v *Martins Bank Ltd* (1932) the customer's wife forged his signature to several cheques, which were subsequently debited to his account. She confessed this to her husband who took no action at that time. After her death, he sued the bank but lost the case because his failure to notify the bank had prevented any action being taken against the forger. The judge in that case stated that the customer had a duty to warn the bank where the customer knew that his signature had been forged.

While the bank may have no right to debit the account of a customer whose signature has been forged, unless the customer is estopped from denying the forgery, this does not affect the rights of other parties. Passing a cheque or bill to other parties means that the transferor is liable to subsequent parties where the drawer's signature is found to be forged. A customer who pays in a cheque which is afterwards returned, 'signature differs' cannot decline to allow the bank to debit his account. While endorsement by the payee is unnecessary in the case of British cheques, the bank will ask the payee of a bill of exchange, a foreign cheque or a travellers cheque to endorse the instrument before it is sent for collection. In that way, the endorsee makes himself responsible for the genuineness of the drawer's signature, the acceptor's signature and the signature of any prior endorsee.

Part 3: Operating the Customer's Account

9 *Banker and Customer*

The definition of a recognised bank has been given in the Banking Act 1979. We have already dealt with the obligations imposed on a banker by the Cheques Act 1957 and the Bills of Exchange Act 1882. The legal protection given to bankers by these two statutes has also been mentioned.

Unfortunately, the various acts do not define a customer in any way. Bankers always use the term 'customer' as opposed to the clients of solicitors, architects and accountants. The difference is that bankers are in a trading relationship with their customers while other professionals work for a fee. In return for this fee, the solicitor or other professional takes instructions from the client and acts on the client's behalf.

The bank's position is very different. It does not hold a customer's money in trust nor is it accountable to the customer for the investment of this money. In the early case of *Foley* v *Hill* (1848) the judge stated 'The banker is not an agent or factor but he is a debtor'. The conclusion to be drawn from this is that the customer is a creditor and before he can become a customer funds must be deposited with the bank.

Mere receipt of funds would make a bank a safe deposit. There is much more to a banker-customer relationship than that. It is necessary to obtain written instructions from the prospective customer to open an account. Although not absolutely essential, it is preferable for these instructions to be given on a printed form of request supplied by the bank.

This form will ask the customer to give full details of his address, occupation, and name and address of his employers. The customer should be asked to supply the names of referees and it is essential that the references are taken up. Although the issue of a cheque book is usually delayed until satisfactory replies are received from the referees, the opening of the account will mark the start of the banker-customer relationship. There is no need for a long period of relationship for a person to be a customer of the bank.

The leading case on this matter is *Ladbroke and Co.* v *Todd* (1914). Todd was an official of the bank which opened the account and Ladbroke and Co. were bookmakers. Ladbrokes posted a cheque for betting winnings to a Mr Jobson. A thief removed the letter from the letter box, forged Jobson's endorsement and opened an account in the name of Jobson. He asked the bank to have the cheque specially cleared as he wished to draw against it as soon as possible. The bank cleared the cheque that afternoon. The following day the thief withdrew the balance. When Ladbroke sued for conversion of the cheque, the judge decided that the thief was indeed a customer of the bank. He would not give the bank the protection of Section 82 Bills of Exchange Act as a collecting bank (now repealed and replaced by Section 4 Cheques Act 1957). The reason given was that the bank had been negligent in not taking up proper references.

In a similar case, *Commissioners of Taxation* v *English, Scottish and Australian Bank* (1920), the Privy Council decided that duration was not the essence of the banker-customer relationship. They felt that any persons whose money had been taken by the bank, on the understanding that the bank would honour cheques, were customers whether their connection were of short or long standing.

The taking of full details of a new account holder and verifying them is a vital part of opening an account. Failure to make adequate enquiries lost the bank statutory protection in *Guardians of St John, Hampstead* v *Barclays Bank Ltd* (1923). This case has already been referred to.

The necessity of getting back full details, not only of the customer's name and address but also of the customer's occupation and the name and address of his employers, was illustrated in the well-known case *Lloyds Bank* v *E B Savory and Company* (1932). Two of the clerks employed by E B Savory and Company, a firm of stockbrokers, stole crossed cheques made out either to other firms of stockbrokers or to bearer. These cheques were paid in at City branches either for the account of one of these clerks at a suburban branch or for the account of the wife of the other clerk, which was kept by her at a country branch. When the frauds were discovered, Lloyds lost the case. They had not obtained details of the first clerk's occupation and employers. They had not received any information concerning the occupation of the lady's husband nor about his employers. Although the case was decided on the grounds of negligence in not making sufficient enquiries when the accounts were opened, it also illustrates the dangers of accepting cheques, in favour of business firms, for the credit of private accounts. These should never be accepted without enquiry. If the credit is intended for another bank or branch, it is safer to send the cheque and credit direct and inform the person paying-in of your action. Since the passing of the Sex Discrimination Act 1975, banks have discontinued the practice of asking lady customers for details of their husband's occupation. The necessity to obtain details of a customer's own occupation and employers is still as important as ever, although less formality is involved these days in opening accounts for wage earners or students.

An enquiry concerning a customer's employers is essential in order to avoid cheques payable to the employer being credited to the customer's account. This principle was illustrated in the *Harding* v *London Joint Stock Bank Limited* (1914) case. A Mr Francom opened an account with the bank on the introduction of one of the customers of the same bank. The first credit to the account was a cheque in favour of the company which employed Francom. The bank manager did not ask who Francom's employers were, he simply suggested that written confirmation should be obtained of Francom's right to the cheque. Francom wrote a letter in the firm's name confirming that it was in order for him to have the cheque. The bank were found to be negligent in not taking the reasonable and proper precautions necessary when opening an account.

If this decision seems rather hard on the bank, consider that of *Lumsden and Company* v *London Trustee Savings Bank* (1971). Blake, an accountant employed by a firm of stockbrokers, opened a deposit account with the bank in the name of Brown. He described himself as a self-employed chemist, recently arrived from Australia. As a reference, the name of a Doctor Blake was given, who was also said to have just arrived from Australia. 'Doctor' Blake gave Brown an excellent reference, which was not surprising as Doctor Blake, Mr Brown and Mr Blake were one and the same man. Blake paid in several thousand pounds worth of cheques signed by his employers in favour of Brown. When the frauds were discovered, the bank was sued and, although they claimed the protection of Section 4 Cheques Act 1957, were found guilty of negligence. It was felt that the bank should have asked for the customer's business telephone number as he was self-employed. Because both the customer and referee were said to have recently arrived from Australia, it was considered advisable for the bank to ask for sight of Brown's passport. Although

Doctor Blake gave a first-class reference, he did not give the name and address of his own bankers and this was not followed up.

1 CONTRACT BETWEEN BANKER AND CUSTOMER

It was pointed out above that the *Foley* v *Hill* case laid down that the bank was a debtor to the customer. This presents some difficulty because it could be argued that the customer is entitled to ask for immediate repayment of his balance at any branch of the bank, irrespective of where the account is kept.

Fortunately for bankers, the judges in *Joachimson* v *Swiss Bank Corporation* (1921) laid down a detailed summary of the banker and customer relationship. In brief form, this is as follows:

(a) Bank undertakes to receive money and collect cheques.
(b) Funds are not in trust for customer but borrowed by bank.
(c) Bank undertakes to repay
  (i) at branch where account is kept
  (ii) during banking hours.
(d) Instructions for full or partial repayment must be in writing.
(e) Bank undertakes to give reasonable notice before closing account.
(f) Customer undertakes to exercise reasonable care when giving written instructions so that the bank is not misled or forgery facilitated.

From this summary it can be seen that there is more to this contract than the normal debtor-creditor relationship. It will also be observed that the bank is not answerable to the customer for the use it makes of the customer's money.

In the case of the normal debtor-creditor relationship it is the responsibility of the debtor to seek out the creditor in order to repay the money owing. Whether the claim against the bank is in the form of a bank note or a bank deposit, it is not the bank's responsibility to offer repayment. The bank is not liable to pay the debt until repayment is demanded. A banker's duty to repay commences when the customer gives instructions in writing to the bank. The customer's written authority usually takes the form of a cheque, but it can also take the form of a letter from the customer to the bank.

The bank's duty to repay can be overridden in a number of circumstances of which the most common are these:

(a) countermand of payment by customer;
(b) notice of death of the customer;
(c) notice of receiving order against a personal customer—one of the stages in becoming bankrupt;
(d) customer becoming mentally incapable of running own affairs;
(e) notice of a petition to wind up a limited company;
(f) receipt of a garnishee order. This is a court order 'freezing' all or part of a customer's credit balances.

2 BANK'S DUTY TO KEEP CUSTOMER'S ACCOUNT SECRET

Although the *Joachimson* v *Swiss Bank Corporation* (1921) case laid down a very full summary of the respective duties of banker and customer, the duty of secrecy was not mentioned. The principle that a bank should not disclose a customer's affairs was confirmed in the *Tassell* v *Cooper* (1850) case. Tassell was a customer of London and County Joint Stock Banking Company and Cooper was the bank's public officer.

Tassell was employed as agent by Lord de l'Isle. Tassell used his account for paying in both private money and funds belonging to Lord de l'Isle. After a disagreement, Tassell was dismissed and Lord de l'Isle asked the bank manager for permission to inspect Tassell's account. This was refused by the branch manager whereupon Lord de l'Isle wrote to the bank's head office and obtained the permission he had previously demanded. Lord de l'Isle then claimed the balance of Tassell's account as a result of which the bank dishonoured Tassell's cheques.

The bank was sued for recovery of the balance, unauthorised disclosure and wrongful dishonour. Tassell won the case on all three counts. The moral of this is not to disclose a customer's affairs. If a third party makes a claim against a customer's account, they should be advised to seek a remedy through the courts.

This principle was restated in *Tournier* v *National Provincial and Union Bank Ltd* (1924). It was alleged by Tournier that the branch manager telephoned Tournier's employers to say that his account was overdrawn, promises to repay had not been kept and that Tournier had issued cheques to bookmakers. The court found that the branch manager had been in breach of his duty in disclosing information and damages were awarded against the bank. The judge in this case laid down four qualifications to the absolute rule of non-disclosure. These are the qualifications:

(a) where disclosure is under compulsion by law;
(b) where there is a duty to the public to disclose;
(c) where the interests of the bank require disclosure;
(d) where the disclosure is made by the express or implied consent of the customer.

In the first instance, when a court order is served on a bank, the bank manager should confine the information given to that limited amount of detail permitted by Section 7 of the Bankers' Books Evidence Act 1879. Since 1952 the Inland Revenue have been able to ask a bank to make a return of deposit account interest paid to customers in excess of £15 in a fiscal year. The full names and addresses of customers are required. The investigating powers of the Inland Revenue were increased by the Finance Act 1976. Little use has been made of these powers so far and, in practice, recent returns have only been asked for the amounts of interest exceeding a higher figure than the statutory minimum. If the Revenue seek further information, the customer and the bank's head office should be informed. At the same time, the Inland Revenue should be told that the customer's affairs are covered by professional privilege and confidentiality will only be broken with the customer's permission or a court order.

The second qualification is more difficult to understand. The judge mentioned a danger to the state but it is unlikely that a prudent banker will consider himself qualified to pass an opinion on such a danger.

In the third instance, the bank is entitled to supply information to a court when they are seeking the issue of a writ to demand repayment of an overdraft. Similarly, if a borrowing customer is unable to repay, the bank is entitled to write to someone who has guaranteed the account to ask for repayment of the amount due under the terms of the guarantee.

The fourth qualification relates to the bank acting as a referee for its customer. The judge expressed the opinion that it is more difficult to state the limits imposed here either as to time or as to the nature of the disclosure. It is generally accepted that replies to enquiries will only be given to other banks and not to other enquirers such as licensed deposit-takers, mortgage brokers, estate agents or building societies.

Another example of disclosure, where the consent of the customer is assumed, is that of a branch manager answering general questions put by an intending guarantor concerning the borrowing customer's account.

The express consent of the customer relates to written permission to give information to an accountant or other professional adviser. Information requested by accountants is usually asked for by means of a standard letter. When replying the bank should be careful not to disclose any more information than is authorised by the customer.

Bank staff should also be careful not to mention any details of a customer's account over the counter where information might be heard by other people in the public space. The same degree of care should be exercised when chatting to customers in restaurants or public houses. The person at the next table may be very interested in your views on your customer's sales target. Extra caution is needed when bank staff talk among themselves in public places. You never know who is listening. Last, but not least, do not mention customers by name even to your spouses.

3 BANKERS' OPINIONS

On a variety of occasions banks are asked to reply to enquiries concerning the financial status of their customers. This is a well-established practice and bankers have always assumed that they have their customers' implied consents to reply to these enquiries from other banks.

Consumer organisations have a different opinion and feel that the customer's prior written consent is required. The banks take the opposite view and believe that, if a customer does not wish the bank to reply to status enquiries, the customer must give written instructions to prevent the bank giving an opinion.

The present state of the law is somewhat unsatisfactory. Banks are not credit reference agencies within the meaning of Section 145 of the Consumer Credit Act 1974. It is not part of the bank's business to collect information for the purpose of making this information readily available to enquirers. The Consumer Credit Act 1974, however, gives consumers considerable rights. They have right of access to the confidential files of credit reference agencies such as Dun and Bradstreet or the United Association for the Protection of Trade. A small fee is payable for a copy of the file on the consumer. This means that any replies to enquiries can no longer be regarded as completely confidential and very great care must be taken to give honest and careful answers to enquiries.

When an enquiry is made on a bank, the bank staff are expected to exercise a duty of care even though there is no contract, or relationship of fiduciary nature, between themselves and the enquirer. In the case of *Hedley Byrne and Co. Ltd* v *Heller and Partners Ltd* (1964) a firm of advertising agents sued the merchant bankers Heller and Partners for negligence. Hedley Byrne had asked their own bankers to telephone Heller and Partners and had also requested their bankers to write to Heller and Partners on two occasions concerning the creditworthiness of a customer of the merchant bankers. Somewhat guarded replies were given to these three enquiries when the merchant bank replied to Hedley Byrne's clearing bank. The replies were headed 'Confidential' and followed by the words 'For your private use and without responsibility on the part of this bank or its officials'.

Relying on the replies given, Hedley Byrne and Co. Ltd entered into a large advertising contract with Heller's customer as a result of which they lost a great deal of money. They sued Heller and Partners Ltd for negligence. The judge found in favour of the bank on the grounds that there was a disclaimer of responsibility in the reply given by the bank.

A more recent case, where the bank relied on a disclaimer, was *Commercial Banking Company of Sydney Ltd* v *R H Brown & Co.* (1972). Even though the Commercial Banking Company had incorporated a disclaimer in their reply, the court held that the opinion expressed had been given fraudulently. The disclaimer clause proved to be no protection and the bank was forced to pay damages.

To summarise the present position of these cases and the Consumer Credit Act 1974, bankers should act in the following ways:

(a) Replies should only be given to other banks or to recognised and reputable credit agencies. Some banks authorise their managers to reply, in general terms, to enquiries from government departments or the Post Office. Enquiries from other sources should be routed through the enquirer's bankers.

(b) The answers given must be honest and reasonable, without any intention to mislead. The reply should be confined to standard phrases without any need to seek any information which is not already in the bank's records. If the customer is a limited company which has given a debenture to the bank, this fact must be stated.

(c) Present practice is not to sign the reply. A standard form should be used which will have information that that bank is not a credit reference agency under Section 145(8) of the Consumer Credit Act 1974 already printed on it. The words 'Confidential—for your private use only' and 'Without responsibility on the part of the bank or any of its officials' are also printed at the top of the same form.

(d) Only initials should be used to identify the customer. Full names and addresses are never shown. If the enquiring banker quotes an incorrectly spelt name such as Browne for Brown, it is usual to answer 'If your enquiry refers to A L B...n he is respectable and considered good for your figures and purpose'. Enquiring banks sometimes give the wrong addresses. The customer's correct address must never be given (remember *Tournier* v *National Provincial and Union Bank Ltd* (1924)). The replying bank should confine itself to the statement 'The address you quote is not shown in our records'.

(e) The bank must strike a reasonable balance between the duty to its customer and the necessity of taking reasonable care. It is not the responsibility of the bank to cast doubts on the customer's creditworthiness. On the other hand, the bank has a duty not to mislead the enquirer by giving too favourable a reply. Normal routine enquiries about hire purchase contracts or building society mortgages are very easy to give a fair reply to. Difficulty usually arises when the bank is asked to express an opinion concerning a large guarantee to be given or a large contract to be signed. If the reply is likely to be a marginal one, it is often advisable to ask the customer to call so that the background to the enquiry can be discussed before an answer is given.

4 ENQUIRIES BY CUSTOMERS OF THE SAME BRANCH

Extra care is needed when a customer of the branch, such as a solicitor or an estate agent, asks you to give information about another customer of the same branch. They should be asked to make a formal request in writing for a specific amount, e.g. likely to be a suitable tenant of leasehold premises at a rent of £2,000 a quarter. The reply given by the bank will incorporate all the usual features.

(a) A printed form will be used with the words 'Confidential—for your private use' at the top. The same reference is shown to the Consumer Credit Act.

(b) Only the initials are used in the reply, which is in the form of standard phrases and unsigned.

Under no circumstance should a banker discuss the reply given with the customer making the enquiry. Any deviations from these strict rules are fraught with danger.

The case of *Woods* v *Martins Bank Ltd and another* (1958) illustrates some of these dangers. Woods was persuaded by Johnson, a manager of Martins Bank, to buy some shares in a company which had an account at the same branch of Martins. Woods asked Johnson whether the company was financially sound and if he should invest £5,000. The manager recommended this course of action and subsequently advised Woods to make further investments in the company. Later on Woods was asked to guarantee another private company and was advised by Johnson that there was no real risk of his being called upon to pay the amount of the guarantee. Subsequently both companies failed. Woods lost approximately £15,000 which he had invested and was compelled to pay £1,000 under the terms of the guarantee.

Woods sued the bank and its manager for negligence and was awarded damages. The manager failed to take reasonable care or exercise the ordinary skill which a bank manager is expected to have. Throughout the whole period of the association between Woods and Johnson, the companies involved in the case were over-trading and there was constant pressure to reduce the companies' overdrafts. The judge held that there was a fiduciary relationship between Woods and the bank and the manager, although not fraudulent, did not advise with reasonable skill and care.

10 *The Customer's Account*

In chapter 9 on the contract between banker and customer we spent some time talking about the duties of a banker in relation to the customer. Unless there are legal restrictions imposed by a court on the conduct of the account, a bank is answerable only to its customer for the funds on the accounts. The customer is the only person whose instructions the bank will follow, although the customer may delegate his authority in writing to an agent. As the bank will be liable to compensate the customer if it does not carry out the customer's instructions in a diligent manner, the customer must reciprocate by giving instructions in a clear and precise manner. These instructions should be given in writing and if the bank is prepared to accept instructions over the telephone, the customer must be asked to confirm these verbal instructions in writing, within a reasonable period of time.

The bulk of the instructions given by customers take the form of cheques. Customers have a responsibility to the bankers to draw their cheques in such a way that fraud is difficult. They must take reasonable care to prevent their bank being misled. This principle was laid down in the very old case of *Young* v *Grote* (1827). In this instance, Young gave his wife five signed blank cheques to be used by her for business expenses. She passed one cheque to Young's clerk to be filled in for wages of fifty pounds. The clerk completed the cheque for fifty pounds, showed it to Mrs Young and afterwards inserted other words and figures so that it now read 'Three hundred and fifty pounds'. The bank paid the cheque for the larger amount and was sued by Young who lost the case because the alteration was not apparent.

This protection given to bankers was reinforced by the case of *London Joint Stock Bank Limited* v *Macmillan and Arthur* (1918). Arthur was a partner in the firm and was asked to sign a cheque for £2 by the firm's clerk. Arthur was leaving the office on his way to lunch and failed to notice that the amount in words had not been written on the cheque although £2 was written in the space for figures. The firm's clerk wrote 'One hundred and twenty pounds' in the space for words and put a '1' and a '0' on either side of the figure '2'. The cheque was cashed for £120 and the firm sued the bank for £118. Macmillan and Arthur lost the case on the grounds that leaving blank spaces on signed cheques is the easiest way by which fraud is facilitated.

If a cheque appears to be complete and correctly filled up in every way, it should be paid, provided that it is regular in all other respects. On the other hand, if there is an apparent alteration which has not been signed by the customer, the cheque should be returned with the answer 'Alteration requires drawer's confirmation'.

1 STOPPED CHEQUES

The bank's customer gives instructions to the bank by signing a cheque. Customers can countermand these instructions by placing a 'stop' on the cheque. If a customer stops a cheque the bank cannot honour the cheque when it is presented for payment.

Section 75 Bills of Exchange Act 1882 states that the duty and authority of a banker to pay a cheque drawn on him by his customer are determined by countermand of payment. Cheques which are stopped should be returned with the answer 'Orders not to pay' if the customer's instructions are given in writing.

When the order to stop payment is given verbally the 'stop' should be accepted and the customer should be asked to confirm in writing. Where telephoned instructions are given to stop a cheque the answer to be given when the cheque is returned should be 'Payment countermanded by telephone. Awaiting drawer's confirmation'. The cheque is likely to be represented within three or four days and it is essential to obtain written confirmation before representation. Only written instructions to countermand payment are really effective as was shown in the case of *Curtice* v *London, City and Midland Bank Ltd* (1908). Curtice purchased some horses and, because they were not delivered as arranged, sent a telegram to the bank stopping the cheque. The telegram was placed in the bank's letter box after the close of business. Although the letter box was cleared on the following morning, inadvertently, the telegram was left behind. In the meantime, the cheque was presented and paid. A day later, the telegram and Curtice's confirmation were removed from the box and the bank advised their customer that the instructions had been received too late to stop payment. In the legal action which followed, it was held that the cheque was not effectively countermanded under Section 75 Bills of Exchange Act 1882 at the time of payment.

The essential details which are required when a customer stops a cheque are these:

(a) date of cheque;
(b) payee's name;
(c) amount;
(d) cheque number.

Many customers are very dilatory in providing this information and it is often advisable to send your customers a printed 'stop' form for them to sign and return. This applies particularly to customers who countermand a cheque by telephone for the first time and who are unsure of the procedure to follow. It is important to get these details right and, in this age of the computer, vital to obtain the number of the stopped cheque. Even in more leisurely days, the number of the cheque was considered the most important piece of identification. This was shown in the case of *Westminster Bank Ltd* v *Hilton* (1926). Hilton issued a post-dated cheque numbered 117,285. The day before the cheque was due, he sent a telegram which asked the bank to stop payment of cheque 117,283 and gave the amount and payee's name. Four days after the date of the cheque, cheque 117,285 was presented and then paid. Two weeks later another cheque was dishonoured for lack of funds. Although Hilton sued the bank for negligence, it was decided that the bank was not negligent as the one certain item of identification is the number of the cheque.

If a cheque book or a number of cheques are lost, the numbers must be obtained from the customer and a 'caution' placed on the computer file. In the event of any lost cheques being presented, the customers should be asked for instructions. Should the customer not be available the cheque will have to be returned with the answer 'Reported lost. Awaiting confirmation'.

A cheque which has been issued for payment of goods and which the payee has accepted with the backing of a cheque card or visa card cannot be stopped, if the following conditions have been complied with:

(a) The card number is placed on the back of the cheque by the payee.
(b) The cheque is signed by the drawer in the presence of the payee.
(c) The amount of the cheque does not exceed £50 and is payment of a single transaction not exceeding £50.

2 DEATH OF A CUSTOMER

The other clause of Section 75 of Bills of Exchange Act 1882 states that the duty and authority of a banker to pay a cheque drawn on him by a customer are determined by notice of a customer's death. It should be carefully noticed that it is the notice of death which determines the bank's authority. Cheques paid by a bank between the date of death and receipt of notice of death can stand. Section 75 only mentions cheques. This means that the bank is entitled to debit the customer's account, even after receiving notice of death, where instructions have been given by the customer:

(a) to purchase Stock Exchange securities;
(b) to order foreign currency;
(c) to send a payment abroad by mail or cable transfer;
(d) to order a foreign draft.

The following action needs to be taken by the bank on receiving notice of the death of a customer:

(a) Stop the account.
(b) Ask to see the death certificate.
(c) Mark any safe custody or security ledger sheets in the name of the customer with a note of the date of death.
(d) Cancel any standing orders.
(e) Return any direct debits.

Any cheques presented after notice of death are returned with the answer 'Drawer deceased'. In a similar fashion any pensions or annuity payments, received by the bank after the receipt of notice of the death of the customer, should be returned to the originators.

With dividend warrants or payments of interest on stock the position is rather more complicated. It is normal practice for banks to continue to credit to an account in the sole name of the deceased customer any dividends, or interest payments on stocks or shares in the customer's sole name. With other dividends they must be placed to a suspense account until the deceased's personal representatives exhibit probate of the customer's will or letters of administration. It follows from this that even where a customer has given a mandate for dividends or interest payments on stock on his sole name to be credited to a joint account, any payments after death must go to a suspense account. In a similar way, where joint stockholders have mandated dividends to a sole account in the name of the deceased, these payments must also be credited to a suspense account until fresh instructions are received.

3 NOTICE OF RECEIVING ORDER AGAINST CUSTOMER

This is one of the steps taken during the process of a person being made bankrupt. A petition will be presented by either a creditor or the debtor himself asking the court to declare the debtor bankrupt. On receiving this petition the court will consider the matter and, if the petition is justified, will appoint an official of the court as a receiver. This official takes over the debtor's affairs and the court makes a receiving order. From the date of this order all the debtor's assets, including the bank account, belong to the receiver.

Details of the receiving orders against the customers are published in a local newspaper near the customer's home and also published in the *London Gazette* and *Stubbs Gazette*. Extracts from these newspapers are sent out by Head Office to those branches of the bank which do not take these newspapers. Depending on negotiations between the debtor and his creditors, the debtor may or may not be made bankrupt but the important date is that of the receiving order.

On information concerning a receiving order being obtained by the bank the customer's account must be stopped. If the current account is in credit and there is a loan or an overdraft in the customer's name, or the customer has a contingent liability, the bank is entitled to set-off the credit balance against the customer's liabilities to the bank. Any surplus funds remaining after this amalgamation are remitted to the official receiver. Cheques presented to the bank on the same day as they hear of the receiving order or at any subsequent time should be returned with the answer 'Refer to drawer'.

This action should be taken because there is no protection for the bank regarding any transactions after the date of the receiving order. The case of *re Wigzell, ex parte Hart* (1921) showed the dangers faced by a bank. Although a receiving order was made against Wigzell in October, this was not published in the *London Gazette*, pending his appeal. The appeal was heard in November but dismissed. Between the date of the receiving order and the date of the appeal, the customer paid funds into the bank and drew money out. The trustee in bankruptcy claimed the funds paid in and would not allow the withdrawals to be deducted. The court decided that there was no protection for the bank under the terms of the Bankruptcy Act 1914 and the funds credited after the date of the receiving order had to be paid to the trustee in bankruptcy.

Section 4 of the Bankruptcy (Amendment) Act 1926 gave some limited protection to bankers. If the banker is able to prove that he did not know of the receiving order and that, on the dates of withdrawals of funds, the receiving order had not been advertised, the trustee can only claim from the bank if the court is satisfied that the trustee cannot recover the money elsewhere. As the bank is almost certainly better able to repay than the debtor himself, who has made the withdrawals, this clause is of limited value.

In *re Byfield (a bankrupt) ex parte Hill Samuel & Co. Ltd* v *Trustee of the property of the bankrupt* (1982) it was said that Section 4 of the Bankruptcy (Amendment) Act 1926 did not apply to payments made after the gazetting. On 5 April 1979 the bankrupt asked the bank to transfer £19,500 to her mother and this was done on that day. Six days earlier, the notice of bankruptcy had been advertised in the *London Gazette* but had not been seen by the bank on the day the £19,500 was transferred out. The bank was compelled to pay an equivalent sum to the trustee in bankruptcy for the benefit of the main body of creditors.

This position is rather different from that before the date of the receiving order. In the case of *re Keever, ex parte Cork* v *Midland Bank Ltd* (1966), the bank obtained protection of Section 45 Bankruptcy Act for transactions up to the date of the receiving order. The customer in that case had an overdraft of £352 and a loan account of £1,000. She paid in a cheque for £3,000 to the credit of her current account and the bank had this cheque specially cleared. The bank received a banker's payment from the paying bank on the following day. The day after the cheque had been credited to Mrs Keever's account, a receiving order was made against her.

The court held that the court had a lien over the proceeds of the cheque and was exempted by Section 45 of the Bankruptcy Act 1914 from paying the whole proceeds to the trustee. They were entitled to deduct the balances of both the loan and current accounts from the amount of the cheque before submitting figures to the trustee.

4 MENTAL INCAPACITY OF A CUSTOMER

The fact that a person is admitted to a hospital as a voluntary patient, in order to undergo treatment for mental disorder, does not mean that he is incapable of running his own financial affairs. In the present day, we do not talk about lunatics or people becoming insane. The only time a customer becomes mentally incapable, according to the Mental Health Act 1959, is when he is compulsorily admitted to hospital on an application signed by two medical practitioners. This state of affairs is not to be confused with the position which arises when a customer enters hospital as a voluntary patient. A banker should not assume that a customer is unable to manage his own finances unless evidence is produced to show that the patient has been compulsorily detained in hospital. After receiving notice of the customer's detention, it may be advisable to ask the medical staff caring for the patient to confirm that the customer cannot look after his own bank account.

The action to be taken when a customer has been compulsorily detained is to

(a) stop the account;
(b) cancel any standing order or direct debit authorities;
(c) cancel any mandates.

The cheques which are drawn by the patient must be returned to the collecting bank. It is not easy to decide what answer to write on these returned cheques. In the case of an account in the patient's sole name, it is better to write 'Refer to drawer' than an answer which would indicate the patient's mental condition. As mental incapacity automatically determines any mandate signed by the patient, any cheques drawn on a joint account should be returned 'Mandate cancelled'.

The banker should advise the relatives of the patient to ask for a Court of Protection order. This order will authorise a person, usually a close relative, to act as receiver. The assets of the patient are vested in the receiver, who will act in accordance with the instructions of the court.

Until a receiver is appointed, it is often arranged to honour cheques drawn by the other party to a joint account, in spite of the cancelled mandate, provided the money drawn is used for the maintenance of the patient. If the joint account holder wishes to draw cheques for other reasons, it is preferable to open a new account in the sole name of that party. It is also possible to agree to honour cheques, signed by a third party authorised by the patient, provided that the funds withdrawn are used for the customer's necessities. The case of *re Beavan, Davies, Banks and Company* v *Beavan* (1912) illustrates this point.

A customer of the bank became unable to manage his own affairs, following a seizure. The bank allowed the customer's eldest son to continue operations on the account for the maintenance of the customer and family. When the customer died, two years after the seizure, the account was overdrawn. Although the eldest son and another son were prepared to repay the bank, the other two of the four executors disputed this. The court decided that the bank was entitled to the principal but could not be paid interest or commission.

In discussing this type of problem with relatives of a patient, the bank should suggest application to the Court of Protection for a receiver to be appointed to manage the financial affairs of the mentally incapable customer.

It would be most unwise for a bank to open an account with anyone who was compulsorily detained in a mental hospital. However, patients do recover and, once a banker has seen evidence that a person who was previously mentally incapable has been discharged from hospital, an account can be reopened. The normal banker-customer relationship is re-established but a certain amount of care is still advisable.

11 *Different Types of Accounts and Banking Operations*

As was mentioned in the section on 'Contract between banker and customer' the case of *Joachimson* v *Swiss Bank Corporation* (1921) laid down a summary of the banker-customer relationship. In the great majority of instances, the relationship is based on a verbal contract between depositor and banker. The bank undertakes to pay on demand or at the end of a fixed period or after agreed notice. In return, the customer undertakes to exercise reasonable care in running the account.

When a customer pays cash into his account or the bank cashes the customer's cheque, when it is presented over the bank counter, only two parties are involved in these transactions. Where a banker is asked to undertake work on behalf of customers and the work involves third parties a different set of rules applies.

Examples of this type of transaction are:

(a) Collecting third party cheques.
(b) Transfer of funds abroad.
(c) Stock transactions.
(d) Arranging insurance cover.
(e) Giving performance bonds or indemnities to third parties at the request of customers.

In these transactions the bank acts as an agent of the customer. Agents are accountable to their principals. They are unable to delegate responsibility and are expected to be competent and diligent. The collection of third party cheques is part of the normal banker-customer relationship for which there is a verbal contract. In the other transactions, the bank must ask for written instructions when it is asked to act as agent for a customer.

Where customers lose share certificates, company registrars usually insist on an indemnity from a bank before issuing duplicate certificates. The Automobile Association and Royal Automobile Club are often asked to give guarantees in connection with the shipping of cars abroad for use by the owners during long stays abroad. It is customary to ask the owner's bank to join in the giving of this type of guarantee. In a similar fashion, builders and contractors are sometimes asked to give performance bonds to local authorities guaranteeing the standard of workmanship. These bonds will be supplied by the builder's bank. With all these cases, the customers are asked to sign a counter-indemnity on the bank's standard form.

1 CUSTOMER'S DELEGATION OF AUTHORITY

Where the customer wishes to delegate authority to a third person who will act as the customer's agent, written instructions should be obtained. These written instructions should be taken on the bank's standard form of mandate authorising delegation of authority. As these instructions will authorise the agent to sign on the customer's account, a specimen signature of the agent should be taken as well as the signature of the customer.

No alteration to the form should be permitted. There can be no limitation on the time the mandate is outstanding and any cancellation of the authority should be given in writing by the customer.

Death of the customer will cancel the authority for the agent to sign on the account. The mandate is also revoked if the customer has a receiving order against him or if the customer becomes mentally incapable.

Death or mental incapacity of the third party will also revoke the mandate. Whether the making of a receiving order against the agent will also cancel the mandate is a matter for judgement. The practical banker will obtain written confirmation from the customer if delegation to an agent is to continue after a receiving order has been made against the agent.

2 POWERS OF ATTORNEY

These are either general powers of attorney or special powers of attorney. They are drawn up by lawyers and the effect is to authorise the donee of the power to act as agent of the donor. The power of attorney must be signed and sealed before it can take effect. It is usual to give a power of attorney before going for a long absence abroad. When a customer gives a power of attorney a copy should be retained and entered in the bank's records.

General powers of attorney give the donees power to act in almost every way in which the donor could act. Special powers of attorney are usually limited to the performance of one specified act. Neither type of power is drawn up to allow the attorney to borrow on the customer's behalf. If the customer wishes the agent to operate the customer's bank account, the bank will consider it desirable to obtain a third party letter of authority. This will be signed on the bank's standard form of attorney and is signed by both the agent and customer to cover operations on the banking account.

Powers of attorney are either revocable or irrevocable. A revocable power can be revoked by either donor or donee giving notice of revocation. Death, bankruptcy or mental incapacity of the donor will revoke the power of attorney, as will death or mental incapacity of the donee. Rather curiously, either a minor or a bankrupt can act under a power of attorney. In the case of the donee becoming bankrupt, the customer's written confirmation should be sought if the power is not to be revoked. Revocation of the power is advisable in these circumstances. Irrevocable powers of attorney can only be revoked with the consent of both donor and donee. Even the death of the donor will not cancel an irrevocable power of attorney without the attorney's consent.

While it is essential for a paying bank to scrutinise very carefully any power of attorney given by a customer, a similar degree of care is expected of a collecting banker. This degree of care was indicated in the case of *Midland Bank Ltd* v *Reckitt and others* (1933). Sir Harold Reckitt gave his solicitor a power of attorney. This enabled the solicitor to draw on Sir Harold's account with Barclays Bank. The cheques on Barclays were drawn 'Harold G Reckitt by Terrington his attorney'. The solicitor issued fifteen cheques for a total sum of around £18,000. These cheques were paid into the attorney's account at Midland Bank. Midland Bank had been pressing the solicitor to reduce his overdraft. When Sir Harold returned from abroad he brought an action against the Midland Bank for conversion.

The court held that the collecting bank had been negligent. The way in which the cheques were drawn showed quite clearly that the money did not belong to the solicitor and yet the Midland Bank accepted these cheques for the credit of the solicitor's private account.

3 MANDATES

A mandate is merely an instruction to the bank given by the customer authorising certain actions. A cheque is a mandate because it is an instruction to the bank. Section 73 of the Bills of Exchange Act 1882 defines a cheque as 'a bill of exchange drawn on a banker payable on demand'. Section 3 of the same Act defines a bill of exchange as 'an unconditional order in writing'. It is the written order which authorises the bank to debit the customer's account.

Written instructions must also be given where more than one person is to sign on a banking account. This requirement has already been noted in the section dealing with a customer's delegation of authority. Apart from private accounts where a third party is allowed to sign, mandates are also required in the following cases:

(a) joint account;
(b) partnership account;
(c) limited company account;
(d) executorships, trusteeships and accounts of administrators;
(e) society, club and church accounts.

4 DIFFERENT TYPES OF ACCOUNTS

4.1 Joint accounts

Unless instructions are given in writing all parties must sign cheques. The instructions given should be on the bank's standard form of mandate. This mandate form will cover the signing of cheques and will also give the bank a good discharge if the balance is paid to the survivor(s) on the death of one party to a joint account.

Although the mandate given to the bank is cancelled on the death of one of the parties to a joint account, the law presumes that each party has a concurrent interest in the whole balance. This means that in common law the legal owners of the balance, after the death of one account holder, are the survivors.

In the case of joint accounts in the names of husband and wife, or parent and child, the doctrine of advancement applies. Under this rule it is presumed that the deceased intended the survivor to have an absolute interest in the joint account balance. While this doctrine is appropriate for husband and wife, the bank would probably seek legal advice if there was a substantial balance standing to the credit of an account where a minor was the sole survivor.

The mandate is drawn up so that all parties accept joint and several liability for any overdraft on the joint account. With joint and several liability each of the account holders can be sued individually for any borrowing outstanding in joint names.

While on the death of one party, the balance can be paid either to the survivors, where a receiving order is made against one party to a joint account, the mandate is cancelled and the account blocked. Similarly, certification that one of the parties is of unsound mind will lead to cancellation of the joint account mandate and stopping the account.

The receipt of a garnishee order by the bank will not operate to stop a joint account unless the order is made in the exact names of all parties to the joint account. In the event of a bank hearing of a dispute between the joint account holders, the customers should be informed that the mandate is cancelled and that all future cheques must be signed by all the account holders. Any signatory to a joint account can countermand payment of a cheque drawn on the joint account, even if he did not sign the stopped cheque. As a matter of courtesy, the bank would ask for confirmation from the account holder who signed the cheque.

4.2 Partnership accounts

A partnership is formed when two or more people carry on a business in common with a view to making a profit. While a partnership deed is sometimes drawn up, setting out the purpose for which the firm is formed, a merely verbal agreement is sufficient to set up a partnership. At one time it was necessary for the partnership to register under the Business Names Act 1916, if the firm was trading under a name other than the names of its partners. This is no longer necessary. The only document which needs to be given to the bank is a partnership mandate. This form will list the names of the partners, the name of the firm, and will give instructions to the bank on how the account is to be operated. It is regarded by the bank as sufficient evidence of partnership.

Any one partner can bind the firm unless the mandate given to the bank states that more than one partner must sign. The mandate will always incorporate a clause laying down joint and several liability for the individual partners. This means that each of the partners is separately liable for any borrowing in the name of the firm.

A normal trading partnership consists of between two and twenty partners. The Companies Act 1967 permitted some exceptions to this rule. Up to fifty partners are allowed in solicitors' or accountants' practices. Provided the permission of the Stock Exchange Council is obtained first, up to fifty people can form a stockbrokers' partnership. Associations authorised by the Department of Industry are also allowed to have up to fifty partners.

A bankrupt cannot be a partner but a minor can. The minor will not be personally liable for his actions until he comes of age and it would be advisable for the remaining partners to give a specific authority to the bank, permitting the minor to sign partnership cheques.

Death of a partner, a receiving order against a partner, or certification of the mental incapacity of a partner will lead to dissolution of the partnership. If the account is in credit, the remaining partners are allowed by Section 38 Partnership Act 1890 to continue operations for the purpose of winding up the old partnership. It is essential, however, for the bank to get a new mandate signed by the remaining partners. Cheques drawn by the dead partner, the partner against whom a receiving order has been made, or the partner who has been compulsorily detained in a mental hospital should be confirmed by the other partners before payment.

If the account is overdrawn, the account must be stopped. This is to prevent the rule in 'Clayton's Case' applying. In the case of *Devaynes* v *Noble* (1816) (known as 'Clayton's Case') the judge laid down that credits to an account were used to reduce debits out, in the order in which they occur. In other words, the first sum paid in provides the funds for the first payment out. It follows from this that any credits paid in after the death, mental incapacity or bankruptcy of a partner would go to reduce the overdraft at the death, mental incapacity or bankruptcy. Clayton was one of the claimants whose claim was considered during the proceedings between Devaynes and Noble.

By stopping an overdrawn account, the bank will preserve a claim against the estate of the deceased, bankrupt or mentally incapable partner. This claim will be on the same footing as that partner's other creditors. There is no need to deduct the value of any partnership security from the total of the bank's claim, when submitting a claim against the partner's private estate.

Any one partner can countermand payment of a cheque even if he did not sign the cheque. As a matter of courtesy, it is usual to ask the original signatory to confirm the countermand of payment, but this is not essential.

Some young bankers consider partnership an old-fashioned form of organisation. This is a misconception. We should remember that in 1973 the Bolton Report found that 60 per cent of all small businesses were either sole proprietors or partnerships. It is impossible for solicitors, accountants, stockbrokers and members of several other professions to form themselves into limited companies without breaking the rules of their professional association. They are, therefore, exempt from the restriction to twenty partners laid down by Section 120 of the Companies Act 1967. Every bank branch has at least one solicitor's, accountant's or chartered surveyor's account and it is essential for the younger banker to understand the basis of conducting a partnership account.

4.3 Limited company accounts

The law governing companies is found mainly in the Companies Act 1948, Companies Act 1967, Companies Act 1980 and Companies Act 1981. The basis of formation of a limited company is that individual shareholders subscribe for shares and their liability as shareholders is limited to the amount of these shares. It is important to realise that the company is a separate legal entity apart from the member and the directors.

This point was clearly laid down in the case of *Salomon* v *Salomon and Company Ltd* (1897). Mr Salomon was the managing director of and majority shareholder in the company. After lending money to the company, he took a debenture which gave him a first charge over the company's assets. Eventually, the company failed. He claimed priority over the ordinary creditors because he held security given to him by the company. Salomon's claim was admitted. The court decided that the company had a separate legal existence, independent from Mr Salomon.

Similar views were expressed by the judges who heard the cases *A L Underwood Ltd* v *Barclays Bank Ltd* (1924) and *A L Underwood Ltd* v *Bank of Liverpool and Martins Ltd* (1924). In these cases the director of a 'one-man' company paid a series of cheques, belonging to the company, into his private accounts with the banks. The banks were held to be negligent and guilty of conversion. As the judges pointed out, the cheques were drawn in favour of the company and were plainly the property of the company. Underwood had no right to pay them into his private account.

Before a bank can open an account for a limited company, it must see the following documents:

(a) Resolution of the board of directors.
(b) Memorandum and Articles of Association.
(c) Certificate of Incorporation.
(d) Certificate to Commence Business (if a public limited company).

4.3.1 Resolution of the board

The shareholders elect a board of directors who appoint a secretary of the company. The directors pass a resolution and a copy, signed by the chairman and the secretary, is sent to the bank. A standard company mandate form, supplied by the bank, will include a specimen resolution and customers are strongly advised to use these standard forms. The mandates are supplied to the secretary in duplicate as the first copy is retained in the company's minute book when the second copy is returned to the bank.

The resolution appoints the bank as bankers to the company and gives instructions concerning banking transactions. Specimen signatures of all signing officials are given on this form.

4.3.2 Memorandum and articles of association

This is a book of rules which is usually prepared by the company's solicitor or accountant. The memorandum of association gives the following details:

(a) Name of company.
(b) Objects of the company, i.e. the purposes for which the company was established. Any act not authorised in the memorandum is 'ultra vires' (beyond the powers of the company).
(c) Capital structure of the company.
(d) Borrowing powers of the company.
(e) Power to give security.

The articles of association supply the following information:

(a) Voting at meetings of shareholders.
(b) Powers and duties of directors.
(c) Any limits on powers of directors to give security.
(d) Any limits on directors' borrowing powers.
(e) Rules for internal administration of the company.

4.3.3 Certification of incorporation

A certificate of incorporation is issued to the company by the Registrar of Companies when the company deposits its memorandum of association and articles of association with the Registrar. The company begins its legal existence when the certificate is issued. No transactions can be allowed on the banking account until this certificate of incorporation has been seen by the bank.

4.3.4 Certificate to commence business

This certificate is issued by the Registrar of Companies when he is satisfied that a newly-formed company, which wishes to register as a public company, has fulfilled the statutory requirements to be a public company.

In the majority of cases companies are private companies before they become public companies. Where a private company is already trading, a certificate to commence business is not issued by the Registrar of Companies as none is required.

4.4 Private companies

Most limited companies are private companies. Any company which does not comply with the definition of a public limited company laid down by the Companies Act 1980 is a private limited company. The Companies Act 1980 now lays down that the minimum number of shareholders in a private limited company is two, but there is no maximum. The minimum number of directors permitted is one, provided an independent secretary is appointed. If a director is also to act as secretary, a second director must be appointed. Although the law allows a private limited company to operate with only one director, it should be noted that the articles of association may stipulate a larger number to form a quorum. The prudent banker will check the articles to make sure that it does not conflict with the mandate given to the bank by the directors. Although there is now no restriction on the transfer of private company shares, these shares cannot be made available to the public by means of an offer for sale.

4.4.1 Table A Companies Act 1948

This is a specimen set of regulations for running a private limited company. Unless the clauses in Table A are excluded by the company's memorandum and articles of association, Table A will have to be adopted as the regulations for the company. Where some of the clauses are excluded, the remainder of the clauses in Table A apply to the running of the company.

The memorandum states the amount which the company can borrow. The borrowing powers of the directors are set down in the articles of the company, which usually state that the directors may exercise the company's borrowing powers.

Unless Article 79 of Table A is excluded, the company is limited to borrowing not exceeding the nominal share capital of the company. This nominal share capital is the amount of authorised share capital stated in the company's memorandum of association.

If the directors' borrowing powers are exceeded, the loans may be ultra vires (beyond the powers of the company). This means that repayment of the borrowing from the bank may be unenforceable and the bank may be in a very vulnerable position.

Article 79 of Table A states that temporary loans obtained from the company's bankers can be excluded from the total when calculating the directors' borrowing powers. While a prudent banker would not shut his eyes to excesses shown on the balance sheet, a bank dealing in good faith with a company is entitled to assume that acts within its powers have been properly performed. This is known as the 'Rule in Turquand's Case' from *Royal British Bank* v *Turquand* (1856). In this case the directors had the power to borrow on behalf of the company and to issue debentures as security. Their deed of settlement (equivalent to the present-day memorandum and articles of association) said that before the directors could borrow or give security the company had to pass a resolution at a general meeting. The directors borrowed in the company's name and gave security to the bank but no resolution was passed. When the company sought to avoid liability on the grounds that no resolution had been passed, it was held that the bank was entitled to assume that the necessary formalities laid down in the memorandum of association had been completed. The bank was not bound to enquire into the internal management of the company.

This protection to banks was extended still further by Section 9(1) of the European Communities Act 1972. The Act states, 'A person dealing with a company in good faith is not bound to enquire into powers of the company nor to look into any limitations on the power of directors'.

In spite of the legal protection available prudent bankers have never relied on it. Where a company wishes to borrow from a bank it is usual to suggest a resolution altering the memorandum and articles of association so that borrowing powers are unlimited. If this is not acceptable to the company it is appropriate to request that a suitable resolution is passed in general meeting. This is especially important in the case of structured lending and the bank will supply a specimen resolution for the shareholders to pass.

As far as the European Communities Act 1972 is concerned this is of little help to a bank. While a trade creditor would not need to examine the company's memorandum and articles of association, it is standard practice for a company's bank to retain a copy when the account is opened. The bank cannot argue that it was unaware of any limitations on the powers of either the company or the directors.

It is still advisable for the bank to verify from the memorandum that the company is not undertaking any operations not mentioned in the objects clause of the memorandum of association. In the very old case *Ashbury Railway Carriage and Iron Company Ltd* v *Riche* (1875), the court found that the company had exceeded their powers. The objects shown in the memorandum were the making and selling of railway carriages and rolling stock. They were engaged to build a railway in Belgium and this was held to be ultra vires.

In the more recent case of *re Introductions Ltd* (1969) a bank was unable to enforce its security or recover its borrowing because the purpose for which the money was borrowed was not shown in the memorandum. The company had been formed to provide services for foreign tourists. Following a change of ownership, the company commenced the business of pig-breeding. The court held that, as the money had been borrowed for a purpose not shown in the objects clause of the memorandum, the bank's security was invalid.

4.5 Public limited companies

New regulations were introduced in the Companies Act 1980 to define a public limited company. The new legislation was introduced to bring the existing company law into line with company law in the remainder of the European Economic Community. At the same time, there was a change of emphasis from the Companies Act 1948. In the 1948 Act a careful definition was given of a private company. Any companies which did not satisfy the conditions laid down were regarded as public companies.

The 1980 Companies Act reverses this emphasis. Public limited companies must now comply with stringent rules and all other companies are private companies.

A public company must satisfy the following conditions:

(a) memorandum of association states that it is a public company;

(b) registered with Registrar of Companies as a public company;

(c) has PLC or Public Limited Company in its name (or CCC if the company's registered office is in Wales);

(d) share capital is not less than £50,000;

(e) minimum number of directors is two;

(f) minimum number of shareholders is two: no maximum;

(g) no restriction on offering shares to the public. (The company usually has a Stock Exchange quotation but this is not essential.)

The following documents are required if a bank is to open an account for a public limited company:

(a) Resolution to appoint the bank as bankers to the company.
(b) Memorandum and articles of association.
(c) Certificate of incorporation.
(d) Certificate to commence business (if a new public company).

In the majority of cases, companies are private companies before they become public companies. A certificate to commence business is not required in these cases provided they fulfil all the legal requirements laid down in the Companies Act 1980 for a public limited company.

Before the Registrar of Companies will accept the private company's re-registration as a public company the company must file, with the Registrar of Companies, one of the undermentioned documents:

(a) a prospectus inviting the public to subscribe for shares;
(b) a statement in lieu of a prospectus.

4.6 Notice of a petition to wind up a limited company

Winding up a limited company is very similar to bankruptcy of a private customer. It can take four forms.

(a) Compulsory liquidation by court order.
(b) Members voluntary winding up.
(c) Creditors voluntary winding up.
(d) Winding up under supervision of the court.

Compulsory liquidation commences when a creditor presents a petition. The petition states that the company is unable to pay its debts. The liquidation process begins at that point and the mandate given by the directors to the bank is revoked by the presentation of the petition. Section 11 of the Bankruptcy Act 1914 states that the notice of the presentation of the petition must be published in the *London Gazette* and a local newspaper. The details are also published in *Stubbs Gazette*. As soon as this information is received by a bank, the company's account must be stopped.

If the court is satisfied with the petitioner's claim, appointment of the Official Receiver as provisional liquidator takes place. A winding up order is then made by the court. The purpose of this order is to sell the company's assets so that the creditors can be fully or partly repaid.

4.6.1 Members voluntary winding up

This takes place when the shareholders of a limited company decide that the company has outlived its useful life. The company is expected to pay its debts in full and the directors have to file a declaration that the company is solvent. A meeting of the shareholders then appoints a liquidator and the directors' powers cease from that time. The mandate given to the bank by the company lapses when the shareholders pass their resolution to wind up the company.

4.6.2 Creditors voluntary winding up

Sometimes the shareholders decide to wind up their company but the directors are unable to make the required statutory declaration. A meeting of creditors is called for the same day or the day following the shareholders' meeting. The meeting of the creditors appoints a liquidator to manage the affairs of the company. The company's mandate to the bank is determined by the appointment of the liquidator.

4.6.3 Winding up under supervision of the court

This type of winding up occurs when the shareholders pass a resolution to wind up their company but a creditor subsequently presents a petition to have the company wound up compulsorily. The presentation of a petition during a members voluntary winding up does not happen very often. The court hears the petition and, if they consider it necessary, instruct the liquidator appointed by the members to continue his winding up either under the supervision of the Official Receiver or under the direction of a committee of creditors.

A banker needs to take great care in all types of liquidation. It is the date of the petition which determines when a company's bank account should be stopped. Under Section 229 of the Companies Act 1980 any winding up order relates back to the date of presentation of the petition.

4.6.4 Garnishee order

A garnishee order nisi is made by a court when a judgement has been given against a debtor with which the judgement debtor has not complied. The garnishee order instructs a third party who owes money to the debtor to pay this money into court for the benefit of the creditor. Presentation of the garnishee order to the bank operates to stop the account, if the customer's account is in credit. In the case of *Fern* v *Bishop Barnes & Co. Ltd and Lloyds Bank Ltd* (1980), it was held that a garnishee order did not attach uncleared effects, unless arrangements had been made with the bank to allow drawings against cheques which had not been cleared. Under Section 38 of Administration of Justice Act 1956, deposit accounts are blocked by service of a garnishee order, in the same way as current accounts are stopped. Savings accounts, where the account holder has a passbook permitting limited withdrawals at any branch of the bank, are not affected by a garnishee order.

The case of *Chine Investments Ltd* v *Jeromniman* (1980) decided that garnishee orders may be made to attach accounts which are denominated in foreign currencies.

After the accounts are stopped, the customer must be advised and, if it is considered desirable, a new account opened in his name. If the customer's account is overdrawn, the garnishee order is inoperative and the account need not be stopped. Where there are credit and debit balances in the same name, the bank can set-off one against the other, pass interest to date, and if the resultant figure is an overdraft, need not stop the account.

The garnishee order nisi includes a summons for the banker (or the banker's solicitor) to appear in court. If the debtor's defence fails, a garnishee order absolute is made. The bank will then pay over the amount of the order to the judgement creditor (or the creditor's solicitors) and the customer's account can be unblocked.

This is a rather cumbersome procedure and the modern practice is for the court to make a limited garnishee order instead of a garnishee order nisi. The limited garnishee order will specify a balance up to a named figure. On receipt of this order, the bank should transfer the customer's credit balance, up to the figure named in the limited garnishee order, to the credit of a suspense account. The bank will await the court's instructions concerning the balance on the suspense account but, in the meanwhile, the remainder of the funds are held at the disposal of the customer.

5 ADMINISTRATORS, EXECUTORS AND TRUSTEES

5.1 Accounts of administrators

Administrators are persons appointed by the court to deal with a deceased's estate in the following circumstances:

(a) where the deceased left no will;
(b) where the deceased left a will but
  (i) did not name an executor; or
  (ii) named an executor who died before him; or
  (iii) named an executor who is unwilling to act.

The administrators are usually the next of kin of the deceased. Letters of administration are granted by the court to enable the administrators to collect the assets of the deceased. This is so that the administrators can pay the debts of the deceased. Any funds remaining after the debts are paid are distributed according to the rules of intestacy. The rules for the distribution of this residue are found in the Administration of Estates Act 1925, which has been amended from time to time by statutes such as Family Law Reform Act 1969 and Family Provision (Intestate Succession) Order 1972. The law makes some provision for the spouse and family but, if people wish their whole estate to be left to their spouse, it is desirable for a will to be made before death.

When the deceased leaves a will but does not name an executor, or names an executor who is unwilling or unable to act, the administrators are granted 'Letters of Administration cum testamento annexo'. This means that the grant is made with the will annexed. In this case the principal legatee is usually appointed administrator and is legally bound to carry out the terms of the will. A grant of administration 'cum testamento annexo' is sometimes made to the guardian of a sole executor when the executor is a minor.

An administrator cannot pass on his authority or delegate power to anyone else. If an administrator dies before winding up the deceased's estate, a fresh application must be made for 'Letters of Administration de bonis non administratis'. This is a grant in respect of property not administered and is usually obtained by the person with the largest interest in the residuary estate.

In the majority of simple estates an application by one administrator is sufficient for letters of administration to be granted. Sometimes a minor will benefit under the rules of intestacy, or beneficiaries will be entitled to the income while they are alive, with the capital passing to someone else on their death. In both these cases, the court will only grant letters of administration to a minimum of two administrators. The maximum number who can be appointed is four.

When a bank account is opened in the name of administrators, all should sign the original mandate which will make them jointly and severally liable for any overdraft. Should bank borrowing be required to pay capital transfer tax, ask for full details of the estate, with gross and net assets, together with the rate of capital transfer tax payable. Any advance fo rthis purpose should be on a loan account with all administrators signing the request to borrow from the bank.

When signing cheques on their current account, administrators may delegate power to sign cheques to one of their number but cannot delegate authority to anyone else.

The bank cannot transfer the balance of the deceased's account or any securities until letters of administration have been exhibited to the bank. If the estate is very small, the bank will pay over the balance of the deceased's account without letters of administration being produced, provided an indemnity is given by the person receiving the balance. The Administration of Estates (Small Payments) Act 1965 authorised the National Savings Bank to pay sums not exceeding £1,500 in estates without executors or administrators. Banks usually follow these guidelines where they are satisfied no capital transfer tax is payable and the correct beneficiary will obtain the funds in the name of the deceased.

In the case of simple administrations, a year is regarded as sufficient time to wind up the estate. After twelve months, the administrators become trustees. If there is a life tenant of the trust or an infant beneficiary, at least two people are required to act as trustees.

5.2 Accounts of executors

Where a customer dies leaving a will and an executor has been appointed, who is willing and able to act, an account can be opened in the executor's name. If there is more than one executor, the bank should ask for an executors' mandate, admitting joint and several liability for any borrowing.

Any advance to pay capital transfer tax should be taken on loan account, with all the executors signing the debit.

When the will is proved to the satisfaction of the Probate Court, and any capital transfer tax has been paid, the executors are given a grant of probate. This contains a sealed copy of the will and is official confirmation that the executors have power to deal with the deceased's assets. On seeing this grant of probate, the bank can transfer the deceased's account and any securities to the named executors, against their receipt.

Executors can delegate authority to one of their number to sign cheques, but the original instructions should be signed by all. At the end of the executor's year the bank shall make enquiries to see if the executors are now trustees and, if so, a fresh mandate will need to be taken.

Should an executor die before the winding up of the estate, the executor's executor will be responsible for the administration of both estates. The chain of executorship means that X deceased has Y as an executor, who in turn has Z as executor of his own will. On Y's death, Z will become the personal representative of both Y and X. This situation does not apply where a number of executors have been appointed to deal with the estate of X. If Y is a joint executor with T and U of X's estate, then T and U will continue the executorship on Y's death.

On the other hand, should Y be the sole executor and he makes no will, or Z is unwilling to act, the principal beneficiary of X's estate applies for 'Letters of Administration de bonis non administrato.'

5.3 Accounts of trustees

The most common form of trust is an undistributed estate or an incomplete administration. A year is normally regarded as adequate to wind up an estate and after that time, the banker should make enquiries with a view to redesignating the executor's or administrator's account as a trust account.

It is also possible for private trust and charitable trust accounts to be opened. Where a trust deed exists, it is preferable for this to be produced when an account is opened. If a trust instrument is produced, the bank should record the details. Sometimes there is no formal trust instrument, but the bank would not decline to open a trust account in the absence of a trust deed.

The mandate taken from the trustees should insist that all trustees must sign. A trustee cannot delegate authority, except in certain special circumstances. These exceptions are laid down by law as follows:

(a) Section 23, Trustee Act 1925 allows delegation of certain powers to professional agents such as stockbrokers, solicitors, bankers and accountants. Where these agents are appointed in good faith, trustees are not responsible for default of the agent. In the case of *re Vickery* (1931) a trustee was held to be guilty only of an error of judgement when employing a solicitor who turned out to be dishonest.

(b) Where delegation is permitted by the trust instrument. This is most unusual and is the reason why the bank must scrutinise the trust deed if it is produced.

(c) Section 25, Trustee Act 1925 (as amended by Section 9, Power of Attorney Act 1971) allows a trustee to delegate authority by means of a power of attorney. This power of attorney must be seen by the bank. Delegation cannot be to a sole remaining trustee, unless it is to a trust corporation.

Although there is nothing in law to prevent a bankrupt acting as trustee, it is very undesirable. The bankrupt trustee should be persuaded to retire from the trust. If he is reluctant to go, the beneficiaries under the trust are able to apply to the Court, under the terms of Section 41, Trustee Act 1925, for a new trustee to be appointed in place of the bankrupt one. Should a new trustee be appointed the bank must obtain a new mandate and ask to see the court order.

Under the terms of Section 25, Trustee Act 1925, if a trustee is incapable of acting by reason of mental incapacity, old age or infirmity, the continuing trustees may appoint one or more persons to be a trustee or trustees in his place. In these circumstances, where new trustees are appointed the bank should ask to see the deed of appointment and also obtain a new mandate.

On the death of a trustee, Section 18, Trustee Act 1925, allows the survivor or survivors to continue to exercise the powers conferred by the trust deed. The bank will ask for a new mandate on the death of one of joint trustees. It is advisable for two trustees to act or a trust corporation to be appointed because a sole personal trustee cannot give a valid receipt for the sale of land under the Settled Land Act 1925.

In the case of charitable trusts, registered for tax purposes with the Charities Commissioners, the trustees must obtain the consent of the Charities Commissioners if the trust is to borrow or charge securities. The bank must ask to see this consent before agreeing to any lending to a charity.

6 SOCIETY, CLUB AND CHURCH ACCOUNTS

6.1 Society and club accounts

A special form of mandate known as a 'Club Mandate' is taken by the bank when an unincorporated voluntary association wishes to open an account. The mandate will give a list of those members who are authorised to sign on the bank account. It will be signed by the chairman and secretary as having been passed by the members in general meeting.

Unless it is an extremely informal association, the society or club will have a printed constitution and a rule book. These two documents should be given to the bank with the mandate. It is unlikely that the rule book will allow any borrowing and no overdraft would normally be allowed, unless personal guarantees were given by leading members.

The bank would usually be asked to open an account in the name of the association, e.g. Thames and Severn Fishing and Sailing Club. Sometimes an account will be opened in a private person's name instead of a club's name, e.g. Henry Hughes re Hemel Hempstead Actors Benevolent Fund. While the account is in the name of Henry Hughes only he can instruct the bank but, because of the designation, the account must be treated as a trust account. While there is no difficulty in accepting cash for this account, difficulties could arise if cheques made payable to the benevolent fund are paid into this account in a private name. It is preferable to seek confirmation from the other members that the account holder can act alone on behalf of the benevolent fund.

6.2 Church accounts

The most usual form of account is that of a Parochial Church Council of the Anglican Church. The Synodical Government Act 1970 laid down the procedure for running parish accounts. The name of the account is always 'Parochial Church Council of . . . Parish'. A mandate is given to the bank, incorporating a resolution of the council. This will authorise the bank to accept the signatures of the treasurer and other elected officers. Before any borrowing is allowed, it is usual to obtain written confirmation from the finance committee of the Diocesan Synod and to ask for personal guarantees from leading council members.

With the Catholic Church accounts can only be opened with the permission of the Diocesan Bishop. The accounts are opened in the names of two or three of the parish priests and they are usually the only persons allowed to sign on the account.

In the case of other denominations the accounts are usually opened in the names of 'Trustees of . . . Church'. The normal trustee mandate is taken and it is usual to have a resolution of a general meeting of the church members authorising the trustees to act on their behalf.

12 Miscellaneous Banking Operations

1 DRAFTS ON DEMAND

There are some transactions such as buying a car, or completing a property purchase, where a customer's cheque is either unacceptable or will take too long to clear. In these cases, the customer will ask his branch manager to draw a draft on the bank's head office. The draft will be in favour of a payee nominated by the customer and, after signature by an authorised bank official, will be handed to the customer or sent to the payee by post. Both the customer and the payee will regard the draft as equivalent to cash, because they know a banker's draft will always be honoured, so long as the bank remains in business.

The drafts are never issued to bearer because that would be equivalent to issuing a bank note, which is illegal in England and Wales for any institution other than the Bank of England.

2 TELEPHONIC TRANSFERS

Customers sometimes want to transfer large sums of money by quicker means than sending a cheque, a banker's draft or a bank girocredit. The banks have a system for the transfer of funds from one bank to another on the same day. This method is widely used by solicitors in completing the purchase of houses on the day laid down in the contract.

The customer wishing to pay the funds out asks his own bank to make a 'same day' transfer. The customer's branch bank then telephones its own head office or sends them a message through its computer network. The head office then pays the other bank's head office and asks them to advise the beneficiary's branch by telephone. When the payee's branch receives the message, it credits its customer's account straight away.

3 STANDING ORDER PAYMENTS

When a customer wishes his bank to pay regular sums such as rates, club subscriptions and mortgage repayments, he signs a standing order authority. This instructs the bank to pay a fixed sum, at regular intervals, to another bank for the credit of the payee's account. The customer benefits in the saving of postage and time, while the bank has the responsibility of remembering to make the payments. Standing order payments are nearly always fed into a computer nowadays. While some payments still go through the Bank Girocredit Clearing, most of the payments are made through the Bankers Automated Clearing by exchange of magnetic tapes between banks. Settlement for transfers is made by an adjustment between accounts which the clearing banks have with the Bank of England.

4 DIRECT DEBITS

This is a slightly different system to the method of standing order payments. A customer signs a mandate, addressed to the bank, authorising it to accept debits to the account from named third parties. These amounts can be either fixed or variable and the dates of debiting can be either fixed or variable. While many private customers give authorities for insurance premiums or local rates to be paid in this way, the system has been used increasingly for trade transactions during the past few years. Many oil companies use direct debits to charge garages for petrol deliveries. Brewers often issue direct debits on publicans' accounts when making deliveries of beer. Most of the direct debit entries are processed on magnetic tapes which are exchanged in the Bankers Automated Clearing.

5 TRAVELLERS CHEQUES

These cheques are issued in denominations of round pounds, e.g. £10, £20, £50. They are drawn on the bank's head office and are signed by the customer to whom they are issued, at the time of issue. Travellers cheques can be cashed at other banks, both in Britain and abroad, at hotels or on ships and aircraft. When presented for payment they are examined to see if they are in order and the customer is asked to counter-sign them. After comparison between the two signatures, sterling is paid over, if cashed in Britain, or the equivalent in foreign currency, if the cheques are cashed abroad.

The advantage of using travellers cheques is that almost all British banks will refund, to the customer, the amounts of lost or stolen travellers cheques, provided that there are no suspicious circumstances. A small commission charge is made when the cheques are issued.

In certain areas of the world, it is difficult to change sterling travellers cheques. British banks will issue their customers with currency travellers cheques in these cases. The currency cheques are drawn on one of the bank's branches abroad or a correspondent bank in the country which the traveller wishes to visit. They are slightly more expensive to buy than sterling travellers cheques. In some cases, correspondent banks will not make refunds for their travellers cheques which have been lost or stolen.

6 FOREIGN TRANSACTIONS

6.1 Notes and coins

Banks are able to supply foreign currencies to holiday-makers and others who travel abroad. In most branches, it is best to allow three working days between giving the order and the date the currency is required. Some large branches which have foreign tills are able to hand out currencies on the spot. You are also able to obtain foreign currencies at airports, some railway stations, and some ferry terminals.

When a customer returns from abroad a bank will buy back any surplus foreign currency. Because of the cost of handling and insurance, the buying rate differs from the selling rate and it is advisable not to bring too much foreign currency back from abroad. This is particularly true of coins, which are often only convertible at a very low rate of exchange.

6.2 Payments

As well as the transmission of funds through their domestic branch networks, the banks are the main means by which funds are transferred abroad. The four principal methods used are foreign drafts, mail transfers, telegraphic transfers and SWIFT.

Foreign drafts are similar to the drafts on demand payable in Britain. Instead of being drawn on the British bank's head office, they are drawn on a bank abroad with whom the British bank has an account. The bank abroad is known as a correspondent bank and will usually be in the same country as the payee. Foreign drafts can be drawn either in pounds sterling or in a foreign currency. Drafts are useful where the bank's customer wishes to write direct to the payee enclosing the money. An example of this type of payment is where an advance payment is being made for holiday bookings. Another instance in which a foreign draft might be used is in payment to a foreign publisher for a book or a magazine.

Mail transfers are payments made abroad on a customer's authority. When customers wish to send funds overseas they can instruct their bank to send the money to a foreign bank, for the payment of this sum to a named beneficiary. The instructions will be sent abroad by airmail. The foreign bank will debit the British bank's account with them and the customer of the British bank will have his account charged with the sterling equivalent of the amount transferred. The foreign bank will then inform the overseas beneficiary of the receipt of the money. There are a number of countries such as Spain and Italy where there are considerable postal delays in the receipt of funds by the beneficiaries. In these cases, British banks recommend that telegraphic transfers should be used.

Telegraphic transfers are similar to cable transfers except that the instructions are sent abroad by cable. A system of coded telex messages is used for this purpose and, in cases of extreme urgency, a telephone call will be made, authenticated by a cipher. Settlement takes place in the same way as with mail transfers. The customer pays the cable charges as well as the sterling equivalent of the foreign currency transfers.

Most payments abroad are now sent through a computerised network. During the past few years the Society for Worldwide Interbank Financial Telecommunication (SWIFT) has developed a computerised system for international payments which will eventually replace mail and telegraphic transfers. Bankers' Automated Computer Services (BACS) is the British agent for SWIFT and around 1,000 international banks are now attached to the SWIFT network.

Part 4: The Financial Environment

13 *Forms of Savings*

When most of us think of savings we remember money put aside for a 'rainy day', bank balances kept to pay for holidays or money kept in a box to pay for Christmas presents. In economic theory, there are wider definitions of savings. The three main sorts of savings are:

(a) Surpluses accumulated by nationalised industries, local authorities and central government.

(b) The undistributed profits of companies, partnerships and sole traders.

(c) The excess of personal income over personal expenditure.

The normal member of the public would probably think of investment as a bet on a horse, buying a bingo card or filling in a football pools coupon. More sophisticated people might define investment as the purchase of government securities or ordinary shares through the stock exchange. To the economist the word 'investment' means that part of a country's gross domestic product which is not used for personal consumption, export of goods abroad, or current expenditure of central and local government.

In its most exact sense, investment, like savings, takes three forms. These are:

(a) Spending by the public sector on airports, roads, schools, hospitals, sewers, power plants, coal mines and other items of a capital nature.

(b) Purchases of new machinery, factories and offices by industrial and commercial firms.

(c) Personal contributions to life assurance, save-as-you-earn contributions, purchase of national savings certificates, regular subscriptions to unit trust savings schemes, additions to bank deposit accounts or building society share accounts, together with compulsory deductions for pension benefits.

With a stable economy, savings and investment should always balance out but investment without compensating savings will lead to inflation.

To the non-economist, the savings they make are their own personal investments. Before considering saving out of income, the bank customer should consider the need to retain a sufficient balance on current account. This will enable the private customer to meet normal living expenses without difficulty and will enable the business customer to have funds available for normal trading expenses. In both cases, if sufficient balances are kept, the payment of bank charges will be avoided. The banks publish personal account tariffs for private account charges. These tariffs show the minimum cleared balances required to avoid paying bank charges. If these balances are not kept, a laid-down scale of charges is applied, off-set by an allowance for cleared credit balances.

Where there is a surplus of current income over current expenditure, the customer should be advised to keep funds on a bank deposit account, a finance house deposit account or a building society ordinary share account. Funds will need to be kept in this form rather than tied-up in longer-term investments for the following reasons:

(a) To iron out the peaks and troughs of expenditure. Extra spending money is needed in the summer holiday period and for buying Christmas presents.
(b) To provide an emergency reserve for unexpected items of expenditure.
(c) To have funds available for favourable buying opportunities. These could occur at the January sales or when increases in indirect taxes are expected.

With bank deposit accounts, finance house deposits and building society share accounts, interest varies from time to time, but press statements are always made when interest rates change. Interest is paid gross on bank and finance house deposits, if less than a year's notice is required. Although it is paid without tax being deducted, the interest is taxable in the hands of the customer. Under Section 17 of the Taxes Management Act 1970 banks and finance houses must give names and addresses of all United Kingdom residents who have been credited with £25 interest in a tax year, if the Inland Revenue request this information from them. In practice, the figure set by the Inland Revenue is now higher than £25.

Building society interest is free of basic income tax. This makes a share account a convenient home for the 'emergency reserve' funds of a standard rate taxpayer. Building society share accounts are unsuitable investments for non-taxpayers such as children and elderly pensioners, eligible for age allowance tax relief. Better gross returns are available elsewhere for these non-payers of tax.

If the income you have is sufficiently great to push you into the higher tax brackets, the interest is grossed-up using this formula:

$$\text{Building society interest received} \times \frac{100}{100 - \text{Standard rate of tax}}$$

Where a building society investor is paying a higher rate of tax, higher rate income tax is charged on the grossed-up equivalent. Let us assume that a taxpayer is subject to 50 per cent income tax on the top slice of his income and that the standard rate of tax is 30 per cent. If he receives £280 a year building society interest, it will be grossed-up in the way shown previously.

$$\pounds 280 \times \frac{100}{100 - 30} = \pounds 400 \text{ (grossed-up figure)}$$

Tax at 50 per cent – 30 per cent will be payable on £400 and an extra £80 tax will be paid as a result of receiving £280 building society interest. The investor's net income will be £200 (i.e. £280 – £80 tax). For this reason, investment in building society shares is not advisable for anyone who is not a standard taxpayer, unless small balances are kept purely for convenience. In some circumstances, an investment income surcharge may also be paid on building society interest received.

Private investors who have surplus funds in excess of £500 should be encouraged to invest at fixed rate for fixed terms with the bank's finance house subsidiary, if the interest offered is competitive.

Where investors have substantial funds available for short-term investment, the bank's treasurer can help here. Sums of money can be lodged with the bank at rates which vary in line with money market conditions. Notice of a change in the rate of interest is always given by the bank.

1 LIFE ASSURANCE COMPANIES

These companies have assets in their life assurance funds which exceed £30,000 million. It is a very formidable mass of money and the investment policies of the life assurance companies are a matter of public comment.

The basic philosophy of life assurance is to provide financial protection for the dependants of the policyholder. In many cases, policyholders are looking for a form of contractual savings as well as protection and a variety of policies can be taken out giving emphasis to a combination of savings and assurance.

The simplest form of life assurance is known as term assurance. With term assurance policies the premiums are payable for a fixed period of years. The sum assured is only payable on the death of the life assured before the end of the term of the life policy. Benefits usually take the form of a lump sum but can sometimes be a series of annual payments. Premiums for this type of cover are extremely small, especially for young policyholders who wish to provide cover for their families at a modest cost.

Decreasing term assurance is suitable for policyholders who wish to protect their dependants against the burden of repaying a building society mortgage, a bank home mortgage loan or a medium-term bank loan. The amount payable on death reduces by annual stages. Premiums are decreased accordingly.

Neither of these types of term assurance are popular because no proceeds are payable if the policyholder survives for the full term. These policies cannot be regarded as contractual savings in the same way as conventional life policies. At no time do term assurance policies ever share in the profits of the life assurance companies.

1.1 Whole life assurance

Although the public are quite prepared to pay out insurance on their houses, furniture and cars, without regarding the premiums as a form of investment, they adopt a different attitude to insuring their lives. They expect to receive a lump sum in return for the premium paid.

The simplest form of this type of policy is known as 'whole life' assurance. In return for premiums paid during the life of the policyholder, a capital sum is payable on the death of the policyholder. Some life assurance companies will waive the payment of premiums after a specified age such as 70 or 75. These whole life policies are a reasonable way of providing life assurance for a young family but they do have certain disadvantages. The impact of inflation is such that a figure which appears to be a large sum at the age of 25 may seem a trifling amount at the age of 75. Another problem is that the premiums are more expensive than comparable term assurance for the same capital sum although the term assurance is limited to a fixed period of years.

The impact of inflation can be partly neutralised by taking out a 'with profits' policy. In return for payment of higher premiums, the policyholder is entitled to a share in the profits of the insurance company. The record of British insurance companies over the past 50 years has been very good and substantial increases have been seen in the bonuses paid when 'with profits' policies mature.

1.2 Endowment assurance

While many people are altruistic enough to pay premiums throughout life in order to provide benefits for dependants, others are anxious to have a lump sum of capital available on reaching retirement age. An endowment assurance policy is often a good compromise between the twin objectives of personal life assurance and contractual savings.

In return for the premiums paid at regular intervals, a lump sum is paid either at the end of term or on prior death of the policyholder. If it is a 'without profits' policy, the maturity proceeds will be a fixed sum. On maturity of a 'with profits' policy, bonuses, which vary according to the profitability of the insurance company, are paid in addition to the agreed capital sum.

The majority of these endowment policies are paid out when the policy-holder reaches 60 or 65. Because of this premiums tend to be higher than comparable whole life policies and the sum assured to be lower.

A hybrid form of policy is called a convertible whole life policy. In return for a fairly small premium, a large capital sum can be assured on a whole life basis. The policy will incorporate an option to change the policy into an endowment assurance after a certain period of time. There is usually a choice of an endowment policy for the same capital sum with payment of a larger premium or a reduced capital sum for the same premium. A fresh medical examination is usually waived on conversion of this type of policy.

1.3 Mortgage protection

This type of policy is a combination of decreasing term assurance and an endowment policy. Because of the reluctance of many policyholders to take out any form of assurance where nothing is paid back, a special type of policy is underwritten. The capital sum reduces over a period of years, more or less in line with the reducing loan. Unlike true decreasing term assurance, with a mortgage protection policy a lump sum is payable at the end of term. For example, with a £20,000 mortgage protection policy, taken out for 20 years, £4,000 may be agreed as the policy maturity proceeds. With genuine term assurance, policyholders do not share in the profits but mortgage protection policies can be either on a 'with profits' or a 'without profits' basis.

1.4 Tax advantages of life assurance

Whether we are discussing term assurance, whole life assurance, endowment policies or mortgage protection policies, the tax position is the same. Relief is given on the premiums paid at half the standard rate of tax. If a direct debit is signed to pay a gross premium of £10 a month, a net premium of £8.50 will be collected, e.g.:

	£
Gross premium	10.00
Tax relief at 15% (half of 30% standard rate)	1.50
Net premium collected	8.50

The tax deducted is claimed by the assurance company from the Inland Revenue and £10 a month is invested by the company on behalf of the policyholder. In the event of the policyholder dying during the period of the policy all the proceeds payable are free of any capital or income taxes. Where the person whose life is assured survives until the end of term, in the case of an endowment policy, the premiums must have been paid for at least 10 years for the proceeds to be free of taxes.

2 PENSION FUNDS

The premiums which policyholders pay to life assurance companies are a direct form of savings. Contributions to pension funds, whether by employees in the case of a superannuation scheme or by employers where there is a non-contributory fund, are forms of indirect savings. Insurance companies are involved to a very considerable degree as the managers or trustees of company pension funds. In some instances, the right to an annuity on retirement is the only personal wealth of any size that an employee will possess. Many large organisations run their own pension funds with investment managers who are directly responsible to the pension fund trustees. A table of some of the largest pension funds is given below. The figures were published in 1982 by the National Association of Pension Funds.

	£ million		
Pension Fund	**Book value**	**Market value**	**Investment income**
The Post Office	—	3,795	234
National Coal Board	1949	—	188
Imperial Chemical Industries	712	—	105
British Rail	—	1,629	99
Electricity Council	—	1,175	88
British Steel	—	1,487	85
British Gas	—	1,034	84
British Petroleum	—	1,046	58
National Westminster Bank	—	831	50
Imperial Group	—	730	40

Total assets of the pension funds now exceed £60,000 million and combined with the £30,000 million owned directly by the insurance companies give these institutional investors considerable powers. Some idea of their influence can be obtained if we compare their growth with that of the London Clearing Banks. In 1956 the sterling deposit liabilities of the clearers were nearly £5,000 million while, at the same time, the combined assets of the insurance companies and pension funds were just over £3,500 million. By 1979 the London Clearing Banks had nearly £33,500 million in sterling liabilities to depositors. In the period up to 1979 the assets of the insurance companies and pension funds had risen to just under £82,000 million. This is a striking contrast and it is no surprise that the apparent lack of disclosure of information and accountability to contributors is a matter of some public concern. There were well-published examples of this when the British Rail pension fund invested in a number of works of art during the 1970s. Other pension fund trustees bought bullion or gold coins during the same decade. Whatever the merits of works of art or precious metals as vehicles for investment, they are unsuitable for pension funds. The retired employee is entitled to a pension based upon final salary. The trustees should, therefore, be looking for assets which will show an increasing income over the years. In order to assist them in this policy, the British government have exempted pension funds from all forms of tax. It follows from this that the trustees should be able to invest contributions to achieve much better results than the contributor could obtain through personal savings.

The private individual is subject to capital gains tax if he realises capital profits above a statutory minimum. Any income from investment of personal savings is also subject to income tax, apart from some investments in National Savings and, in the case of standard taxpayers, building society interest.

The deduction of pension contributions from salary for investment in a pension fund is not only a form of indirect savings it is also compulsory under the employee's conditions of service. All the members of the working population have to be provided with pensions when they reach retirement age. The state scheme gives minimum benefits but if an employer wishes to contract out of the state scheme, both for employer and employees, the private scheme set up must offer pensions which are at least as good as those under the state scheme.

2.2 Personal pension plans

Self-employed people are in a difficult position. They are compelled to make contributions to the state scheme but the benefits they obtain may be well below the income they are currently earning. The state scheme will only give them the basic retirement pension and, as self-employed people, they obtain no benefits such as payment of a capital sum on retirement, which is available with most private schemes.

The special difficulties of self-employed persons saving for their old age are allowed for in the substantial tax concessions given to those who provide for their own pensions. Provided their contributions are used to purchase deferred annuities, payable from the date of retirement, 100 per cent relief is given, up to certain limits which change from time to time. Because these contributions are allowed as deductions from business profits, the self-employed person is investing money at a large discount. The discount is the rate of tax paid on the top slice of the contributor's business profits.

Take the example of a man aged 50 who has made a profit in the year of £19,000. On the top band of taxable income, 45 per cent will be paid in tax (figures as the tax year 1982/83). If a contribution of £3,800 (20 per cent of £19,000) is made to a retirement annuity plan, managed by an insurance company, full relief is given. The total of assessable income is reduced from £19,000 to £15,200. The net cost to the self-employed person will be:

Gross contribution payable	£3,800
Tax relief given (45%)	£1,710
Net cost of insurance premium	£2,090

In return for a net drain on resources of £2,090, the contributor will have £3,800 invested for him by the insurance company. The income earned by the insurance company is not taxed while held by the insurance company nor are there any assessments to capital gains tax in respect of capital profits accruing to the insurance company.

The contributor has the right to commute part of the pension for a lump sum amounting to three times the figure of the annual annuity payable. With all these advantages, it is little wonder that self-employed retirement annuities have been the fastest growing part of the insurance business during the past few years.

3 NATIONAL SAVINGS

Savings which are placed directly with the British government are administered by the Department for National Savings. The director of savings runs this department under the general supervision of the Treasury. A wide range of securities is available to the public by means of sales through Post Offices and banks. With the competitive rates of interest given and the tax concessions available for investment in National Savings, these securities provide powerful rivalry to the banks and building societies.

3.1 National Savings Bank

This was formerly known as the Post Office Savings Bank and was started in 1861. Through the network of post offices and sub-post offices it provides a nationwide machinery for the handling of small savings. There are over twenty million active accounts. The majority of depositors with the National Savings Bank have what are known as ordinary accounts. These accounts can be opened by anyone aged seven or upwards, with a minimum deposit of 25p. The maximum balance permitted on ordinary accounts is £10,000. Interest is allowed at 3 per cent per annum on balances below £500. For balances over £500, interest is paid at 6 per cent per annum. The first £70 of National Savings Bank interest is tax free. This means that if you had a deposit of £3,000 in a National Savings Bank account you would only pay tax on £110 a year of this interest.

	£
Balance of £3,000 at 6% per annum—interest	£180 a year
Exempt interest	70
Taxable interest	£110

All National Savings Bank interest is paid gross, that is without tax being deducted.

Up to £100 in cash can be withdrawn on demand but larger sums require a few days notice.

3.2 Investment accounts

Savers who wish to obtain a higher rate of interest than that available on ordinary accounts can open investment accounts with the National Savings Bank. The minimum deposit is £1 and the maximum balance allowed on any investment account is £200,000. Interest on these investment accounts is taxable but the National Savings Bank credit interest without any tax being deducted. The rate of interest allowed is highly competitive with other deposit takers such as banks and building societies, although it varies from time to time in line with other money market rates. One main disadvantage which investment accounts have is that a month's notice must be given before withdrawals can take place.

3.3 National savings certificates

Substantial sums are raised for the government by means of issues of national savings certificates. These securities are intended for long term savers. The first issue was made in 1916 and a variety of issues have been made since that time. The current issue (1983) is the 26th issue. Although the terms vary from issue to issue, the basic principle remains the same. No interest is payable but the certificate grows in value the longer the period for which it is held. The capital growth is equivalent to a compound interest rate of around 8 per cent over a five year period, in the case of the 26th issue, although the previous issues gave an even more favourable return. These yields are completely free of capital gains tax, income tax and investment income surcharge. This makes the grossed-up return very attractive for taxpayers and, because of this, limits are placed on the amounts which can be held. The current limit for the 26th issue is £5,000 but this is in addition to any holdings of other issues of national savings certificates.

3.4 Index-linked national savings certificates

In 1975 the Department for National Savings issued a new form of national savings certificate called the 'retirement issue'. They were nicknamed 'Granny Bonds' because they were only available to men of 65 years of age or more and to women who were 60 or over. The feature of this retirement issue was that there was no fixed capital appreciation on the lines of normal national savings certificates. Instead of this, the value of the certificates was changed in line with the government's retail price index. During periods of inflation, they proved to be extremely sound investments. £1,000 invested in the retirement issue certificates in 1975 had grown to £2,130 in 1980. This return is equivalent to compound interest at the rate of 13 per cent a year. An added attraction was the fact that the profit made was not subject to any form of British tax. The retirement issue was withdrawn in November 1980 and replaced by the second index-linked national savings certificates.

The later issue certificate can now be bought by anybody but with the fall in the rate of inflation it is a less attractive investment than many other forms of savings. Up to £10,000 of second index-linked national savings certificates can be purchased in units of £10 each. The certificates must be held for a year before they increase in value. At the end of the first year they are revalued in line with the increase in the retail price index since the date of purchase. In the unlikely event of the retail price index falling during the time the certificates are held, the original purchase price of the certificates can always be repaid.

After the first year is finished the certificates are revalued on a monthly basis in line with the retail price index. This revaluation is based on the new value, not the original purchase price. An example should make this clear.

	£
100 units of £10 each purchased at cost of	1,000
Increase in retail price index during first year (8%)	80
Value at end of first year	1,080
Increase in retail price index during second year (10%)	108
Value at end of second year	1,188
Increase in retail price index during third year (5%)	59
Value at end of third year	1,247

At the end of five years a bonus of 4 per cent on the original purchase price is paid. This is additional to the index-linked increase in value and, like the index linked appreciation, is exempt from all forms of British tax. In November 1982, the government said a special bonus of 2.4 per cent would be paid to holders who held index-linked national savings certificates for more than one year. This was to counteract the withdrawal of funds caused through the slowing down of inflationary increases.

3.5 Premium savings bonds

These are another form of bond issued by the Department for National Savings. They were first introduced in 1956 but have never been as popular as National Savings Certificates or National Savings Bank accounts. Premium savings bonds are not securities which produce either income or capital growth. The modest notional interest of 7 per cent a year allowed on the bonds is placed in a prize fund.

Drawings are made each weekend by means of a computer known as Ernie (Electronic Random Number Indicator Equipment). The first prize in the weekly draw is for £100,000 and there are second and third prizes for £50,000 and £25,000 each. Once a month a special draw is made with a top prize of £250,000. There are also a number of smaller prizes in the monthly draw ranging from £50 to £10,000. The total sums paid out each month come to around £8 million. All the prizes are exempt from any form of British tax.

3.6 National savings income bonds

In order to be more competitive with banks and building societies, the Department for National Savings has now introduced a monthly income bond. The minimum deposit accepted is for £2,000 while the maximum permitted is for £200,000. Interest rates vary from time to time in line with money market conditions, but the director of savings has said that these interest rates will remain fully competitive. The interest is calculated on a daily basis and once a month a warrant is sent by post or credited to the bondholder's bank account. No tax is deducted but these payments must be included in the bondholder's tax return.

The disadvantage of these bonds is that full interest is only paid on withdrawals if you give six months notice and only then if the bonds have been held for a year. Penalties are imposed for cashing the bonds during the first year or for only giving three months notice of withdrawal. National savings income bonds are only useful for those who can put capital away and forget about it.

3.7 National savings stock register

The Department for National Savings provides a service for those who wish to purchase British Government Stocks. In the strictest sense of the word, these purchases are not savings as the national savings stock register deals with purchases and sales of stocks which have already been issued. This may sound 'hair-splitting' to a private investor who may be making a choice between leaving money in a deposit account with a bank, retaining a balance with a building society or switching funds into government securities.

There are considerable advantages to using the national savings stock register.

(a) Forms of instructions to buy or sell are available at any Post Office.
(b) Interest is paid gross, i.e. no tax is deducted, but the figure must be included in the stockholder's tax return.
(c) The commission charges are much lower than dealings through the Stock Exchange. While stockbrokers' commissions are subject to value added tax, the Director of Savings will pay VAT on commissions arising from dealings in stock on the national savings stock register.
(d) No limit on the amount of stock which you can hold or which can be sold at any one time.

These are the disadvantages of using the national savings stock register:

(a) Not all securities issued by the British government are included in the register.
(b) A limit of £5,000 on a purchase of any particular stock on one day.
(c) Instructions cannot be given to buy or sell at a specified price or on a named day. With orders being sent by post to the Bonds and Stock Office in Blackpool while the dealings are on the London Stock Exchange, there may be delay in executing orders.
(d) The Director of Savings will not give advice on the time to buy and sell or the price at which transactions should be arranged.

Unlike purchases of ordinary shares, which attract ad valorem stamp duty at the rate of 2 per cent on the purchase price, no stamp duty is paid when government securities are bought. There is no capital gains tax on the proceeds of sale of government securities held for more than twelve months. Capital gains tax is always assessable on the disposal of ordinary shares, although small gains are exempt from capital gains tax.

3.8 Index-linked save-as-you-earn

Although there were contractual savings schemes run by the Department for National Savings from 1969 onwards, the present index-linked scheme has been operating since 1975. A five-year contract is signed to pay a fixed sum each month. The minimum monthly subscription is £4 and the maximum £50. Payment can be made by deduction from earnings, standing order transfer from a bank account, or handing cash over a Post Office counter.

Each monthly contribution is revalued in line with the change in the retail price index. The first contribution is revalued by comparison with the index five years earlier. The last contribution is revalued by comparison with the index figure for the previous month. As an alternative, instead of obtaining repayment at the end of five years, the savings can be left with the Department for National Savings for a further two years. Revaluation of the contributions continues between the end of the fifth and seventh year but no further monthly payments need be made. At the end of seven years, an additional bonus equal to two monthly contributions is paid when the savings are repaid.

If repayment is requested within a year of the start of the contract, no interest is payable. Should repayment be asked for before the end of five years interest at the fixed rate of 6 per cent per annum is paid. All interest, capital appreciation or bonuses are exempt from British tax.

While this is a highly attractive form of contractual savings during a period of rapidly rising prices it is a much less desirable investment when the rate of inflation is falling.

4 BUILDING SOCIETIES

Building society share accounts are very popular homes for the savings of the public. Some of the funds are raised from deposit account holders who, in return for a lower rate of interest, are entitled to priority of repayment in the event of the society going into liquidation. In 1974 the British government lent £300 million to the building societies. During the next four or five years these appeared on the societies' balance sheets as official loans. Another source of finance was tapped by the Anglia Hastings and Thanet Building Society in 1979 when they borrowed £20 million in the wholesale money market in order to finance increased mortgage lending. This society later merged with the London and South of England Building Society and is now known as the Anglia Building Society.

In this merger it was following a pattern set in the building society movement over the past twenty years. At the end of 1965 there were 605 building societies. This number was reduced by various amalgamations to 287 by the end of 1979. Further mergers since that time have reduced the numbers even more. Alongside this concentration in numbers has gone a tremendous growth of funds deposited by the public. A simple table will show the rate of expansion.

Date	Total of shares and deposit accounts (thousand million)
1962	£3.5
1965	£5.5
1970	£10.1
1975	£22.5
1979	£46.1

During the same period the increase in the deposits with the clearing banks did no more than keep pace with inflation. The only years since 1962 in which the clearing bank deposits increased by a larger percentage than the increase in building society deposits were 1973 and 1974. In these two years the government first of all imposed restrictions on the rate of interest which banks could pay to small savers and then lent the building societies £300 million on favourable terms. The increased loans which banks are granting for house purchase are part of a campaign to hold on to their share of the market for retail deposits. Building societies traditionally had a monopoly of mortgage-type finance and would-be borrowers were asked to become shareholders first.

4.1 Building society share accounts

This is the most usual way in which people invest in building societies and 90 per cent of a society's liabilities are usually in this form. They are a very convenient account to hold for day-to-day transactions. Any cash or cheques paid in to the account will earn interest from the day following their credit. Most societies allow cash withdrawals of up to £250 on demand and the majority of societies will issue cheques for up to £2,500 on request. The maximum balance allowed on a joint account is £60,000 and the permitted maximum balance allowed on an individual account is £30,000. The rate of interest allowed varies from time to time and is, by arrangement with the Inland Revenue, 'basic income tax paid'. This makes a share account an attractive savings vehicle for the standard tax payer. Where there is a liability to a higher rate of tax the interest payment is grossed-up. If we assume that a taxpayer, who is liable to pay 40 per cent on the top slice of his income, receives interest of £70 a year from his building society share account, his liability will be calculated as in the following example, when 30 per cent is the standard rate of income tax.

		£
A	Building society interest received (Basic income tax rate paid 30%)	70
B	Grossed-up interest $(£70 \times \frac{100}{100 - 30})$	100
C	Tax payable (£100 x 40%)	40
	less tax already accounted for (£100 x 30%)	30
	Additional assessment	10

4.2 Regular savings accounts

These are available for members of the building society who wish to enter into a contractual savings scheme. An agreement is made to pay a fixed monthly sum which can be a maximum of £100 or a minimum of £1. As long as these regular contributions continue, interest will be paid at a higher level than the interest paid on ordinary share accounts. One withdrawal of any sum of money can be made in each calendar year without losing the extra interest. In circumstances such as saving for a holiday, a car, or a deposit on a house, regular savings accounts are an invaluable aid to self-discipline. Interest is paid in a 'basic income tax rate paid' manner.

If monthly payments stop or more than one withdrawal is made in the calendar year, the interest rate is reduced to the normal rate paid on an ordinary share account. The total invested on regular savings and ordinary accounts combined must not exceed £30,000 (or £60,000 if a joint account).

4.3 Save-as-you-earn accounts

This scheme is on similar lines to the national savings index-linked save-as-you-earn scheme except that the agreement is fixed in money terms. The saver agrees to pay the society between £1 and £20 a month for a five-year period. At the end of these five years, the society will pay a bonus of fourteen monthly subscriptions if the contributions are withdrawn. Should you decide to leave the savings with the society for another two years, another bonus of fourteen monthly subscriptions is added at the end of seven years. This table will make the position clear.

	Monthly contribution	5 year bonus	Total at end of 5 years	7 year bonus	Total at end of 7 years
A	£4	£56	£296	£56	£352
B	£9	£126	£666	£126	£792
C	£20	£280	£1480	£280	£1760

As these five and seven year bonuses are regarded as capital accretions rather than income, they are not 'grossed-up' for taxpayers paying more than the standard rate of income tax. These bonuses are exempt from capital gains tax and save-as-you-earn contributions do not need to be added to other building society accounts in order to arrive at the figure for the maximum permitted investment.

4.4 Term shares

A minimum deposit of £500 or £1,000 is required, depending on the society. Some societies have bonds which carry a fixed rate of interest and are repayable at a fixed time, usually one to three years ahead. Almost all societies have fixed term shares where the interest varies but is always greater than the interest paid on ordinary shares. With certain societies withdrawals are permitted from these fixed term share accounts but three or six months notice must be given. No interest is paid during the period of notice on the amount of money withdrawn.

4.5 Other share accounts

At one time, ordinary share accounts and deposit accounts were the only services which building societies offered to investors. In the past few years, a bewildering range of accounts has been available. The extra flexibility has shown the building societies to be imaginative competitors of other deposit-taking institutions.

Accounts can now be opened with interest paid on a regular monthly basis. Provided minimum deposits are retained, which vary from society to society, bonus accounts are available combining higher interest than that paid on ordinary shares with withdrawals available at short notice. Some society accounts combine a form of life assurance with a regular savings scheme. Alliance Building Society even has an account where interest paid varies to the same extent as the retail price index.

The building societies have shown by their expansion during the past twenty years that they are capable of providing formidable competition to the Department for National Savings and to the banks. They are much less directly competitive with the life assurance companies who have continued to grow at a fast rate in spite of the fairly modest competition given by save-as-you-earn and other subscription schemes.

5 SAVING ACCOUNTS AT BANKS

5.1 Deposit accounts

Most savers who use banks have deposit accounts. These can be used for deposit of both cash and cheques but, because cheque books are not issued with deposit accounts, only cash withdrawals are allowed. Standing order payments cannot be made from deposit accounts, but instructions can be given for the transfer of funds to the customer's current account. Seven days' notice of withdrawal is required but withdrawals are usually permitted without notice provided there is a seven day loss of interest.

Interest is paid without deduction of tax, although this interest is taxable. Rates of interest vary from time to time but a statement is always made to the press whenever there is any change.

The accounts are fully computerised and periodic statements are sent to customers on the same lines as the statements sent to current account customers.

In the early 1960s, most of the retail deposits collected through the branch networks of the banks were current accounts. With the substantially higher rates of interest paid during the past twenty years, this position has now reversed. Customers are very interest-rate conscious and will keep the minimum balances on current accounts needed to avoid bank charges. Any surplus funds are transferred to deposit account to take advantage of the high returns offered. This process was slowed down between 1973 and 1975 when the government prevented the banks giving competitive rates of interest to small savers. During those three years the 'leakage' of funds from current accounts was to building society share accounts rather than to the banks' own deposit accounts.

5.2 Regular savings accounts

Higher interest is paid on regular savings accounts than is allowed on normal savings accounts or branch deposit accounts. In a similar manner to other bank accounts, interest is calculated on a daily basis and is paid without tax being deducted at basic rate of income tax. This makes a regular savings account very attractive for young students or other non-taxpayers, as the gross return is usually above the net return paid on building society subscription share accounts. The regular saver must agree to save a minimum of £10 a month but there is no maximum figure. One monthly subscription can be missed within a six-month period without losing the benefit of the higher interest rate. In just the same way, there is no interest penalty if one cash withdrawal is made during any six-month period.

5.3 Mortgage savings plan

Some banks have variations on the regular savings plans. The mortgage savings scheme states that, in return for regular subscriptions, the saver is guaranteed a mortgage. Under the Barclays scheme a saver is guaranteed a mortgage of up to ten times the balance in the mortgage savings account. The minimum balance to qualify must be £1,000 and the account must have run for at least a year. A maximum of £30,000 is placed under the guarantee given to the saver. In certain circumstances, however, this figure can be increased up to a maximum of £40,000. The agreed figure is conditional on the mortgage not exceeding 95 per cent of the price or valuation of the property.

The arrangements for payment of higher interest, missed contributions, and cash withdrawals are similar to those for regular savings accounts.

National Westminster Bank has a mortgage saver account which is aimed at those who want a short-term savings account with a considerably higher interest. Although the rate of interest will vary in line with the interest on other savings and deposit accounts, there will be an added bonus of 2¼ per cent per annum.

An agreement is made to transfer at least £100 a month from current account at any bank to the mortgage saver account. The saver must undertake to save for a minimum of eighteen months and a maximum of thirty-six months. In return a mortgage of up to £30,000, against normal security, is guaranteed up to six months after the monthly subscriptions have ceased.

5.4 Monthly income accounts

Salaried persons are used to dealing with their financial affairs on a monthly basis. On retirement, they are frequently given a lump sum payment as part of their pension benefits. With normal investment, income accrues on a quarterly, half-yearly basis, and sometimes income varies as to amounts paid and times payable. To overcome these problems of matching monthly expenses with monthly revenue, the banks have introduced monthly income accounts for those who are approaching retirement or who have already retired. Interest on the amount deposited is paid without any deduction of tax. It is very attractive, therefore, for people living abroad or old persons who are non-taxpayers. The interest is transferred at the end of each calendar month to the depositor's current account.

A month's notice is needed for any withdrawals from the monthly income account and a minimum balance of £2,000 is stipulated by most of the banks. Interest will vary from time to time, in line with the interest paid on other deposit accounts but at a higher rate than other accounts. National Westminster Bank have given an assurance to those who have monthly income accounts that they intend to maintain the interest on these accounts at a higher level than the rate paid on ordinary deposits.

6 UNIT TRUSTS

These are intended for the long-term investor. Because the value of the underlying securities fluctuates in line with Stock Exchange prices, the unit trust holder might find the value of his savings reduced when he comes to sell. For that reason, it is good investment policy always to have liquid funds available in bank accounts, national savings securities or building society accounts to meet foreseeable or emergency expenses. In that way, the investor avoids being forced into a sale of securities which might involve a loss of capital.

Unit trusts are managed by banks, including trustee savings and merchant banks, insurance companies and professional management companies such as M & G. These trusts are set up by means of a deed between the managers and a corporate trustee, such as a bank or insurance company, which holds the securities. The trust deed must be authorised by the Department of Trade and Industry, which also controls the charges made.

Investments are made by the managers in a wide range of company shares. Unit trusts are a better way for a small investor to buy ordinary shares than through a stockbroker. There are heavy expenses such as stamp duty and commission charges which make a direct purchase of shares worth less than £800 disproportionately expensive. The theory of unit trust management involves a large number of small investors merging their savings. These funds are invested on their behalf by the trust managers and the securities purchased are held by the corporate trustee.

A very wide spread of risk is achieved by investing in a large number of British companies and, in addition, purchasing shares of companies registered abroad. In this way the investor not only obtains a range of securities spread throughout a number of industries but also has a share of investments in different geographical areas of the world.

Although the income from unit trusts is likely to be lower than the income from fixed interest securities, the long-term investor is likely to find that, over a five or six year period, his capital will keep pace with inflation. For the person with between £500 and £15,000 surplus funds, in addition to liquid assets, who can leave these surplus funds invested for at least five years without disturbance, unit trust investment is less risky than purchasing a number of shares in a small group of public companies.

Apart from lump sum investment, unit trust managers, including the banks, have regular monthly savings plans. These are particularly suitable for elderly savers or those who are uncertain about their future income. There are a number of advantages to regular savings plans.

(a) Monthly subscriptions can be stopped at any time and the investor can take the units purchased up to that date.

(b) The investor is able to ignore fluctuations in stock exchange prices and does not need to consider the timing of purchases.

(c) The whole of the monthly subscriptions is used to buy fresh units.

(d) If the investor's circumstances change, the monthly payments can be altered without any penalty.

A variation on the regular savings plan is to have the monthly subscriptions invested in unit trusts, combined with life assurance relief. A small part of the subscription, usually between 5 per cent if you are young and 15 per cent if you are older, is used to pay the premiums on life assurance cover. The remainder of the monthly payments are invested by the managers in the purchase of shares for the unit trust. The unit-linked life assurance schemes have considerable benefits for the investor.

(a) The saver does not need to worry about the problem of timing the purchases.

(b) The policy holder has life assurance cover for a sum which is usually a multiple of the monthly subscription.

(c) Tax relief is given. At the present time, this amounts to 15 per cent of the gross payment. This means if you sign a contract to pay £25 a month, the net sum payable is £21.25 (£25 – £3.75).

There are disadvantages to this type of policy. If you cash in your investment before the end of ten years, the Inland Revenue may 'claw back' some of the tax relief you have been given on the premiums. Premiums must be paid by standing order and must be maintained on a regular basis. For the elderly saver the amount taken to pay the life assurance portion of the premium may be as much as the tax relief given.

For the comparatively young saver this is a good way of saving over a very long period. Because of tax relief it is possible to invest more than you can pay. If a man aged thirty takes out a fifteen-year policy with gross premiums of £10 a month, the figure would work out on the following lines:

Total annual gross premiums (12 x £10 a month)	£120
Total invested by unit trust managers (95% of £120)	£114
Total premium paid by investor (tax relief of 15%)	£102

For net annual premiums of £102, the investor has £114 a year invested for him. At the end of the fifteen-year period he will obtain the units purchased with the premiums (15 x £114). These should have increased in value over this time. During this period, he will also have been given life assurance (15 x £120) of £1,800 in addition.

Sales of the lump sum investments in unit trusts, regular savings or unit-linked life assurance can be easily arranged over the counters of branch banks. As well as having displays of material relating to unit trusts available in their branch networks, the banks advertise this particular service in the press. Where people already have Stock Exchange securities, they are invited to exchange these for investments in unit trusts in order to get the benefit of a wide spread of a risk and the expert knowledge of the bank's investment managers.

7 THE STOCK EXCHANGE

Small private investors who wish to buy government securities would be well-advised to confine themselves to purchases of those issued by the Department of National Savings, through banks or post offices. These include the British government stocks on the national savings stock register, which can be purchased more cheaply than through the Stock Exchange.

Where private investors wish to invest in equities, they should consider the unit trusts, managed by banks or insurance companies, if their holdings are likely to be modest. The larger investor might well use the services provided by the clearing banks and merchant banks in the field of investment management.

The wealthy private customer or the company treasurer with substantial surplus funds to invest will seek the services of a stockbroker. A stockbroker is a member of the Stock Exchange who acts as an agent for the investor. A commission is charged for the purchases and sales which the stockbroker carries out on behalf of his principal. Stockbrokers are also employed by companies to advise on the price and timing of new issues of shares.

The rules of the London Stock Exchange prevent the stockbroker buying and selling shares except through a stockjobber. The stockjobber is only allowed to deal with brokers or other jobbers. In theory, jobbers are always prepared to buy and sell shares. In practice, this is sometimes difficult, especially where small company stocks are involved. Stockjobbers obtain the capital they need by borrowing from the banks against the security of the stocks which they have purchased through the Stock Exchange.

To support the activities of selected jobbing firms, eligible banks are now allowed by the Bank of England to include money at call, lent out to approved gilt-edged stockjobbers, in the ratio of 5 per cent which they need to keep between money at call and eligible liabilities.

By the middle of 1980, the number of jobbing firms had fallen to seventeen. Many critics have claimed that this reduces the effectiveness of a competitive market.

Although the British government borrows from the public, largely by issues of long-term stocks through the Stock Exchange, and companies issue new shares through the Stock Exchange, the stock market is concerned with second-hand securities in the overwhelming majority of its transactions. For the efficient operation of a market, based on transactions in already issued securities, you need a system of 'trading posts' where brokers deal with each other, such as is used abroad, or a large number of well capitalised jobbing firms who act as the wholesalers of the market.

The institutional investors, who now dominate dealings on the Stock Exchange, tend to enter into transactions which strain the capital resources of the jobbing firms. Through the activities of pension fund trustees and insurance companies, most of us are indirect investors on the Stock Exchange. Direct investment nowadays is largely confined to wealthy private individuals.

Investments should not be made in stocks of money which the investor cannot afford to lose. The quotation of a share on the Stock Exchange does not guarantee an investor against loss, although the Stock Exchange Council requires quoted companies to provide more detailed information than the statutory requirements of the various Companies Acts.

Some companies cannot comply with the requirements of the stock market needed for a full quotation. In some instances, these shares can be dealt with in that section of the stock market known as the 'unlisted securities market'.

Competition to the unlisted market is provided by the 'over-the-counter' market run by M J H Nightingale and Co. Ltd. Prices of the shares traded in the market run by Nightingales are quoted daily in the *Financial Times*. It is not necessary to go through a broker in order to buy or sell shares on the 'over-the-counter' market.

14 *Interest Rates*

Interest is the price paid by those who want 'money now' to savers prepared to exchange 'money now' for 'money in the future'.

The main demand for loanable funds comes from industrial and commercial companies, central and local government, together with professional firms. The principal supply of loanable funds comes from private individuals.

While the fixing of a rate of interest is an attempt to reconcile the demand and supply of loanable funds, the needs of savers and borrowers differ. Savers want to have security combined with liquidity (i.e. the ability to realise funds quickly with a minimum of capital loss). Borrowers, on the other hand, are primarily concerned with borrowing for as long as possible on the easiest terms.

1 DIFFERENT TYPES OF RATES OF INTEREST

Some rates are administered rates which are widely publicised by the financial institutions concerned. Examples of administered rates are bank rate and minimum lending rate, both of which were used by the Bank of England to signal its intentions to the financial markets. Other examples of administered rates are the base rates published by leading banks, the building society mortgage rate recommended by the Building Societies Association and the finance houses rate announced by the Finance Houses Association.

Market rates are those rates of interest which are determined simply by the need for funds and the willingness of investors to supply these funds. Examples of these rates are Treasury bill rate, London inter-bank offered rate and eligible bank bill rate. Treasury bill rate is the discount offered by the government to savers who take the promissory notes issued by the Treasury to cover its short term borrowing needs.

London inter-bank offered rate is the interest paid in the inter-bank market when banks borrow and lend to each other. Eligible bank bill rate is the rate of interest on bills of exchange which have been accepted by banks whose acceptances command the finest rate of discount. Commercial companies are the main group who finance themselves through the sale of bills and discount houses are the main purchasers. Eligible bank bills are desirable investments because the Bank of England is always willing to discount them.

2 STRUCTURE OF INTEREST RATES

The three main factors which influence interest rates are

(a) risk;
(b) liquidity;
(c) expectations.

The careful saver is always risk-averse. This means that he will be prepared to accept a lower rate of interest on a government security than one paid on a loan to a small industrial company.

However creditworthy its directors, the small local building society is likely to find it difficult to attract funds and thus be forced to pay higher interest to savers than the interest paid by the largest building societies such as the Alliance, Anglia and Nationwide building societies.

In just the same way, the clearing banks find it easier to attract funds on deposit than small finance houses. The rates paid by the clearing banks on their interest-bearing deposits are nearly always the lowest in the market and act as the 'marker' for other short-term rates.

Liquidity means the ability to obtain cash for your investment without capital loss. If a deposit can be repaid on demand or within a very short time, the interest allowed is likely to be much lower than a fixed deposit due to mature in twelve months time. Similarly, the saver who invests in a three year building society term share will expect a much higher rate of interest than that paid on an ordinary share account, to compensate for the loss of liquidity.

In some cases the asset can be passed on to someone else and liquidity is assured in these circumstances. An example of this type of asset is the range of British government securities which can always be sold for cash on the stock exchange. Other examples are Treasury bills or eligible bank bills which can always be re-discounted at the Bank of England. Because of their high liquidity, assets such as these earn much lower interest than fixed term loans to an unquoted private company.

Expectations of future interest rates also influence present rates. In normal circumstances, long-term investments yield higher interest rates than short-term investments. If short-term rates are expected to fall, the reverse applies. This is because an investor who buys a long-term security now is guaranteed a high yield for as long as the security is held. A saver who deposits money with a bank for a month may obtain a high rate now but when the money is reinvested in a month's time, a much reduced income may be available on the new investment.

Below are examples of charts showing the term structure of interest rates. The first chart (Figure 14.1) illustrates the way in which rates on money deposited with the bank rise as the term lengthens. In a similar fashion, higher income is obtained by the bank investing in assets with a longer term.

The second chart (Figure 14.2) shows a term structure for the yields on eligible bank bills, when the rates are expected to fall in the near future, and another line showing yields when short-term rates are expected to rise in the near future.

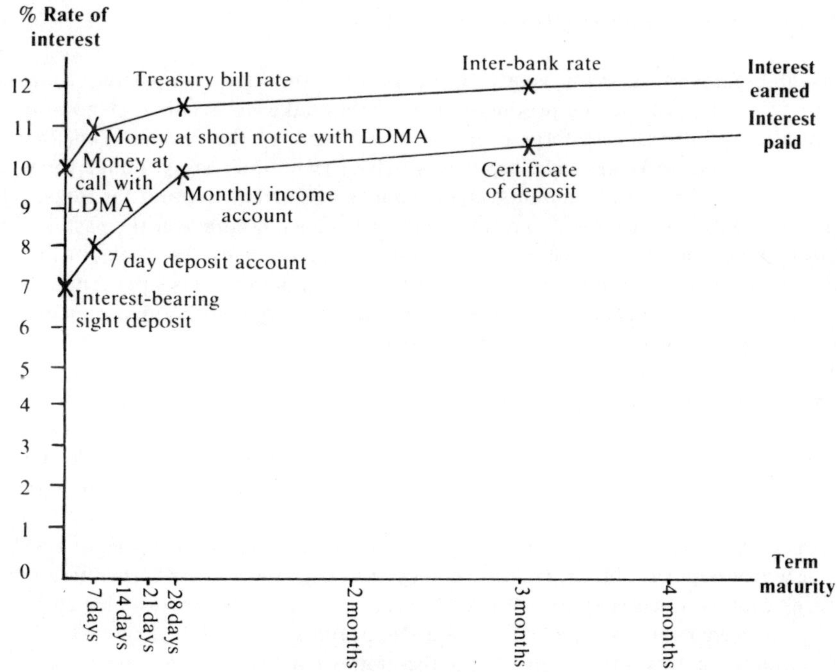

Figure 14.1

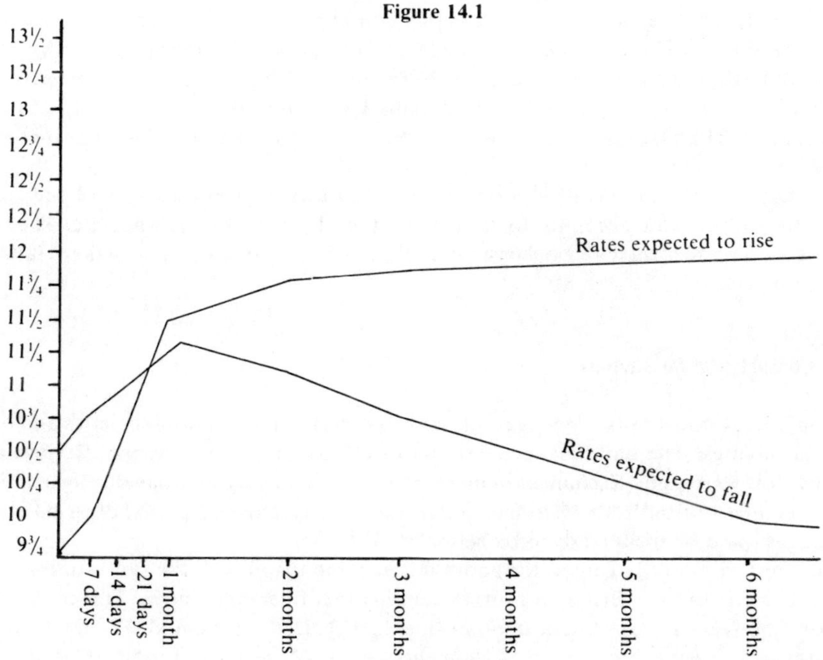

Figure 14.2

3 EFFECT OF INTEREST CHANGES ON BANKS

Although Figures 14.1 and 14.2 give a representation of the relationship between interest-bearing deposits and income-producing assets, they take no account of non-interest bearing demand deposits. A large proportion of a bank's liabilities are in the form of current accounts. These are sight deposits which carry no interest. Although the banks still have very substantial amounts in the names of current account customers, the proportion of current accounts to total liabilities has been falling over the past decade.

A very large part of these current accounts are invested by the banks in income-producing investments or advances. It costs the banks approximately 9 per cent a year to service these current accounts and, unless more than 9 per cent is obtained from income-producing assets, the costs of running the current accounts must be recovered through bank charges.

When interest rates rise, the banks will earn a higher income from their very short term money, although this extra profit may be off-set by capital losses on long-term investments. More interest will be charged to those borrowing customers whose loans have been agreed at a variable rate i.e., a percentage figure over the bank's base rate or London inter-bank offered rate.

At the same time, the banks will pay higher interest on interest-bearing deposits. Many of these will be deposits obtained in the wholesale markets. If very short term interest rates are rising rapidly, it may pay large borrowing customers, who borrow at 'blue chip' rate, usually 1 per cent over base rate, to borrow up to the full amount of their agreed limit. The funds obtained in this way are invested in the money market at a slight margin over the interest paid on the borrowing. Because of this 'round-tripping', as it is called, banks need to be able to respond very quickly to changes in interest rates by altering their own base rates. Unlike the old bank rate system, used by the Bank of England until 1972, when bank rate fixed interest rates for all other rates, bank base rates are only one group of rates among many. The base rate changes tend to follow market rates rather than the other way round.

The banks still gain overall in a period of rising interest rates because of the large proportion of current accounts to total liabilities. By contrast, falling interest rates squeeze the 'endowment' effect of large totals of current accounts and lead to sharp falls in bank profits.

3.1 Competition for savings

Falling interest rates cause 'leakages' of bank deposits to the building societies and into national savings. The building societies and the Department for National Savings are equally slow to respond to changes in market rates. The interest they pay during a period of falling rates is usually above other similar rates just as, during a period of rising rates, the interest paid by them tends to be below market rates.

If interest rates in the United Kingdom fall in comparison with the rest of the world, funds are likely to leave Britain for investment in other financial centres. This could take the form of overseas investment in other financial centres. This could take the form of overseas investment by the investment managers of pension funds or insurance companies. It might also take the form of a reduction in the level of bank deposits held by British banks in the names of non-residents. In a similar fashion, higher interest rates in

Britain, compared with the rest of the world, will attract foreign deposits to the United Kingdom and encourage British investors to keep their funds at home.

3.2 Other effects of interest rate changes

Borrowing customers of banks will benefit from falling interest rates, unless they are borrowing fixed rate loans. They are likely to consider investment in stock, purchases of fixed assets and the taking on of fresh workers, if a profitable opportunity presents itself. High interest rates are going to increase the burden on most borrowers, discouraging fresh investment and leading to lay-offs of workers.

Interest rates which are below world levels may lead to a fall in a country's exchange rate. While this will reduce the price of exported goods, thus stimulating exporters' output, it will also increase the price of imported raw materials and will increase manufacturing costs.

Where interest rates are higher than world levels, they will keep the exchange rate higher than it would otherwise be. Export prices will be kept high, reducing the demand for these export goods abroad. Import prices will be kept low, stimulating a demand for imports from abroad. In following an interest rate policy, it is very hard for a government or a central bank to achieve a balance between the conflicting interests of exporters, importers, manufacturers and consumers.

15 *Definitions of Money Supply*

The items included in the figures for money supply are not identical throughout the world. This does not mean that one system is better than another, only that comparison is difficult. The Bank of England uses several calculations of the money supply, but the main definition used in government targets and the one which symbolises money supply in the financial press is Sterling M_3. In the March 1982 budget the Chancellor of the Exchequer announced that targets would be set in future for M_1 and PSL_2, as well as for £M_3. The various definitions are given below:

M_0 = Notes and coins in circulation + the credit balances on accounts held by banks as bankers deposits with the Bank of England.

M_1 = Notes and coins in circulation + sight deposits with British banks in the names of UK residents in the private sector – 60 per cent of items in transit through the clearing.

Notes: (a) Deposits in the private sector are all deposits apart from those in the names of government bodies or other banks.

(b) After a cheque is credited to a customer's account, it will be some time before that cheque is debited to the account on which it is drawn. Until the transaction is complete, the balances will be swollen by funds not belonging to the drawer. To allow for this distortion, 60 per cent of the total of cheques being cleared is deducted from the amount of sight deposits. Similar adjustments are made for bank giro credits and standing order payments going through the clearing system.

M_2 = M_1 + interest-bearing deposits with UK banks of up to £100,000 in the name of any one customer, which are repayable within one month or less. (This symbol fell into disuse in 1971 and was not used at all during the rest of the 1970s. In June 1982 the Bank of England re-defined M_2 so that it measures what are described as 'transaction balances'.)

M_3 = M_2 + all other deposits with British banks held by residents of the United Kingdom.

£M_3 = M_3 – UK residents' deposits with British banks in other currencies. (Since exchange control restrictions were lifted in 1979, it is no longer necessary to obtain Bank of England permission to open an account which is denominated in a currency other than sterling. This has led to a large increase in the amounts deposited in this way and, to avoid complications, Sterling M_3 is now used as the main money supply target rather than the simpler M_3.)

PSL_1 *(Private sector liquidity one)* = M_3 + deposits with local authorities and finance houses + Treasury bills and bank bills.

Notes: (a) Local authorities accept short term deposits to cover their expenditure until rates demands are paid. Finance houses accept short term deposits to lend out for the hire purchase or leasing of vehicles and other machinery.

(b) Treasury bills or bank bills can be turned into cash by selling to the Bank of England. A Treasury bill is a short-dated promise to pay on a fixed date. A bank bill is a document covering a commercial debt which the bank have agreed to meet on the due date.

PSL_2 = PSL_1 + shares and deposits with building societies + deposits with National Savings Bank + National Savings Certificates.

Notes: (a) Although not money in the strict sense of the term, PSL_2 is the definition which most members of the public would choose to describe money. With the rapid expansion of the building society movement in recent years, combined with the increasing range of transmission services offered by some building societies, PSL_2 may be a more useful guide to the future growth of the money supply than M_1 and £M_3.

(b) The figure for PSL_2 excludes all shares and deposits with building societies which have an original maturity of more than one year. Save-as-you-earn contracts are also excluded.

1 METHODS OF CONTROL OF BANK DEPOSITS

The Bank of England gives informal guidance from time to time and also uses the method of buying and selling securities to control the total of deposits in the banking system. Detailed analysis of these methods is the province of the monetary economist. The practical banker must, however, be familiar with alternative methods used at the present time and also with other methods used in the recent past.

1.1 Cash ratio

This is the oldest and most familiar of the controls. If banks create deposits by lending money or buying securities, they must obtain cash to maintain the accepted ratio between cash and deposits. The banks kept a 10 per cent ratio between cash and deposits up to 1946. This cash figure used to include not only the coins and notes they kept in their tills but the balances they retained at the Bank of England. Between 1946 and 1971 this ratio between cash and deposits was reduced to 8 per cent.

The system known as 'Competition and Credit Control' was introduced in 1971. Coins and bank notes were excluded from the figure of cash in calculating the new ratio. This meant that only the balances kept at the Bank of England were taken into the calculation of the new ratio. The cash ratio under 'Competition and Credit Control' was fixed at 1½ per cent of eligible liabilities and applied to the clearing banks alone. The clearing banks felt that the exclusion of bank notes and coins from the figures used in the cash ratio was most unfair, especially as only the clearing banks were obliged to keep to the 1½ per cent ratio between their balances at the Bank of England and their eligible liabilities. Under the system of 'Competition and Credit Control', 'eligible liabilities' were defined as sterling deposits minus any money at call lent to discount houses and also minus any funds lent to other banks in the inter-bank market.

New arrangements were proposed in the Bank of England paper *Monetary Control – Next Steps* published in March 1981. Following discussion with interested parties the Bank of England published a paper *Monetary Control Provisions* on 5 August 1981. This gave details of the new cash ratio to be applied as from 20 August 1981.

A new monetary sector was defined consisting of recognised banks, licensed deposit takers, National Girobank, the Bank of England's own banking department and the Trustee Savings Banks. All recognised banks, licensed deposit takers and National Girobank must now hold funds on a non-operational, non-interest bearing account at the Bank of England, equivalent to ½ per cent of their eligible liabilities. The banking department of the Bank of England is not expected to comply with the Bank's controls. Trustee Savings Banks are exempt from this requirement until they receive approval as recognised banks under the terms of the Banking Act 1979, when they will be expected to maintain this ½ per cent cash ratio.

In the calculation of eligible liabilities, the following items can be deducted from the total of sterling deposits:

(a) funds lent by banks and licensed deposit takers to discount houses or other institutions in the new monetary sector;
(b) secured money at call lent to money brokers and gilt-edged stock jobbers.

Where members of the London Discount Market Association are concerned they can deduct, from the total of their sterling deposits, any deposits with them from institutions in the new monetary sector as well as secured money at call from money brokers or approved gilt-edged stock jobbers.

Because of the special difficulties of Northern Ireland a ¼ per cent cash ratio applies to banks operating in that area. This special ratio will only be applicable to sterling deposits of the branches in Northern Ireland and is currently being reviewed by the Bank of England.

The clearing banks are expected to maintain, on a voluntary basis, adequate operational funds on ordinary accounts at the Bank of England. These deposits at the Bank of England will continue to be used for cash withdrawals and clearing purposes.

1.2 Liquidity ratio

Up to 1963 the clearing banks were expected to keep a ratio of 30 per cent between their liquid assets and their deposits. The formula was worked out on this basis:

$$\frac{\text{Cash + Money at call + Bills discounted}}{\text{Deposits}} = 30\%\ \text{Minimum}$$

As you will remember from the previous section, the cash ratio up to 1946 was kept at 10 per cent. It follows from this that the sum of money at call and bills discounted was 20 per cent of deposits. In 1946 the cash ratio was reduced to 8 per cent but the liquidity ratio remained at 30 per cent. This meant that the sum of money at call plus bills discounted increased from 20 to 22 per cent of deposits.

Between 1963 and 1971 the liquidity ratio was reduced to 28 per cent. As the cash ratio was maintained at 8 per cent, the figure for money at call plus bills discounted could be reduced from 22 to 20 per cent of total deposits. With the introduction of 'Competition and Credit Control' in 1971 the liquidity ratio was replaced by a reserve assets ratio.

Unlike the liquidity ratio which only applied to the London clearing banks, the reserve assets ratio was applicable to a larger range of institutions.

1.3 Reserve assets ratio

Instead of being based on total deposits the reserve assets ratio was expressed as a percentage of eligible liabilities (as defined above in the cash ratio section). The minimum figure stipulated for banks was 12½ per cent of eligible liabilities. A figure of 10 per cent was laid down for the finance houses who were subject to reserve assets requirements. In place of the liquid assets which were used for the liquidity ratio, prior to 1971, the reserve assets were carefully selected by the Bank of England. The group of assets selected was as follows:

(a) balances with the Bank of England;
(b) money at call with the discount houses;
(c) local authority bills eligible for re-discount at the Bank of England;
(d) commercial bills eligible for re-discount at the Bank of England;
(e) British government and Northern Irish Treasury bills;
(f) British government stocks with one year or less to maturity;
(g) stocks guaranteed by the British government with one year or less to maturity.

The introduction of the reserve assets ratio was hedged about with qualifications. Apart from the discriminatory impact of the 12½ per cent ratio imposed on the banks as opposed to the 10 per cent imposed on the finance houses, the clearing banks were penalised by the exclusion of coins and bank notes from the total of reserve assets. Because of their substantial involvement in money transmission, the clearing banks' holdings of non-income producing cash were much higher than those of other financial institutions.

A further element of discrimination was the Bank of England's ruling that the London clearing banks, and only the London clearing banks, must maintain a minimum of 1½ per cent of the eligible liabilities in credit balances at the Bank of England. Although this 1½ per cent figure was included in the 12½ per cent reserve asset ratio, non-clearing banks could have the whole of their 12½ per cent ratio in income-producing securities.

Short-dated securities with less than a year to maturity, issued by or guaranteed by the British government, were included in a control ratio for the first time. While this decision widened the choice available for the investment of liquid funds, another decision of the Bank of England counteracted this. Although there was no limit, apart from normal prudence, to the amounts of commercial bills which could be held, the Bank of England would only allow a proportion of available bills, up to a maximum of 2 per cent of eligible liabilities, to be held as reserve assets.

1.4 Eligible banks

The system of reserve ratios introduced in 1971 was scrapped in 1981. A new monetary sector was set up with a larger group of institutions coming under Bank of England supervision. The details of the new non-operational balances have been mentioned in the cash ratio section. At the same time the Bank of England invited recognised banks to apply for eligibility. Those banks who were selected were institutions whose acceptances the Bank of England undertook to discount. In return for this slightly higher status than the rest of the monetary sector, these eligible banks undertook certain obligations. In August 1983, the Bank of England requested that an average of 5 per cent of their eligible liabilities would be lent at market rates as secured money at call to money brokers and gilt-edged jobbers and/or secured money at call or short notice to discount houses. Of this figure, a minimum of 2½ per cent of eligible liabilities must always be kept as secured loans made to members of the London Discount Market Association.

1.5 Special deposits

On the banking department section of the Bank of England's weekly return there is a space for special deposits. This item is placed between public deposits and bankers deposits.

When the Bank of England calls for special deposits, a bank has to lodge a percentage of its deposits on a 'frozen' account at the Bank of England. A low rate of interest, usually Treasury Bill rate, is allowed. The system was introduced in 1958 but prior to 1971 only applied to the London and Scottish clearing banks. Amounts called for varied between 1 and 2½ per cent of deposits. Before 1971, the rate asked of the Scottish banks was usually half the percentage called from the English banks.

The effect of the special deposits scheme was to make the banks short of liquid assets and led to the following results:

(a) restrictions on new bank loans;
(b) subsidiaries of banks bidding for new deposits in wholesale markets. This has the effect of forcing up interest rates;
(c) banks lending against commercial bills instead of in the form of advances.

In 1971 the special deposits scheme was extended to cover all banks and deposit-taking finance houses. Clearing banks were allowed to bid for wholesale funds directly but the reserve assets ratio prevented too large a switch into commercial bills. Calls for special deposits, however, still led to restrictions on lending combined with increased short-term interest rates.

The new 1981 system has not replaced special deposits. The scheme remains in force and applies to all institutions in the new monetary sector whose eligible liabilities exceed £10 million.

1.6 Supplementary special deposits

This scheme was in force between November 1973 and June 1980. It was otherwise known as the 'differential special deposits' system or 'the corset'. Unlike special deposits, which were based on total deposits, the corset related to interest-bearing deposits or IBELS (interest-bearing eligible liabilities). A target was set by the Bank of England for the maximum permitted increase in the growth of interest-bearing eligible liabilities. Penalties were imposed on a progressive scale as the permitted maximum was exceeded. This penal system was to prevent the banks bidding for new deposits in the money markets but it had the effect of penalising the efficient institutions who were growing more quickly. If interest-bearing deposits exceeded the permitted level, non-interest-bearing supplementary deposits had to be placed with the Bank of England.

The scheme was operative during the whole seven-year period except for a few months at the end of 1975 and the beginning of 1976 and again at the end of 1977 and the beginning of 1978. Penalties were imposed at the following rates:

Excess growth of IBELS over specified level	**Non-interest-bearing deposits required**
(a) 3% or below	(a) 5% of excess
(b) 3% to 5%	(b) 25% of excess
(c) above 5%	(c) 50% of excess

The savage penalties imposed on banks which increased their interest-bearing deposits effectively prevented banks competing with each other or with other financial institutions on price. It led to the banks being less eager to increase their lending and diverted borrowing into other channels not subject to Bank of England controls. Instead of taking loans from the banks, many companies at this time financed themselves by bills of exchange. When these bills were accepted by banks they became 'bankers acceptances'. These bills were taken into the banks' bill portfolios and were included as part of the reserve asset ratio, up to a figure of 2 per cent of eligible liabilities. The extent of the 'bill leak' combined with other ways of obtaining finance, such as borrowing abroad with the ending of exchange controls in 1979, led to the abandonment of the supplementary special deposits scheme. In *Monetary Control – Provisions* published by the Bank of England in August 1981, the Bank announced that the scheme has been allowed to lapse.

2 QUALITATIVE CONTROLS ON LENDING

These selective credit controls on bank lending have been imposed by the Bank of England from time to time. Guidance from the Bank on how the clearers should lend is the chosen way of discriminating between borrowers. At the present time, the commercial banks are asked to favour exporters, import-savers, and productive investment in manufacturing industry. In addition, the banks and finance houses were asked to discriminate against private persons, property companies and purely financial transactions. The government's terms control instructions concerning hire purchase contracts are now in abeyance. When these instructions were operative, lending bankers were asked by the Bank of England to apply the same rules concerning minimum deposits and maximum repayment periods in the making of personal loans to private individuals.

Selective controls are unpopular for a variety of reasons. Professional bankers consider it unethical to have to discriminate between equally creditworthy borrowers. It is particularly hard to turn down personal customers who provide a large proportion of bank deposits. Unwillingness to help these personal customers when they needed to borrow has led in the past to some leakages of deposits to other institutions.

The banks have tried to rectify this problem of loss of deposits to the building societies by entering the house mortgage market themselves. Concern has been expressed by the Bank of England who issued a notice on 20 January 1982 to banks, insurance companies, and building societies. These institutions were asked to ensure that funds advanced against mortgages of houses should be used only for the purchase or improvement of residential properties. Where properties were being exchanged or mortgages were being transferred to another lender, the size of the mortgage should not be increased unless the standard of housing was increased or the new property was to be improved. In a speech a few days later the Governor of the Bank of England elaborated on this theme. He said that there was a danger that funds provided on favourable mortgage terms could be used to finance an expansion of cheap consumer credit.

There are a variety of parallel markets for credit and a refusal by the banks to lend to personal customers will not prevent borrowers obtaining funds elsewhere. This was the situation in the 1960s and early 1970s when personal borrowers sought from the 'fringe' lenders and finance houses the funds they could not obtain from their own bankers.

3 QUANTITATIVE CONTROLS ON LENDING

Lending ceilings were imposed for the first time in 1955. This meant that banks were not allowed to increase their advances by more than a specified percentage over a given period. The figures varied from time to time but this method of direct control over the activities of the banks was applied with extreme severity between 1965 and 1971.

A limit of 5 per cent increase in advances was imposed in 1965 and again in 1966. No increase was permitted in 1967 while a limit of 4 per cent increase was applied in 1968. At the end of 1968 the Bank of England called for a 2 per cent reduction within four months, with the exception of loans to shipbuilders and exporters. Most borrowing customers had agreed overdraft limits in force at the time, subject to review once a year. As a result, the reduction of 2 per cent proved impossible to achieve and a severe penalty was imposed on the banks. At that time banks had to lodge frozen deposits with the Bank of England known as 'special deposits'. These deposits could not be withdrawn but some interest was paid on the balances. The penalty imposed by the Bank of England was a unilateral reduction of a penal nature in the amount of interest paid.

This action led to a complete distortion of the credit market. These controls stifled competition between clearing banks and meant that they had to introduce a system of rationing of loans. Many institutions, such as the 'fringe' bankers, were not subject to such strict controls and lent freely during this period. The over-extension of these institutions, on an inadequate capital base, was one of the causes of the eventual financial collapse of the secondary banking sector in 1973. This system of quantitative credit controls was dropped by the Bank of England in 1971. A new system called 'Competition and Credit Control' was introduced which ended in 1981.

16 *Factors Influencing Money Supply*

The qualitative and quantitative controls on lending imposed on the banks by the Bank of England were based on the theory of credit creation. This theory suggests that bank lending creates bank deposits. As bank deposits are now the most important element in the money supply, control of bank lending should control the money supply. The government's restriction of bank lending in this way is part of its monetary policy which also includes control of interest rates.

Since 1981 the Bank of England's main method of carrying out monetary policy has been through its control of interest rates. The Bank of England is able to influence very short-term interest rates through its operations in the money market. Its agent, Seccombe Marshall & Campion, a member of the London Discount Market Association, carries out these open market operations on the Bank of England's behalf.

A purchase of bills, mainly banks' bills but also including Treasury bills, will push interest rates down. This is because the purchase of these bills will have the dual effect of simultaneously reducing the supply of bills available and also increasing the total of bankers' deposits with the Bank of England.

The banks are reluctant to leave surplus balances with the Bank of England as these balances earn no interest. They will either bid for the bills on offer in the money market or lend surplus funds to discount houses or the inter-bank market as money at call. Whatever action they take results in a fall in interest rates.

Sales of bills by the Bank of England will result in a rise in short-term interest rates. Settlement for these bills will involve a reduction in the total of the bankers' deposits at the Bank of England. At the same time, the supply of bills available in the market will be increased. The reduced supply of cash, combined with the increased supply of bills, will lead to a fall in the price of bills, thus pushing up the yield on these bills. The banks will also be withdrawing money at call from the discount houses and the inter-bank market, leaving them short of funds.

When the Bank of England wishes to influence long-term interest rates, they can ask the government broker, a senior partner in the stockbroking firm of Mullens & Co, to buy or sell government securities on the London Stock Exchange. Most of the stocks held in a bank's investment portfolio are securities issued by, or guaranteed by, the British government. By the rules of the Stock Exchange, settlement for these securities is on a 'cash basis'. Purchases of gilt-edged securities by the government broker have the same effect as purchases of bills by the Bank of England's agent in the money market. Payment for these stocks results in an increase in bankers' deposits at the Bank of England. The banks could lend out money at call to the discount houses or purchase bills but, if they already have enough liquid assets, they will purchase government securities. Increased demand for these securities will lead to a rise in price, a fall in yield and a fall in long-term interest rates.

If the government broker sells gilt-edged securities through the Stock Exchange this will result in a reduction of bankers' deposits held at the Bank of England. Banks could call in money lent out at short notice to the discount houses and the inter-bank market or they could sell bills. By the new rules for monetary controls introduced in August 1983, banks are not permitted to allow their ratio between their eligible liabilities and total money lent to discount houses, approved stock jobbers and approved moneybrokers to fall below 5 per cent. A reduction in the level of money at call might compel the banks to sell investments in order to restore the required money at call/eligible liabilities ratio. Sale of investments could lead to reduced prices for government stocks and higher yields combined with higher long-term interest rates.

When the government broker buys gilt-edged securities it will usually be confined to the purchase of stocks with less than three months to go before redemption. This is to acquire sufficient stock to avoid a dislocation to the market when large quantities of stock are repaid. Issues of government stock are made in totals of between £500 million and £2,000 million. If the whole of a £2,000 million stock was repaid to the public on the same day, the money market would have large quantities of money for investment and interest rates would fall rapidly. In order to prevent this, the Bank of England will try to buy up as much as possible of the maturing government stock, in advance of the redemption date.

Sales of gilt-edged securities are usually of medium-dated or long-dated 'tap' stocks. When a government stock is offered for sale to the public, it is very unusual for all of it to be taken up. A large proportion of the stock is left in the Bank of England's hands and held with the remainder of the securities which are shown under 'issue department' on the weekly state. As and when the Bank of England wishes to push up interest rates, it will instruct the government broker to sell part of these 'tap' stocks. The price at which the government broker is prepared to deal is regarded as a signal to the stock market of the Bank of England's intentions.

1 PUBLIC SECTOR BORROWING AND THE MONEY SUPPLY

When taxation from all sources equals government expenditure the central government's budget is said to be balanced. Included in the government's spending are grants or loans to local authorities plus loans and subsidies to nationalised industries. If the total spending on all these items exceeds the amount raised in taxes there is said to be a 'public sector borrowing requirement'. This PSBR, as it is called, must be covered by borrowing as quickly as possible.

One possible way of covering this shortfall is to issue notes or mint coins. Both represent interest-free loans made by the public to the government. Past British governments have never used the issue of token coins or inconvertible bank notes as a method of government finance. They have always taken the view that sufficient coins and notes should be issued to meet the requirements of the banking community for satisfying the demands of the public and traders.

A second way of covering the deficit in government receipts is to issue various government securities to the general public. The main forms of central government debt are:

(a) Securities issued through the director of national savings.

(b) Gilt-edged securities issued by the Bank of England and dealt with on the Stock Exchange and through the national savings stock register.

(c) Treasury bills.

(d) Certificates of tax deposit.

If the securities issued through the director of national savings such as premium savings bonds, national savings certificates and National Savings Bank deposits are equal to the difference between government revenue and expenditure, there will be no increase in the money supply. Figure 16.1 should make this clear.

Figure 16.1: Flow of funds during one month

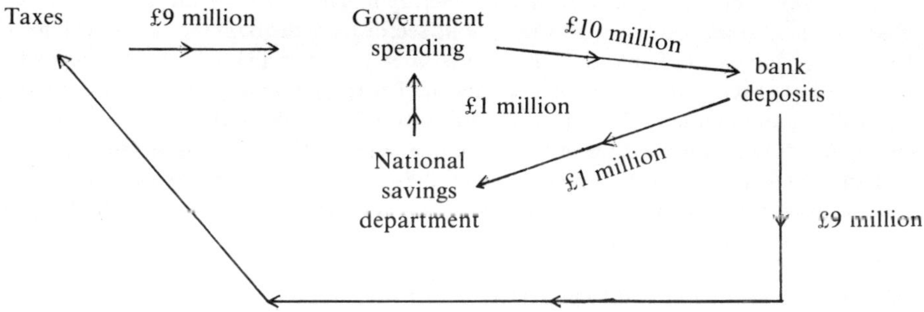

There will be no increase in bank deposits caused by government borrowing so long as the public's investments in national savings are the same as the difference in government spending and revenue. During the financial year 1981/2 the amount raised for the government by the department for national savings was 48 per cent of the public sector borrowing requirement (PSBR). The national savings total for that year was £4,230 million. About half of this total was raised through the issue of index-linked national savings certificates. Although these index-linked securities are less popular with lower rates of inflation, the government has still indicated that a substantial part of the current PSBR will need to be met from the issue of national savings.

Issuing gilt-edged securities through the Bank of England is a way of financing the shortfall in government income. To the extent that these securities are issued to the general public there will be no increase in the Sterling M_3 definition of money supply. A simple diagram demonstrates this (Figure 16.2).

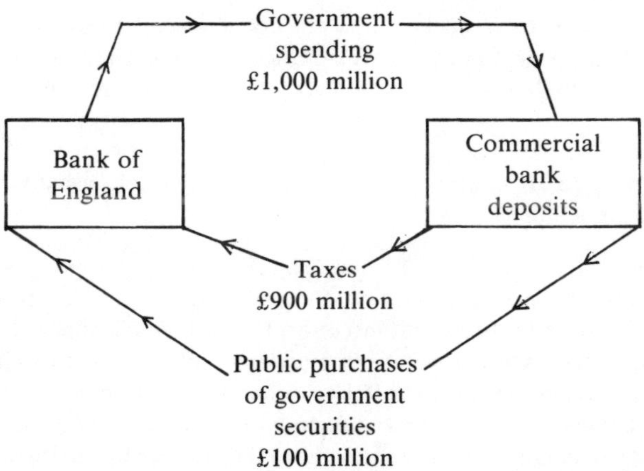

Figure 16.2

To the extent that government expenditure cannot be covered by a combination of an increase in the note issue (currency inflation), sales of national savings or issues of government securities, there will be increased borrowing from the banking system (credit inflation). The increased borrowing can take the form of 'ways and means advance' by the Bank of England, loans from the commercial banks taken by government departments, local authorities or public corporations, or the issue of Treasury bills to the banking system. 'Ways and means advances' are overnight overdrafts which are always for relatively small sums. Borrowing by the public sector from the banking system will have the effect of increasing bank deposits on the lines shown in the 'creation of deposits' section, that is each loan creating a new deposit. The total of bank deposits are the most important component of the figure for Sterling M_3, which is the target set by the government for the control in the growth of money supply. With the issue of Treasury bills the banks have a desirable liquid asset which they can turn into cash at any time by re-discounting at the Bank of England. The possession of these liquid assets will enable them to expand their deposit base by granting loans.

Through the workings of the Exchange Equalisation Account any balance of payments deficit will cause the Bank of England to sell foreign currencies, under a system of fixed exchange rates. The Exchange Equalisation Account will receive sterling in exchange which the Bank of England will invest in 'tap' Treasury bills. This will reduce the government's need to borrow from the banking system and thus have a contracting effect on the money supply. Under a system of floating exchange rates, the Exchange Equalisation Account rarely intervenes in the foreign exchange market. Any pressure from speculators is met by

(a) allowing exchange rate to fall;
(b) allowing interest rates to rise

if there is a balance of payments deficit.

In the event of a balance of payments surplus, the central bank, operating under a freely floating system, will permit

(a) falling interest rates
(b) rising exchange rates.

Changes in non-residents' bank balances are not allowed to influence money supply targets as these non-resident holdings are not included in Sterling M_3.

A simple formula to describe the major factors influencing movements in Sterling M_3 would be:

Change in $£M_3$ = PSBR – Sales of government securities to non-bank private sector + Changes in bank lending

As far as PSBR is concerned this can be altered by changes in government expenditure and changes in the amounts raised in taxation. Sales of government securities will be greatly influenced by interest rate changes. If interest rates are high it is likely to be easier to sell government debt than when interest rates are low. With regard to changes in bank lending, the government can use quantitative or qualitative credit controls. They are also able to use 'open market' operations to influence interest rates, but bank lending tends to be unresponsive to changes in interest rates unless the rates are pushed up to crisis levels.

2 WHOLESALE MONEY MARKETS

In addition to the traditional money market involving the Bank of England, the London discount market and the commercial banks, there are a number of parallel money markets. They are called parallel money markets because the Bank of England does not undertake to act as 'lender of last resort' to operators in these markets who get into financial difficulties.

Because of the severe restrictions placed on the expansion of the banking system during the 1950s and 1960s, borrowers needed an alternative source of finance. They found this alternative in the parallel money markets. The borrowers in these markets were able to raise funds by offering lenders a higher rate of interest than was available from the commercial bankers, who were reluctant to increase deposits during the periodic 'credit squeezes' in those two decades.

2.1 Local authority market

Local authorities are responsible for about one-third of the spending of the public sector. Nearly 60 per cent of the total of local government spending is covered by direct grants from the central government. While most of the remainder is met from local rates, there is still a substantial shortfall which must be met by borrowing.

Borrowing is the usual method of meeting capital expenditure on roads, houses and schools. Long-term loans would be raised for these purposes. Because of the uneven flow of income from rates, local authorities are compelled to borrow short-term loans. Local government treasurers can either borrow from the central government or from independent sources, but all loans for capital projects must have the approval of the central government.

The local authorities' loans market was established in 1955 when local authorities were asked by the Treasury to borrow in the open market instead of from the Public Works Loans Board. This was an early attempt to keep down the level of the central government's budget deficit. The local authorities' loans market is still very active and, although not as large as the inter-bank market, it is still a substantial competitor for private sector funds.

Most of the lending to the local authority market is provided by banks and other financial institutions. The local authority debt which is financed through the local authorities' loans market is:

(a) Money at call.
(b) Money at short notice.
(c) Short-term local loans.
(d) Local authority bills.
(e) Local authority bonds.

In addition to the funds raised by local authorities through this market, there is also a very substantial market for 'yearling' bonds and other local authority securities on the stock exchange.

2.2 Inter-bank market

This large and very important market is a means by which banks can adjust their liquidity. All the major British banks, together with many overseas banks and secondary banks, operate on a considerable scale in the inter-bank market. Many companies outside the banking industry, such as finance companies, insurance companies, pension funds, industrial and commercial concerns, also lend to the inter-bank market. The main reason why the inter-bank market developed, however, was to provide an easy mechanism for large-scale movement of bank deposits. There are five main money brokers who act as intermediaries between borrowers and lenders. All inter-bank lending is unsecured and the transactions which take place in this market involve the taking and lending of large bank deposits. Deals are arranged by telephone and most transactions are on an overnight or short-term basis (up to three months). Some transactions are for a fixed term, usually between three months and five years. When banks lend to customers for a fixed term of five years, for example, they will often obtain a matching deposit from the inter-bank market. The bank's borrowing customer will be charged a varying rate of interest, which will be a small percentage above rates in the inter-bank market. The sums involved in inter-bank transactions go from a minimum of £250,000 up to several million pounds.

2.3 Inter-company market

The severe restrictions on bank lending in the 1960s caused difficulties for companies who were unable to obtain adequate credit from the banking system. Money brokers matched companies who had surplus funds with those who had liquidity problems. When the market started in 1969 it was a large, active market but now that bank credit is freely available for credit-worthy companies, its importance has diminished.

The main lenders to the inter-company market are the banks although other financial institutions and commercial companies still use the services of money brokers to place surplus funds in the inter-company market. Interest rates are marginally higher than in the inter-bank market and the lending terms range from a month to three years.

2.4 Finance house market

This is another market which was very large in the 1960s but has since contracted. At that time the finance houses had great difficulty in obtaining all the funds they needed from the banking system. The finance house market was established to attract the deposits to finance the growing businesses of the finance houses. The term of deposits in this market range from overnight up to fixed periods of six months.

The banks are now the main lenders in this market although pension funds, insurance companies and other commercial companies use the finance house market as an outlet for surplus funds. Almost all the major finance houses are now subsidiaries of clearing banks. These finance house subsidiaries can now obtain almost all their borrowing requirements from their parent banks and, as recognised banks, can obtain short-term funds from the inter-bank market. As a result, the demand for funds through the finance house market has dropped and the rates seen in this market vary in line with rates in the inter-bank market.

2.5 Euro-currency markets

Euro-currency deposits are funds lodged with banks outside their currency of origin but still denominated in their original currency, e.g. Euro-sterling in Paris or Frankfurt, Euro-dollars or Euro-marks in London.

Paris is the main financial market for Euro-sterling, while London is the main market for lending and accepting bank deposits in currencies other than sterling. The Euro-currency market dates back to the middle of the 1950s. Over 80 per cent of the transactions in the London Euro-currency market are in Euro-dollars because the American dollar is the currency which is most freely available.

Although all the major British banks are involved in the market, the main dealers in the Euro-currency markets are American and Japanese banks. The dealing unit is a minimum of a million dollars. This money is lent and borrowed on an unsecured basis. Most of the money lent is at call or short notice but some of the loans made are for periods up to five years. Massive totals of funds are dealt with in the Euro-currency markets. As well as overseas and British banks, multi-national companies are also major operators in the Euro-currency markets. Many foreign governments have borrowed from the Euro-currency markets as a way of providing themselves with short-term finance.

There have been times when major American banks have borrowed in the London Euro-dollar market and then transferred the funds back to the USA in order to meet domestic demand for loanable funds. On one or two occasions, British corporations have obtained Euro-currency funds, which they have converted into sterling to meet pressing financial needs.

As well as the very active market in Euro-currency bank deposits, US dollar certificates of deposit are also freely traded in the Euro-currency markets.

2.6 Euro-bond market

This term is used to describe the international market in bonds where both the capital and interest are payable in Euro-currencies. The issuing houses are international banks and the majority of bonds issued are in Euro-dollars. The Euro-bonds issued and payable in London are issued on behalf of foreign governments and foreign corporations. They are always fixed interest securities and are usually long-term bonds. Although they are not quoted on the London Stock Exchange, they can be traded on the secondary market, if the amount is relatively small, or in the Euro-currency market, in the case of a very large transaction.

2.7 Foreign exchange market

This is not a physical market like the Stock Exchange. The foreign exchange market consists of all the major banks in London together with some foreign exchange dealers. This group arranges transactions between themselves over the telephone. In dealing with other banks abroad they will use telephone, cable and telex to communicate.

Although there are some minor transactions in foreign notes, the negotiation of currency bankers drafts, and the purchase and sale of travellers cheques, the overwhelming volume of transactions consists of transfers of bank deposits between various financial centres. This is the reason why banks are the most active traders in the foreign exchange market although large multi-national companies also operate in this field.

A 'spot' rate is quoted for the purchase or sale of bank deposits for immediate delivery. This sometimes causes confusion in the public's mind because these rates differ from the tourist rates at which banks will buy or sell coins, notes, or travellers cheques.

A forward rate is quoted by the bank when it is asked to agree a rate now for the purchase or sale of foreign currency either at a fixed future time or within an agreed period in the future. Banks will quote forward rates in most currencies. These rates are not identical with spot rates but will enable traders to calculate their future earnings or expenses in foreign currencies, without being concerned about exchange rate fluctuations in the meantime.

2.7.1 *Influences on exchange rates*

A country's balance of trade can greatly affect the market's view of present exchange rates. If the value of exports increases faster than the value of imports into the country, there will be a greater demand for that country's currency, leading to an appreciation in the rate of exchange.

Similar reactions can result from movements in the balance of payments. Heavy capital outflows caused by the ending of exchange controls or by political uncertainty can lead to increased demand for foreign currency. This will cause a depreciation in the home country's rate of exchange.

The comparative costs of production in two different countries will also influence the market's view of the correct rate. Different inflation rates will be adjusted by movements in exchange rates. High rates of inflation will lead to a fall in exchange rates until the purchasing powers of the trading currencies are roughly equal. Low inflation rates compared with other countries should lead to an appreciating exchange rate.

Central bank intervention can sometimes have a dramatic effect on the rate of exchange. A central bank will intervene in the market by buying or selling its own currency if it wishes to avoid violent changes in the country's exchange rate. The bank will buy its own currency when exchange rates are moving adversely. This method of operation involves the central bank in selling its reserves of foreign currencies in the market.

If a country's exchange rate is rising rapidly, the central bank may try to stabilise the rate by selling its own currency. The central bank will receive foreign currencies in exchange which are added to the bank's foreign currency reserves.

2.7.2 *Influences on forward exchange rates*

The factors mentioned in the previous section relate mainly to dealings in spot rates. Forward rates are affected by these factors but are also strongly influenced by speculation and by differences in interest rates between financial centres.

In the case of spot dealings, the purchaser of a currency must provide funds straight away. Similarly, a seller of a currency must be able to give immediate delivery to the purchaser. With a forward contract, the customer does not need to pay for or make delivery until the end of the agreed period. This makes forward dealings the favourite method of speculation in the foreign exchange market. Most speculation takes place by selling forward a currency which is expected to depreciate and buying forward a currency whose exchange rate is expected to rise. Both methods enable a profit to be made when the contracts mature provided the speculator has guessed correctly.

If the currency which has been sold forward has depreciated in value during the period of the contract, it can be bought at a cheaper rate to deliver at the end of the term of the contract. Similarly, the currency which has been bought forward can be sold at a profit at the end of the term, if it has appreciated in value in the meantime.

Where interest rates in a country are low, that country's interest rates will stand at a premium in the forward market. High interest will lead to a country's currency being quoted at a discount in forward markets. Examples will show that a premium means dearer relative to sterling, while a discount means cheaper relative to sterling.

The golden rule in spot rates where the home currency is fixed is:

BANK BUYS HIGH — BANK SELLS LOW

e.g. US$ 1.49 — US$ 1.50
Bank buys at US$ 1.50 to £1 and sells US$ 1.49 to £1.

Forward quotations would look something like this:

Spot	US$ 1.4995 –	US$ 1.5005	Cents	Cents
Deduct premium	.0026 –	.0022	0.26 –	0.22 premium 1 month
Forward rates	1.4969 –	1.4983		

Bank sells dollars for one month forward at 1.4969.
Bank buys dollars for one month forward at 1.4983.

			Centimes –	Centimes
Spot French Francs	11.655 –	11.665	2.70	– 4.70 discount 1 month
Add discount	.027 –	.047		
	11.682 –	11.712		

Bank sells francs for one month forward at 11.682.
Bank buys francs for one month forward at 11.712.

A bank which sells a currency forward will match that contract with a spot purchase of that currency and place this sum on deposit with a correspondent bank abroad. Funds placed in a centre with low interest rates will mean a loss of profit compared with a similar investment in London. When currency is bought forward there is a corresponding spot sale. If the funds are brought back to London from a centre with high interest rates, there will be a similar loss of earnings. The forward rates quoted by the banks will allow for these differences in interest rates.

2.8 Financial futures market

The financial futures market opened at the Royal Exchange in the City of London in September 1982. It is known as the London International Financial Futures Exchange or LIFFE for short. The market's aim is to provide financial institutions and industrial companies with the facilities to hedge against the risks involved when exchange rates for currencies change or there are changes in interest rates.

Currency risks are covered by contracts in terms of:

(a) £ Sterling - US$
(b) Swiss Franc - US$
(c) Japanese Yen - US$
(d) Deutsche Mark - US$

The exchange rate between the pound and the dollar is familiar to most people. The other three rates are known as dollar cross rates. Although these cross rates are quoted in the financial press, they are not so widely known as the Sterling-Dollar rate.

The contracts available to cover interest changes are confined to just three rates.

(a) 3 months Euro-dollar deposit
(b) 3 months Sterling deposit
(c) 20-year Gilt-Edged stock

Members of the London International Financial Futures Exchange are drawn from a wide variety of financial institutions, some commercial companies and private individuals. Only members of the exchange or their authorised representatives are allowed to deal on the floor of the exchange. This means that company treasurers who wish to cover themselves against unexpected interest rates movements or changes in the exchange rates must deal through members if they require cover through LIFFE.

Trading is conducted by members quoting prices verbally in open dealings. This gives every member the opportunity to participate in a transaction and is a guarantee that the same price is quoted, irrespective of the size of the deal. Once a deal is made on the floor of the exchange, details are passed to the clearing house. A major part in this is played by the International Commodities Clearing House Limited (ICCH) which is owned by the London clearing banks. The details of the transaction are passed to the clearing house by the buyer and seller and checked by the clearing house staff.

An initial margin, which is a small percentage of the nominal value of the contract, is then paid to the clearing house by both seller and buyer. The clearing house then takes over the deal and provides a contract to each of the members involved. A diagram of the operations involved is given below (Figure 16.3):

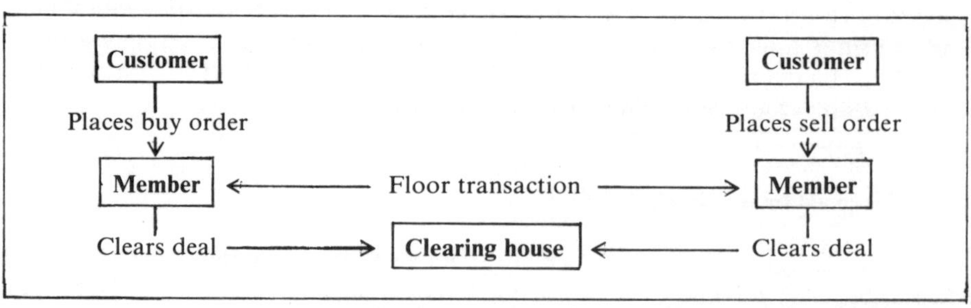

Figure 16.3

Each buyer and seller is also responsible for a daily settlement of any changes in trading prices. In the event of loss on any daily revaluation, a call is made by the clearing house for payment of a 'variation margin'.

Examples of instances where a financial futures contract could be taken out are:

(a) Agreement in principle is reached for a long-term loan to an industrial company from a pension fund for buying fixed assets. The company secretary sells a 20-year gilts contract until the rates on the loan are agreed. The company then buys back the 20-year gilts contract and any profit or loss will counteract changes in rates between agreement in principle for the loan and fixing the loan terms.

(b) A company which expects to receive substantial funds in six weeks time may want to invest them in a certificate of deposit on receipt. Not wishing to run the risk of volatile interest rate changes, the company buys a three months sterling deposit contract. When the money is received the contract is sold back. Any interest rate changes are counterbalanced by the profit or loss on the three months contract.

(c) When a British company's subsidiary abroad plans a capital investment overseas, they may wish to finance it by raising money through local money markets abroad. The planned use of appropriate currency contracts will enable the company to estimate costs with greater certainty.

Unlike a forward exchange transaction, which is a legally binding contract between bank and customer, financial futures contracts can be reversed at any time by entering into a matching contract with another party. Around 95 per cent of all contracts are 'closed out' before delivery takes place.

Part 5: Related Banking Services and Lending

17 *Banking Services*

1 EXECUTOR AND TRUSTEE SERVICES

As well as looking after customers' finances while they are alive, the banks are prepared to look after a customer's estate on death. The trustee department of a bank is well qualified for this role and has the professional skill to wind up an estate more efficiently than a private person is likely to be able to do.

If a person dies without leaving a will, the estate has to be distributed according to certain legal principles, known as the 'rules of intestacy'. Although the next-of-kin can apply for letters of administration for the purpose of paying debts and winding-up the estate, distribution of the residue must be made strictly according to law. In these circumstances, it is often advisable to suggest that the next-of-kin authorise the bank's trustee department to apply for letters of administration on behalf of the next-of-kin.

In the circumstances where the deceased left a will, but the executor is unwilling or unable to act, an interested party must apply for a grant of 'letters of administration *cum testamento annexo*'. The person who applies is usually the principal beneficiary under the will. It is worthwhile emphasising the security, skill and impartiality which the trustee department of a bank can show in these instances. The appointment of the bank as administrator should be carefully considered by all parties involved.

Where an administrator dies before completing the administration of the estate, it is necessary to apply for 'letters of administration *de bonis non administratis*'. Application is usually made by the person with the largest interest in the residue of the deceased's estate. This is another instance in which the advantage of the bank being appointed can be stressed to all those interested.

It is preferable for people to make a will in order that their wishes can be known when they die and their estate can be distributed in accordance with these wishes. Banks have been acting as executors for their customers for many years now and this service is a logical extension of the other banking services provided during a person's lifetime. When a customer makes a will appointing the bank as executor, he knows that he will obtain security, confidentiality and impartiality to a greater extent than is possible with a private executor.

2 TAXATION SERVICES

The practice of offering taxation advice varies between banks. In some banks, there are separate tax branches. In other banks, the tax branches form part of the network of branches which make up the trustee department.

Since the tax reforms of the 1960s, tax law has become very complicated. Capital transfer tax, capital gains tax, development land tax and the investment income surcharge combine to make the preparation of anything other than a simple annual income tax return a very complicated business.

The bank's tax managers are able to submit annual returns for private customers and also to negotiate with the Inland Revenue concerning their customers' liabilities for the various taxes. They are also expert in claiming the allowances which can be off-set against a person's income. Where a customer is reluctant to commit himself to an annual service, the tax manager will provide a consultancy service. This is particularly useful when a customer has a difficult 'one-off' problem.

While the salaried employee, whose tax is deducted under PAYE, is unlikely to benefit from using the bank's tax services, the following groups will find the tax branches of the bank very helpful:

(a) people with large dividend incomes;
(b) investors with income from overseas;
(c) employees working abroad for part of the tax year;
(d) owners of tenanted properties;
(e) people who are wholly or partly self-employed.

The self-employed include not only those working for a fee but also sole proprietors and partnerships. The tax services provided by the bank for this group are more specialised than the services for private taxpayers. They include preparation of VAT returns (if required), keeping books of accounts and preparing balance sheets and income and expenditure statements.

3 TRUSTEE APPOINTMENTS

In the winding-up of some estates a time may come when the executors become trustees. When there are beneficiaries who are minors or other beneficiaries who are entitled to receive the income for life from the estate, two trustees are required. This will present difficulties where there is a sole executor and the bank is well suited to act as a trustee of a residuary estate where there are minors or life tenants.

Parents sometimes create trust funds for children and grandparents will often set up trust funds for grandchildren. The bank can offer the advantage of continuity in comparison with the appointment of personal trustees and this aspect should be stressed to those customers who are contemplating this type of discretionary settlement.

Many people are aware of the impact of capital transfer tax which will be payable on their death. In order to overcome part of the problem, they will take out a life policy, on their own life, for the benefit of wife and/or children. The life policy proceeds will form a separate estate and will not be lumped together with other assets when the amount of capital transfer tax is being assessed. There are considerable advantages in the bank being appointed as trustees of the life assurance policy proceeds, particularly where a single parent has taken out a life policy for the benefit of children.

Banks are also happy to act as trustees of company pension schemes. As well as providing continuity and security to the pensioners and contributors, the bank's investment managers are also available to offer advice on investment of the pension fund.

Trustees of unit trusts are another useful role which can be played by the bank's trustee department. While the investment policy of the unit trust fund is in the hands of professional managers, the law states that an independent corporate trustee must be appointed to hold the trust securities. Banks are ideally suited for these appointments.

4 CREDIT CARDS

Another important service provided by the banks is the issue of credit cards. The two main cards used in Great Britain are Access and Barclaycard. This type of card was first used in America as a way of paying for goods and services by producing a plastic card signed by the cardholder. Because of the convenience of payment, this system of credit cards has now spread throughout the world. Barclaycard is linked up with the Visa international network, while Access has similar arrangements with MasterCard and Eurocard. Barclaycard is run as a department of Barclays Bank while Access is run by the Joint Credit Card Company. The ordinary shares in the Joint Credit Card Company are owned by Lloyds Bank, Midland Bank and National Westminster Bank. Williams and Glyn's has a small holding of the preference capital of the Joint Credit Card Company.

Yorkshire Bank issue Barclaycards to their customers while the Co-operative Bank issue their own cards with the Visa symbol. Trustcards are issued to customers of the Trustee Savings Banks and also carry the Visa symbol. British Airways have a credit card which is part of the Visa network. Bank of Scotland cards also form part of the Visa group.

Figure 17.1: Example of credit card

Clydesdale Bank, Coutts and Co, Northern Bank, Ulster Bank and Royal Bank of Scotland issue Access cards to customers of their banks. Building societies are also extending their operations into the credit card field. National and Provincial Building Society customers have facilities for the issue of Access cards through the Access department of National Westminster Bank. Nationwide Building Society have a similar scheme for the issue of Access cards to their customers through Midland Bank. In neither case does the building society member have to maintain a bank account. When the cardholders receive the credit card statement they will be able to settle in cash through the building society branch or authorise a debit to their building society account. Abbey National Building Society have asked Co-operative Bank to issue Visa cards to Abbey National cheque-save account holders. Similar arrangements are available for settlement of these Visa accounts to those made by National and Provincial Building Society and the Nationwide Building Society for their members with Access cards. The issuing banks arrange the pre-determined credit limit for each cardholder.

The participant institutions are split into two quite distinct groups:

Visa group
Abbey National Building Society (through Co-operative Bank)
Bank of Scotland
Barclays Bank
British Airways
Co-operative Bank
Trustee Savings Banks
Yorkshire Bank

Access group
Clydesdale Bank
Coutts and Co
Lloyds Bank
Midland Bank
National and Provincial Building Society (through National Westminster Bank)
National Westminster Bank
Nationwide Building Society (through Midland Bank)
Northern Bank
Royal Bank of Scotland
Ulster Bank
Williams and Glyn's Bank

To pay for goods in a shop, or to pay for some form of service, the cardholder will hand over his credit card to the retailer. The card is then put into the imprinter machine with a voucher for the amount to be paid. After the details on the card have been printed on the voucher, the voucher is then signed by the cardholder and the signature is compared with that on the card. In order to obtain funds for his Visa vouchers, the retailer will pay these vouchers into a branch of one of the participant banks of the Visa group. The retailer's account is credited straight away through the Bankgiro clearing. To obtain funds for Access vouchers, the retailer pays into a branch of one of the participant banks of the Access group. Similar arrangements are made for the retailer's account to receive immediate credit through the Bankgiro clearing.

Both types of vouchers are sent to the accounting sections of the card companies. Monthly statements are sent to the cardholders showing the minimum payment which must be made within twenty-five days. On balances which are outstanding more than twenty-five days after the date of the monthly statement, interest is charged at published rates which vary from time to time, in line with market conditions.

Cash can be drawn from a participant bank with the use of either a Visa or an Access card. Interest is charged on these cash withdrawals from the day the cash is taken until the amount of the withdrawal is repaid.

The same cash withdrawal facilities are available through automated tills outside bank premises. Barclaycard holders obtain funds through Barclays machines while Access cardholders obtain funds through automated tills run by the bank which issued the Access card.

4.1 Charge cards

Apart from Access and Visa cards, there are other cards which are used mainly by businessmen for travel and entertainment expenses. The two principal cards in this category are American Express and Diners Club. Both these cards are widely used throughout the world. National Westminster Bank has a 49.7 per cent interest in the United Kingdom operations of Diners Club, while American Express has links with Lloyds Bank. Both companies charge a membership subscription which varies according to the type of membership. There are different rates for personal membership, joint membership (e.g. husband and wife), or company membership.

Figure 17.2: Example of charge card

The cards are used by members for hotel, garage, restaurant and travel expenses and can also be used in some other retail establishments. The vouchers which the members sign are sent direct to the card companies who submit monthly statements to their members. The members are expected to settle their accounts without delay and both American Express and Diners Club reserve the right to charge interest on overdue accounts.

American Express have also issued a Gold Card, which is intended for business travellers with high incomes. The Royal Bank of Scotland and Lloyds Bank have arranged to issue some of their selected customers with American Express Gold Cards.

In order to obtain a share of the charge card market, Midland Bank have issued qualifying customers with the Midland Bank Gold Mastercard. An annual fee is paid by the cardholder and it is not intended to be used as a credit card. Cardholders are asked to settle their bills within twenty-five days of receiving their statement, otherwise interest may be charged. At the present time, the issue of Midland Bank Gold Mastercards is limited to customers of Midland Bank and its subsidiaries. This is in contrast to Access,

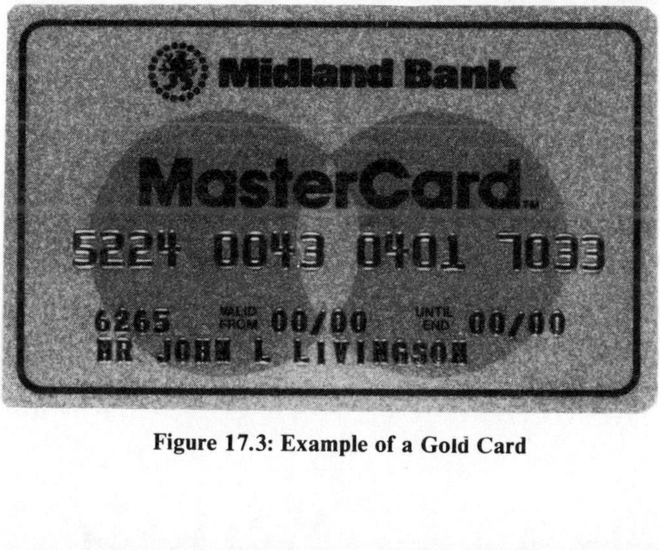

Figure 17.3: Example of a Gold Card

American Express, Diners Club and Visa cards where you do not need to be a customer of a sponsoring bank in order to make an application for a card.

Barclays Bank also now issue a charge card called Premier Gold Card. It works in the same way as the Midland Gold Mastercard. These Gold Cards are similar to a Diners Club card in not having a fixed spending limit. Because of their active participation in the United Kingdom operations of Diners Club, National Westminster Bank probably feels that any of its high-spending customers are already adequately catered for.

4.2 Automated teller cards

A customer who is unable to reach a bank during banking hours can be supplied with an automated teller card. Some customers also order a card to cover emergency requirements of cash. Customers are not limited to their own branch but can use the automated teller service, where machines are available, at any branch of their own bank.

The automated teller machine is directly linked to the bank's central computer. When the customer inserts his plastic card, he is asked to tap out his own personal number on the machine's keyboard. He then keys in the amount of cash required. Cash withdrawals are not limited to a fixed sum but, by arrangement with the customer's own branch manager, can be made up to an agreed maximum during any one week or any one day. If the cash required by the customer is within the agreed limit, the machine delivers the cash ordered. The card is returned at the same time and, even if the limit has been exceeded, the card is still returned, although no cash is provided.

Because of its direct link with the bank's central computer, the automated teller machine is able to debit the customer's account straight away. In addition, customers can request details of their accounts and can order cheque books or statements to be sent to them. While all automated teller machines are at present on bank premises, future development of this system is likely to lead to some of them being situated in places such as large stores, airports or railway stations.

National Westminster and Midland announced at the end of 1982 that they would link their automated teller machines some time in 1983. Customers are able to draw cash from any machine in the combined network. Ordering of statements, cheque books or balances of accounts will only be possible through a machine operated by the bank which issued the card. Eventually it is hoped to link Clydesdale Bank and Northern Bank, Midland Bank subsidiaries, to the combined network of automated teller machines.

Barclaycard holders can use their cards to obtain a cash advance through a Barclaybank machine. The maximum cash advance on any one day is £100 and this is subject to the amount being within the cardholder's credit limit. After inserting the card, the cardholder keys in his personal number and then punches in the amount of cash required. A 1½ per cent handling charge is made for cash advances. The Barclaybank machine can also be used to check the credit available on the Barclaycard account but no charge is made for that service. The cash advance service is available to any Barclaycard holder and is not limited to customers of Barclays Bank.

Access cardholders are able to draw up to £50 a day from automated teller machines of the bank which issued the Access card. As with any Access card cash advance, the cardholder will be charged interest from the day the money is drawn.

5 CHEQUE CARDS

These cards guarantee the payment of cheques which do not exceed £50 in settlement of a single transaction. The guarantee is conditional on the following:

(a) the cheque is signed in the presence of the payee;
(b) the signature on the cheque must correspond with the signature on the card;
(c) the payee writes the card number on the back of the cheque;
(d) the sorting code number on the cheque must correspond with the sorting code number on the cheque card;
(e) the cheque is dated before the expiry date on the card.

Cheque cards are intended for use mainly as shopping cards. The shopper is able to take immediate delivery of small purchases in shops without the necessity of paying over cash. The retailer has the advantage of guaranteed payment and does not incur bad debts in taking cheques backed by cheque cards, provided the laid down conditions are observed.

In addition, cheque cards can be used to obtain cash. The cardholder signs a cheque in the presence of the paying cashier who compares the signature of the drawer with the signature on the card. By these means, cheques up to the value of £50 per day can be cashed at almost all banks in Great Britain and Ireland.

Visa cards are intended to be used not only as a credit card, with an arranged credit limit, but also as a cheque guarantee card for shopping purposes. Cash can also be obtained by cashing a cheque with a bank in the Visa group, using the Visa card for identification purposes.

The banks advise cardholders to keep their cheque books and cheque cards separately. This is to avoid the substantial losses which have occurred because of the fraudulent use of cheque cards.

Between 1974 and 1983 £50 cheque cards could be used abroad at any bank displaying the Eurocheque symbol. The British banks suffered heavy losses through the use of stolen cheque books and cheque cards abroad and from May 1983 the use of the £50 cheque cards has been limited to the British Isles.

It is important to realise that the issue of a cheque card does not give a customer unlimited credit. Although the bank must pay all cheques backed by a cheque card, provided the requirements of issue have been complied with, the customer must seek permission from the bank before overdrawing his account. Failure to seek this prior permission can be held to be the obtaining of funds by misrepresentation, making the customer liable to criminal proceedings under Section 16 of the Theft Act 1968.

In the case of *Regina* v *Kovacs* (1974) the customer's account was already considerably overdrawn. The bank wrote to her asking that no more cheques should be issued and soon afterwards a bank official called to ask for the return of her cheque book and cheque card. The customer claimed that she no longer had these and two months later issued two more cheques. The court decided that she had obtained a pecuniary advantage by deception and she was found guilty.

The similar case of *Metropolitan Police Commissioner* v *Charles* (1976) involved a customer who had an overdraft limit of £100. While gambling one evening he issued twenty-five cheques for £30 each in payment of gambling chips. All the cheques were backed by his cheque card. The bank were obliged to honour these cheques, thus increasing the overdraft well above the agreed limit. The customer was found guilty of theft by deception in that he recklessly represented that he had the necessary permission to issue all these cheques backed by his cheque card.

While criminal proceedings were felt to be appropriate in these two cases, if a bank feels that there is any prospect of obtaining repayment of their lending, it is more likely to begin civil proceedings to obtain recovery of the customer's borrowing.

The decision in these two cases was followed by the House of Lords in the case of *Regina* v *Lambie* (1981) which involved a credit card fraud. The bank asked for return of the credit card, after the cardholder had used it beyond the agreed limit. The credit card was not returned. The holder continued to use it and she was convicted of theft on the grounds that she acted dishonestly in representing to a shop that she was authorised to use the credit card.

6 EUROCHEQUE ENCASHMENT CARDS

These new cards were first issued in April 1983. They are for the convenience of customers of British banks travelling overseas and will enable holders of Eurocheque encashment cards to obtain cash abroad. The cards are intended for use at any bank displaying the Eurocheque (EC) symbol. While the member banks of the Eurocheque scheme are domiciled in Europe, some other banks in non-European countries have also agreed to cash cheques backed by a Eurocheque encashment card.

To make a cash withdrawal the customer hands his cheque book and Eurocheque encashment card to the paying cashier. The customer is asked to sign the cheque in the presence of the paying cashier and, in certain countries, the customer may need to produce his passport. Although the cheque will be drawn in sterling, foreign currency will be handed over, at the current rate of exchange.

There are a number of important differences between the Eurocheque encashment card and the £50 cheque card. These are listed below.

£50 cheque card	**Eurocheque encashment card**
Valid for two years.	Valid for one year.
Renewed automatically.	Only renewed on application.
Maximum encashment permitted, £50 a day.	Maximum encashment permitted, two cheques of £50 each day, cashed at the same time.
Only available for use in British Isles.	Solely for use outside British Isles.
Must be used with a cheque bearing the same sorting code number as the card bears.	Must be used with a cheque bearing the same customer's account number as the card bears.
Also available for guaranteeing purchases of goods and services.	Cannot guarantee cheques in shops, stores, hotels, etc. abroad.

18 Other Banking Services

1 INSURANCE SERVICES

In offering advice on insurance matters to a customer, a bank is acting not as an insurance underwriter but as an insurance broker. The major banks now have their own insurance departments which are staffed by experienced insurance specialists. Unlike an insurance agent, who works for one company, or a local insurance consultant, whose contracts are usually limited to just a few companies, the insurance departments of the banks are in constant communication with all insurance companies.

The insurance departments of the banks will investigate all possibilities before making a recommendation to one of their customers. Because of its size, range of contacts and professional skill, the insurance department of a bank is usually able to provide the most economical premiums for the right type of insurance cover for any of its bank's customers.

Personal customers can be assisted in finding the life assurance which is most suitable for their requirements. There are a great variety of policies available and not all of them are equally appropriate for every customer. Although many people regard life assurance as a form of contractual savings, the principal function of insuring your life is to give financial security to your dependants on your death. Convertible whole life policies or whole life policies with a lump sum payable on death can give this security as long as the life cover is frequently increased to keep pace with inflation. Term assurance or mortgage protection policies, where the sum assured is paid on death during a fixed time, are very cheap and are appropriate where there is a substantial borrowing outstanding.

Most conventional life assurance policies are drawn up to pay a lump sum at the end of a fixed time or on the policy holder's earlier death. They are known as endowment policies and are a combination of life cover and a savings scheme. The majority of endowment policies and a few whole life policies are 'with profits' policies. This means that, in return for payment of a slightly greater premium, the policy holder shares in the profits of the insurance company. On the maturity of the policy, a bonus is paid in addition to the lump sum assured. Although not a perfect hedge against inflation, the 'with profits' policy makes some attempt to compensate for the reduced value of the sum assured, caused by rising prices over the period of insurance.

The bank is also able to help customers who wish to insure their houses, the contents of their houses or their other valuable items. Many people continue to insure their goods at cost value. The correct figure for which they should be insured is replacement cost. This is an area in which the domestic branch banker can provide considerable assistance.

With business customers the banks can obtain premises insurance for factories, shops and other commercial buildings. Employers' liability insurance, public liability insurance and motor insurance are just three of the many types of cover which a bank can provide.

Personal sickness policies, personal accident policies and travel insurance are examples of policies which are equally useful to personal customers or business people.

The greatest scope for expansion of the banks' insurance business in recent years has occurred through the sale of pension policies. These can be either company pension schemes or self-employed retirement annuity policies. There must be at least two people who will benefit under a company pension scheme and the premiums must be paid by a limited company. With self-employed retirement annuities, the policies are for the benefit of sole proprietors or partners in a firm. The premiums payable under the self-employed schemes must be paid by the person who will benefit. There are very considerable tax advantages in both types of pension policies. In addition to acting as an insurance broker when these policies are taken out, the bank is also willing to act as the trustee of company pension funds. Before any approach is made for the bank to be appointed as corporate trustee of a company pension scheme, the advice of the bank's trustee department should be sought.

2 HIRE PURCHASE AND LEASING

Although there are other finance houses active in the provision of finance for the acquisition of equipment, the subsidiaries of the clearing banks play a dominant role in this market. Funds are provided for any item of a capital nature, including purchases of farm buildings and factories.

Most private individuals will be familiar with the hire purchase agreements which are signed when a shopper wishes to obtain credit for the purchase of a television set or automatic washing machine. The purchaser undertakes to make fixed monthly repayments over a fixed period. In return, the seller gives the purchaser an option to buy, for a nominal sum, at the end of the fixed period.

The form of industrial hire purchase used by companies is known as 'lease purchase'. It is not to be confused with outright leasing and is best regarded as instalment credit. The finance house buys the capital asset for the industrial company and hires it to them for an agreed fixed time. The asset remains the property of the finance house until the last instalment is paid, when the hirers will exercise their option to buy at a nominal sum.

Although the finance house will insist on the payment of a deposit by the industrial company, lease purchase has tax advantages. The capital allowances on the equipment are made available to the company obtaining the finance, as soon as the agreement has been signed. This makes instalment credit an attractive option for very profitable companies with heavy tax assessments.

Leasing is based on the theory that a company makes a profit by using an asset instead of merely owning it. The concept of leasing is basically quite simple. We pay rent to British Telecom for the use of our telephones and most people pay money under a rental agreement for the hire of a television set. These types of leases are known as operating leases. Banks usually confine their activities to finance leases. With a finance lease, the asset is owned by the bank's subsidiary and they obtain the capital allowances from the Inland Revenue. The lessee pays a rent for the use of the asset and, in addition, undertakes to maintain and repair it. The leasing agreement is drawn up in such a way that the cost of the asset is repaid before the end of the useful life of the asset.

No deposit is required for a leasing agreement and this makes such a contract particularly attractive to companies with cash flow problems. The bank's finance house subsidiary is unlikely to finance a leasing contract for a total sum of less than £5,000. Any companies which wish to finance the purchase of assets for less than this amount should be asked to enter into an industrial hire purchase contract.

3 FACTORING

Subsidiary companies of the banks are now very active in the factoring of book debts. The locking up of working capital in slow-moving debtors causes difficulties for most companies. Newly-established or fast-growing companies are particularly badly affected. Delays in payments of money owed to a company can cause havoc with its cash flow.

Factoring tries to overcome these problems by providing these services:

(a) 100 per cent credit insurance to safeguard the company against loss through bad debts.

(b) Sales accounting services which include keeping the sales ledger, processing invoices and paying funds to the company at an agreed date after issue of invoices.

(c) Credit control which includes responsibility for collection of debts due from slow payers.

A small commission on turnover is charged and many companies find that the quicker and more efficient collection of debts is enough to solve their cash flow problems. Those companies which are still short of funds can obtain immediate finance at the date of issue of their invoices.

The factoring company will provide funds for 80 per cent of the value of the invoices, with the remainder, less factoring charges, being paid across on settlement of the invoices. Interest is charged at normal overdraft rates on this advance payment facility which is provided against the factored book debts.

4 ADVISORY SERVICES FOR IMPORTERS AND EXPORTERS

Importing goods is not usually as hazardous an operation as exporting and the difficulties which the importer encounters are usually fewer in number than those encountered by the exporter.

Importers will often benefit from advice given by the bank's specialists in the overseas department. Unless they are familiar with all aspects of the documentation involved in foreign trade and the supplier is prepared to send the documents direct to the importer, it is advisable to suggest that the bills of lading and other papers are routed through the bank's overseas department.

Finance may be required until the imports are sold. This help could take the form of a conventional loan or overdraft. It may take the form of a produce advance which means that the supplier will receive payment as soon as the goods are imported. The bank will have the security of the goods until they are sold, at which time the produce loan will be repaid.

Less usual methods of providing finance are the acceptance by the bank of bills of exchange issued by the supplier or the payment of promissory notes issued by the importer.

With exporters, the bank's specialist can advise on the risks involved in foreign trade. Status enquiries can be made concerning the buyer overseas. Information can be given about import restrictions or exchange control regulations in the foreign market. If it is thought desirable, a forward sale of the expected currency proceeds might be advised. As far as political or natural hazards are concerned, the bank can either advise on credit insurance or, if the exporter's turnover is large enough, suggest factoring. In some instances the bank may suggest the exporter obtaining indemnities from the Export Credits Guarantee Department. The bank will arrange for the exporter's documents to be sent to the buyer's bank for release against payment or acceptance of bills of exchange. If finance is required, the accepted bills can be discounted. The bank can also advise the exporter on the advantages of a confirmed irrevocable letter of credit so that payment is guaranteed for the goods exported. Both importers and exporters can be given information concerning foreign currency borrowings or foreign currency deposits, preferably through the branches of the bank in overseas countries.

5 COMPUTER BUREAU SERVICES

The computer networks of the banks are used not just for processing their own accounting and cheque clearing systems but also for standing order and direct debit payments, automated cash withdrawals and factoring of book debts. There is still a great deal of unused computer capacity and the banks actively seek customers who wish to make use of the bank's computer facilities.

The one which is most cost-effective is the service provided by the bank as registrar. The names and addresses of company shareholders can be stored on computer files and arrangements made for the bank to pay dividends, send out annual reports, issue allotment letters and register transfer deeds. As well as keeping the shareholders' register, the bank would also issue fresh share certificates.

Similar facilities are available for small and medium-size building societies, clubs and charitable organisations. The bank's registrar keeps a register of shareholders, members or subscribers as the case may be. Half-yearly interest warrants can be posted by the bank in the case of building societies. Where clubs and charities are concerned, reminders can be sent out about overdue subscriptions and the membership records up-dated.

The bank's computer bureau will also provide computer time for accountants or stockbrokers, if arrangements are agreed in advance. Specialised accounting procedures are available through the computer bureau for insurance brokers, solicitors, stockjobbers, stockbrokers, architects and similar professional partnerships.

Sales ledger services are provided through the bank's computer bureau subsidiary. A full accounting service is provided for the sales side of a company's operations. Sending out statements to customers, keeping records of the sales ledger accounts on the computer, providing debtor totals and other up-to-date management information are among the ways in which the computer bureau can assist. The benefits of full utilisation of computer time can be made available to small companies. They are saved the heavy capital expenditure which would be involved in undertaking their own purchase of computers. Considerable benefits will also accrue in the economies possible in the use of office space and supervisory time.

Purchases ledger services are also available through the bank's computer bureau. The bought ledger operations are on similar lines to the sales ledger services and the same economies of scale are possible. Most trading companies are likely to have a larger number of debtors than creditors. Because of this, fewer companies will be able to make use of the purchases ledger services provided. The computer bureau recommend that the company processes 150 invoices a month for the computer service to be a viable alternative to manual accounting.

6 NIGHT SAFES

These are used by retailers who wish to deposit cash and cheques outside banking hours. The safes are mounted on the outside wall of the bank and the retailer is supplied with a key. After the safe is opened by the retailer, he will place a wallet containing money and cheques in the night safe. When the night safe is closed the wallet will go down a chute into the bank's internal safe.

Wallets can be either locked or unlocked. If they are locked, the customer collects the wallet next day and opens it himself to pay in the takings. Unlocked wallets are opened by two members of the staff of the bank and the contents are then credited to the retailer's account. Unlike automated teller machines, the night safes are not linked to a computer. If a retailer places money in the night safe at 4pm on Friday afternoon, the funds will not be credited to his account until Monday morning.

7 SAFE CUSTODY

When customers leave items at the bank and there is no agreement that they should be held as security they are said to be held in safe custody. Examples of the type of items which may be held are:

(a) Locked suitcases.
(b) Sealed parcels and envelopes.
(c) Locked deed boxes.
(d) Wills.
(e) Deeds.
(f) Share certificates.

A small commission charge is usually made when locked boxes and cases or sealed packets and parcels are left with the bank for deposit in the safe. A receipt is usually issued for this type of item. The customer is always advised to insure anything of value and, if necessary, the bank can arrange to insure through its own insurance broking subsidiary.

Where documents of title, national savings certificates, birth certificates and similar items are deposited it is usual for the bank to supply the customer with a list of the documents which are being held in the customer's name.

When any articles are deposited in joint names, in the names of limited companies or partnerships, or by executors or trustees, the bank should be careful only to allow withdrawals in accordance with the mandate which is held.

The main risks involved in providing this type of service for customers are claims for damages because of

(a) Negligence.
(b) Conversion.

As far as negligence is concerned, it appears to make no difference if a specific charge is made when an article is deposited in safe custody or if the service is free. The bank is expected to take the same care of a customer's property as it does of the bank's property, whether or not it is acting gratuitously.

Conversion means depriving the true owner of this property by carrying out an unauthorised act. This act of conversion would occur when a bank inadvertently delivered safe custody items to the wrong person.

19 A Bank's Lending Services

Lending of money is a major service provided by banks. The main groups of advances to customers are overdrafts, loans and structured loans.

1 OVERDRAFTS

With overdrafts the borrowing is taken on current account. Interest is calculated on a day-to-day basis, even though the rate is expressed as a percentage over the bank's base rate, which is always published as x per cent a year.

An agreed limit is given, indicating the maximum borrowing the customer can take at any one time. The limit is subject to fairly frequent review but the borrowing is said to be repayable on demand. Overdrafts are a relatively cheap form of borrowing, particularly for businesses, because interest is charged only on the amount borrowed.

2 LOANS

These are granted where the borrowing is likely to be less fluctuating than with an overdraft on current account. The amount agreed is transferred from the loan account to current account and a standing order authority is usually signed to repay by agreed instalments by transfer from current to loan account. Interest is also calculated on a daily basis and, like the overdraft, is repayable on demand.

3 STRUCTURED LENDING

The most common form of structured lending is the personal loan. These loans are made available towards the purchase of motor-cars, household furniture, kitchen equipment, television sets, video recorders and similar goods. At one time guidance was given to the banks by the Department of Prices and Consumer Protection. The banks were not allowed to exceed the limits on amounts to be lent and periods of repayment required given in the Department's [illegible] purchase regulations. These restrictions have now been withdrawn.

Security is not normally required for these loans which carry interest at a slightly higher rate than other loans. A form of insurance cover is included in the cost, because the bank will cancel the outstanding loan if a borrower dies before the personal loan is repaid and the borrowing is in sole name. The rate of interest does not vary during the time the borrowing is outstanding. The amount of interest is added to the principal when the borrowing is taken. The total is then divided by the number of months in the repayment period. Instructions are then taken from the customer to transfer this figure each month from the current account to the personal loan. An example will make this clear:

Amount borrowed	£200
Interest at 7% per annum for 2 years	£ 28
	£228

Monthly repayment $\frac{£228}{24} = £9.50$

A small arrangement fee may be charged on the setting up of the personal loan.

Other structured loans include:

(a) Borrowing by qualified professional men to buy a share in a practice.

(b) Purchase of land, machinery, or breeding herds by farmers.

(c) Business development loans made to companies to enable them to acquire fixed assets such as buildings and plant.

The basic method of granting these types of loans is the same as that used for personal loans. An agreement is signed for a fixed sum of money to be lent by the bank, at a fixed rate of interest and for a fixed term.

Unlike personal loans, loans to businesses do not have any form of insurance cover but a two-tier structure of interest rates applies. Where borrowers lodge security a lower rate of interest is charged than is charged on unsecured structured loans.

A commitment fee is usually charged to the business borrower when the structured loan agreement is signed.

4 BRIDGING LOANS

Houseowners often need temporary finance when moving house. It is very difficult for the purchase of the houseowner's new house and the sale of the houseowner's old house to take place at the same time. When there is likely to be a gap between the purchase and sale dates, the bank will be asked to allow the customer to borrow. The amount of loan agreed is limited to the amount of money likely to be received by the customer's solicitor, after the existing house is sold.

So that the customer can obtain tax relief on the interest paid, it is always preferable to arrange for the borrowing to be taken on a loan account. The interest rate is agreed before the borrowing is taken and a commitment fee is charged when the bridging loan limit is agreed. As security, the customer's solicitor will be asked to give the bank an undertaking to pay the net proceeds of the sale to the bank.

Sometimes concurrent completions can be arranged for the purchase and sale. In these circumstances, the customer may only need a bridging loan for the amount (usually 10 per cent of purchase price) required on exchange of contracts. The same procedure is followed as for a large bridging loan.

5 VENTURE CAPITAL

Either directly, or through their finance house or merchant bank subsidiaries, the banks now have schemes for financing businesses by other means than as creditors. Businesses, whether sole traders, partnerships or limited companies, which require funds for the acquisition of fixed assets can negotiate either a sale of part of the equity stake in the business or borrow in the form of convertible loans. These convertible loans pay a slightly smaller rate of interest than normal loans but the bank has the right to convert the loans into ordinary capital if the business is profitable. There is a fixed time limit before which the option to convert the loan must be exercised by the bank.

These venture capital schemes are carefully drawn up to allow the original owners to retain control of their businesses although the agreement usually allows the bank the right to appoint a director to the board of a company in which they have ordinary shares.

6 HOME MORTGAGE LOANS

Banks have been competing very strongly for the house mortgages which building societies used to monopolise. Although practice varies between individual banks, it is possible for a borrower to find banks who will lend as little as £5,000 at one end of the market and as much as £150,000 at the other end of the market. Normally advances of up to 90 per cent of valuation or purchase price (whichever is lower) are made for properties costing up to £40,000. Between £40,000 and £75,000 the loan figure is usually 85 per cent while between £75,000 and £150,000 borrowers are usually limited to 80 per cent of cost or valuation figure.

Security consists of a first legal mortgage over the property. The titles to the property should be freehold or leasehold with at least 40 years of the term to run after the mortgage has been repaid.

Banks normally lend up to two and a half times gross annual income of the main earner and will also consider adding the gross annual income of the other joint borrower to the sum advanced.

The minimum repayment term for these loans is 10 years and the maximum 25 years. The borrower is expected to arrange the borrowing in such a way that it will be repaid by the anticipated age of retirement. Banks offer the options of either a repayment mortgage or an endowment mortgage.

Repayment mortgages are similar to building society mortgages. Instalments are paid monthly and include both capital and interest. With endowment mortgages, interest only is debited on a monthly or quarterly basis. The loan is expected to be repaid from the proceeds of a suitable endowment policy. Some banks insist on a mortgage protection policy where repayment is not being arranged by means of an endowment assurance. Even where this is not insisted on, a reducing term assurance is advisable.

In all circumstances, an index-linked comprehensive insurance policy should be taken to cover the house in security. Insurance of the contents of the borrower's house is also advisable.

7 BUDGET ACCOUNTS

Bills come in at irregular intervals while most people are paid on a monthly or weekly basis. The budget account is a method of matching the outflow of household expenditure with the regular pattern of income.

Annual expenses such as season tickets, car insurance, house insurance, car tax and television licence are added to quarterly bills such as telephone, electricity and gas charges. It is not advisable to include items such as local rates which can be paid by monthly standing order. Significant savings can be made, however, by paying for items such as television rental, life assurance premiums and rail season tickets on an annual basis.

The total expenses arrived at are divided by twelve, after a small commission charge has been added. A standing order is set up to transfer this figure (one twelfth of annual expenses) from current account to budget account each month. A separate budget account cheque is issued and the customer is free to use this cheque book to pay the bills on the schedule of annual expenditure, as and when the bills arrive. Unsecured borrowing will occur from time to time but no interest is charged, if the overdrafts are kept to a reasonable proportion of the total annual expenditure. This is an example of a budget account schedule:

	£
Car tax	85
Car insurance	75
Season ticket	500
Water rates	60
Telephone	160
Gas	220
Life assurance	250
House and contents insurance	180
Electricity	195
Club subscriptions	65
Holidays	210
	2,000
Commission (£10 on first £200 and 1% on residue)	28
	2,028
Monthly standing order transfer (£2,028 ÷ 12)	169

8 LEGISLATIVE CONSTRAINTS ON BANKS

The increased demand for consumer protection at the beginning of the 1970s led to the passing of legislation. The two acts which have had some impact on banking operations are the Fair Trading Act 1973 and the Consumer Credit Act 1974.

Until recently banks had not been accused of acting unfairly. This changed in 1977. Taking advantage of the Fair Trading Act 1973 a number of garages complained to the Office of Fair Trading. The garages felt it was unfair that credit card customers and cash customers should pay the same price.

The Monopolies and Mergers Commission was asked to investigate. In 1980 they reported that there was nothing wrong in differential charges. As a result, a number of petrol service stations began adding surcharges to credit card vouchers. In 1981 the Minister for Consumer Affairs expressed the opinion that it would be more convenient for the consumer if there were no surcharges. The system of surcharges has now been abandoned because the garages found that imposing a surcharge reduced turnover. In addition, they found that handling large quantities of cash was less cost-effective than dealing with credit cards or charge card vouchers.

Since the passing of the Consumer Credit Act 1974, no unsolicited mailing of credit cards has been permitted. This legislation has significantly changed the methods employed to launch Barclaycard in 1966 and Access in 1972.

Another effect of the Consumer Credit Act 1974 is that credit card companies may be liable for any defects in goods and services purchased with a credit card. This liability is limited to goods and services which are priced between £30 and £10,000. Substantial funds were re-imbursed by credit card companies in 1982 to cardholders who had used their credit cards to purchase holidays or airline flights in advance from Laker Airways and who had not taken the holidays or flights before Laker Airways collapsed.

The lending banker must exercise a certain amount of caution because of the constraints imposed by the Consumer Credit Act 1974. The main effects have been to aim for 'truth in lending' and to prevent aggressive canvassing of loans. Fortunately there are considerable exemptions at present. The main exemptions are:

(a) No restriction on lending to limited companies.

(b) Any borrowing of £5,000 and above is not affected by the Act.

(c) Overdrafts (this exemption was confirmed by an amendment made by the Banking Act 1979).

The main bank loans affected are consumer credit agreements up to £5,000. The true cost of credit must be disclosed on any loan agreements below £5,000. The bank could be held responsible for any misrepresentation when the borrower signed the agreement and the borrower might escape liability on those grounds.

Canvassing for loans is restricted to trade premises. The description of trade premises refers to the bank's own offices and also to the prospective borrower's premises if the banker is there by invitation. If a lending officer of the bank is asked to talk to a company's employees on that company's business premises, it is advisable to ask for the invitation to be in writing.

Telephone communications and written communications are exempt from the Consumer Credit Act 1974. It is, however, illegal to send a minor a written communication inviting him to seek information about consumer credit. If a bank official is asked to give a talk to school children, bank lending should only be mentioned in the most general terms. Discussing overdraft facilities with existing customers is permitted anywhere. The talks do not need to be on trade premises. Local golf courses or the saloon bars of local public houses are not ruled out as venues!

It says a great deal for the good sense and discretion of bank officials that there have been no actions brought against them under the Consumer Credit Act 1974.

20 Principles of Lending

The basic question which a bank must ask when a customer or prospective customer wishes to borrow is 'Can the borrower repay at the time and in the way agreed?' In order to assess the chances of obtaining an affirmative answer to this question the manager must keep a number of points in mind. A list of these points is given below:

(a) Character.
(b) Competence.
(c) Capital.
(d) Connection.
(e) Security.

1 A CUSTOMER'S CHARACTER

Although a banker will always try to assess the reliability of a customer or a potential customer, honesty and integrity on their own, although important, are insufficient. A record of prudence over a period of years is a better guide to a customer's creditworthiness than your personal opinion of his probity. Customers who have been able to keep their promises in the past are better credit risks than a new customer, however honest, who is branching out in a fresh venture.

2 A CUSTOMER'S COMPETENCE

Another question that a banker must ask when a loan is requested is 'Are the potential borrowers competent business people?' However good the business may be at actually making goods, building houses, or producing food, are the owners financially sophisticated? At the very least, the banker must satisfy himself that the business is making sufficient profits to find both interest charged and the agreed capital repayments. While the customer may believe the business to be profitable, the cautious banker will insist on a cash flow forecast for a reasonable time ahead, with the servicing of the bank borrowing included. When medium-term loans are granted, ask your customers to produce quarterly management accounts and send the copies to the bank.

3 A CUSTOMER'S CAPITAL

The security of the depositor's money must be a bank's first concern. Although the banks now have schemes for providing venture capital, the funds for these operations should be raised from money belonging to the bank's shareholders. It is seldom advisable for a bank to risk its depositors' funds by making 100 per cent advances towards the cost of a new project, however creditworthy or capable the borrowers might be. If the borrower has funds of his own in the scheme, not only will the bank have a margin of cover against loss, but the borrower will be more prudent, knowing his own capital is at risk.

As a general rule, the bank expects its contribution to be matched pound for pound by the borrower, especially with a new business or the buying of land for development. In some cases, such as short-term seasonal loans, the banks will lend more than 50 per cent of the required amounts and, in the case of building work, it is customary to lend up to 66.6 per cent of the estimated final building costs.

With all borrowing, a banker will assess the private means of the customer in addition to ascertaining the borrower's stake in the business. All partners in a borrowing partnership are fully liable for their firm's debts and the prudent banker will seek information about the partners' private assets. Where small limited companies are concerned, the directors should be asked to give personal guarantees and the figures for the directors' loans to the company should be given to the bank at frequent intervals.

4 CONNECTIONS

When banks are faced with a request for a loan, they should ask three additional questions, apart from the checks on character, capability, capital, and security. These are as listed below:

(a) Which business accounts is the proposed borrower associated with?
(b) How many of the borrower's family bank with you and what is the value of these accounts?
(c) Are you likely to lose these business or family accounts if the proposed advance is declined?

The researches undertaken may show that there are valuable business or family accounts with good credit balances held by people associated with the proposed borrower. In that event, it may be an acceptable risk for a banker to make a modest personal loan available rather than risking a refusal to lend which may lead to the loss of valuable credit balances.

5 SECURITY

The taking of security does not turn a bad advance into a good one. If the bank is reluctant to lend on an unsecured basis, it is better to decline the advance, even if adequate security is to be given. The borrower ought to be capable of repaying the borrowing, without the bank being forced to realise the security lodged. With third-party security, it is even more essential to be satisfied with the soundness of the borrowing. If you have to seek repayment by calling up the third-party security, it is likely you will lose not only the goodwill of the borrower but also that of the person who lodged the security. A good rule for a banker to observe is that if there is any doubt about the lending, the advance should not be made. No bank ever lost money by not lending!

Why then is security taken? The first reason is to cover the bank against loss in the event of unforeseen circumstances which prevent the borrower repaying the loan. The second reason is to emphasise to the borrowers that they share the risks undertaken by the banks. This is a form of insurance for the lending banker and will make the borrowers act in a more prudent manner if the borrowers' own assets are at risk.

There are times when it is right for a bank to insist on securities. When a bank is asked to lend to a small private company, personal guarantees should be obtained from the directors. Where a well-to-do customer asks the bank to lend to the customer's child (aged 18 or over), on the strength of the family connection, it is reasonable to ask for a guarantee to be given by the parent.

In both cases, the guarantors should be asked to show the same confidence in their company or child respectively which they have asked the bank to show.

6 BASIC ENQUIRIES CONCERNING LENDING

Even after assessing character, competence, capital, connections and security, the banker is still left with the task of asking certain vital questions and ensuring that adequate answers are received from the borrower. Most of these questions should be on the lines of who, when, where, why and how much. The interviewing banker should never ask questions which are capable of yes or no answers. The enquiries that are made should encourage the borrower to provide information to enable the lending banker to reach a decision.

6.1 Who are you?

This is the first question to ask. While it may seem superfluous in dealing with an established customer, it is not irrelevant in two cases, however. The question will not be put directly when a lending officer is asked to interview an existing customer. When approached by a new borrower, even if by a customer who is already in account, the banker will research the history of the account before the interview.

If a banker is asked to take over borrowing from another financial institution, a more direct approach is needed to find out the borrower's background. Bank statements and, if appropriate, audited accounts should be asked for.

Sometimes a customer who is well-known to the branch manager seeks a larger loan than the manager is able to grant on his own authority. When making a request to his head office concerning this customer's lending proposition, the branch manager will be careful to introduce the customer in this first report to head office. The history of the account and any background information will be commented on. In subsequent reports, the manager will merely refer to previous correspondence by way of introduction.

6.2 Why do you want the money?

A banker should never accept vague generalisations such as:

(a) It is needed for expansion.
(b) It is required for working capital.
(c) We need it for normal trade requirements.

A lending officer who grants the loan to the bank's customer should be able to justify the borrowing on its own merits. Therefore, the borrower must be precise as to the reason why the money is required because the lending officer needs to be convinced that the extra borrowing is not being used to finance the difference between the borrower's expenditure and income.

6.3 What will the money be used for?

This may sound as though it is identical to the last question but it goes right to the heart of the banker's business. An agreement to lend the money is insufficient. The bank has to ensure that the funds are spent on the project for which agreement was obtained. Supervision of the lending is always essential. In so many instances the bank finds that overdraft limits are negotiated to enable a business to purchase equipment and the funds are used to finance day-to-day expenditure instead.

6.4 How much is needed?

Most customers fall into two categories:

(a) Those who only have a vague idea of what to ask for.
(b) Those who try to tailor their request to
  either (i) what they think the bank will be happy to lend;
  or (ii) the maximum they think a branch manager can lend without going to his head office.

Both these approaches are disastrous. They will end up with a borrower whose business is restrained by an inadequate borrowing figure and there will be constant pressure to exceed the limit which the bank has granted.

The bank manager should ask the borrower for a cash flow forecast. This will show the amount which is expected to be paid into the customer's account and the amount expected to be withdrawn. The difference will show up as an increase (or decrease) in the total of bank borrowing. Payments in are subdivided between receipts from debtors and cash sales. Payments out are subdivided between settlement of money owed to trade creditors and disbursements for overhead expenses. If the customer is unable to prepare a cash flow forecast, the bank manager should provide advice on how this is done.

Sometimes borrowers are unwilling to produce cash flow forecasts. In those circumstances, the branch manager should prepare a forecast from the information available. This will give an indication of the highest figure the borrowing is likely to reach and this is the limit to discuss, if all other conditions are satisfactory.

The old maxim 'If in doubt, don't lend!' still applies. If a banker is not confident that the customer can keep within the revised limit and repay the borrowing in due course, the banker should explain to the borrower why he feels it to be in the borrower's best interests to decline to grant the borrowing that is being requested.

6.5 When will the advance be repaid?

The customer's cash flow forecast should give an indication here. The borrower's word should never be accepted without confirmation. A lending officer must use his judgement to assess the probability of the income of the borrower being sufficient to repay in the manner and the time suggested.

6.6 Where will repayment come from?

If you believe that the borrower's forecasts will not work out and that they cannot repay without difficulty, do not lend the money. Even the most creditworthy borrowers sometimes run into problems. Murphy's Law (anything which can go wrong, will go wrong!) applies just as much in banking as in any other industry. Therefore, the bank takes security to protect the depositors' money against unexpected events. Except for small, short-term, self-liquidating loans, borrowers should be asked to put up some form of security. Guarantees given by directors to secure the borrowing of their companies are particularly desirable. This requirement is not because of the assets behind the guarantee but because it shows a degree of commitment by the directors concerned.

In the case of 'one-man' companies, where the sole director is also the main shareholder, an assurance policy on the director's life should be assigned to the bank. This will enable bank borrowing to be repaid without difficulty on the director's death.

7 SOME ACCOUNTING TERMS

7.1 Liquid assets are

(a) Cash.
(b) Current accounts with banks.
(c) Items which can be quickly and easily turned into cash with a minimum of capital loss, e.g. bank deposit accounts or short-dated government stocks.

7.2 Current assets are

(a) Liquid assets.
(b) Assets which are regularly turned into cash at fairly short intervals, e.g. debtors, stock and work-in-progress.

7.3 Fixed assets

These are items which are used in business operations to produce profit.

(a) Freehold and leasehold premises.
(b) Plant.
(c) Machinery.
(d) Motor vehicles.
(e) Fixtures and fittings.

The customer should always be asked to arrange full insurance cover for all fixed assets as well as current assets such as debtors, stock and work-in-progress.

7.4 Intangible assets

These items on the balance sheet represent purchases made in the past which are not represented by physical possessions, which is why they are called 'intangibles'.

(a) Copyrights.
(b) Licences.
(c) Goodwill.

(d) Patents.
(e) Shares in unquoted subsidiary companies.
(f) Goodwill.
(g) Suspense accounts re marketing programmes.
(h) Debit balances on profit and loss accounts.

7.5 Current liabilities

A list of the main items which are payable on demand or in the near future is given below:
(a) Bank overdrafts.
(b) Trade creditors.
(c) Current tax payable.
(d) Bills payable.
(e) Directors' loans.
(f) Dividends payable.
(g) Short-term loans.

7.6 Working capital (often known as net current assets)

This figure is found by subtracting the total for current liabilities from the figure for current assets. It is a common fallacy to think that a bank provides working capital. If an increased bank overdraft limit is used to finance more stock or a larger figure for debtors, working capital is unchanged. Current assets and current liabilities will have increased by identical amounts. Where an increase in the current account overdraft is used to finance fixed assets, working capital is reduced. Current liabilities will have increased while current assets remain the same. A lending banker will compare a customer's current assets with current liabilities in order to judge the customer's ability to repay over a period.

7.7 Long-term liabilities

These are amounts repayable at a fixed date or after a long period of notice.
(a) Structured loans from the bank.
(b) Mortgages.
(c) Debentures.
(d) Loan stocks.
(e) Convertible loans.
(f) Deferred taxation.
(g) Hire purchase.

7.8 Shareholders' funds

Any money which has been subscribed by the shareholders or retained by the company out of its past profits.

(a) Capital.
(b) Reserves.
(c) Credit balances on Profit and Loss account.

7.9 Company's net worth

This is a figure which tries to assess what the company is worth to an outside purchaser. It is found by deducting the figure for Intangible assets from the total for shareholders' funds. The net worth of an individual share can be found by using the following formula:

$$\frac{\text{Shareholders' funds MINUS Intangible assets}}{\text{Number of shares issued by company}}$$

Another term used to describe a company's net worth is 'surplus tangible assets'. The figure for surplus tangible assets can be arrived at by this method:

Surplus tangible assets = Total assets MINUS (Total Liabilities + Intangibles)

The figure for surplus tangible assets or company's net worth is an important one. It is all that stands between the company and insolvency. A bank would be most unwise to lend more than this figure without security. If more than the company's net worth is requested by way of a bank loan, ask the company to give security. In addition, the directors should be asked to lodge collateral security to their guarantees and they should also be requested to postpone the loans they have made to the company. A very simple company balance sheet will illustrate some of these terms.

Balance sheet

Current assets				
	£		£	
Stock	500			
Debtors	200			
Bank	400	} Liquid assets	1,250	
Cash	150			
Current liabilities				
Trade creditors			750	
Net current assets			500	Working capital
Leasehold property			8,500	} Fixed assets
Plant, fixtures and fittings			4,000	
Goodwill			600	Intangible asset
			13,600	
Capital, authorised and issued			100	} Shareholders' funds
Profit and loss account			2,300	
Directors' loans			9,000	Current liability
Hire purchase			2,200	
			13,600	

This is how the audited figures could be produced, although some variations are encountered in practice. Some adjustment is required for assessment by a banker.

The company's net worth is £1,800 (shareholders' funds – intangible asset). We arrive at the same figure for surplus tangible assets.

If we take the figure for total assets this is

£ 1,250	Current assets
£12,500	Fixed assets
£ 600	Intangible asset
£14,350	Total assets

From this total we deduct

£ 600	Goodwill	Intangible asset
£ 750	Trade creditors	Current liability
£ 9,000	Directors' loans	Current liability
£ 2,200	Hire purchase	Other liability
£12,550		

£14,350 – £12,550 gives us £1,800 as the company's surplus tangible assets but the calculation for the company's net worth is a much easier one. Directors' loans present a problem. If we add them to trade creditors and deduct current assets it shows that the company has a deficiency of £8,500 in its working capital. The best advice to give the company is to change its directors' loans into share capital.

Hire purchase figures are not usually regarded as current liabilities. The company has received 'money now' in exchange for 'money later'. The 'money now' has been used to purchase plant and as long as regular payments are made under the terms of the agreement it can be regarded as a long-term liability.

7.10 Going concern

The net worth we have calculated is based on the company's value as a going concern. A very different position arises if a company ceases to trade. Because of this, prudent bankers often re-calculate the balance sheet as if the company were a 'gone concern', with the assets sold off at a break-up value. Our re-calculated figures would look like this; a very different picture from the previous accounts.

Balance sheet

Current assets

		£
Stock	(50%)	250
Debtors	(80%)	160
Bank	(100%)	400
Cash	(100%)	150
		960

Current liabilities

	£		
Trade creditors	750		
Hire purchase	2,200	2,950	(now payable)
Net current deficiency		(1,990)	
Leasehold property (60%)		5,100	
Plant and figures (25%)		1,000	
Goodwill		NIL	
Total assets		4,110	

21 *Trading Accounts*

Unless an adjustment is made in the company's accounts for the difference in the value of stock at the beginning of the financial year and the end of the financial year, a fair figure cannot be shown for profit. A simple trading account would look like the one illustrated below:

Trading account for the year ended 31 March

	£		£
Stock at beginning of year	73,000	Sales	1,608,000
Plus: Purchases	527,000		
	600,000		
Less: Stock at end of year	52,000		
	548,000		
Wages, power and other manufacturing costs	658,000		
Cost of trading	1,206,000		
Gross profit	402,000 (25% of sales)		
	1,608,000		1,608,000

The trading account will show the direct costs to the business of items such as labour costs and the purchases of materials. These costs are sometimes called variable costs because they increase or decrease in line with sales.

They differ from the fixed costs, or overheads, such as rates, rent, insurance, depreciation of machinery, interest on fixed debentures or bank loans and maintenance of plant and machinery which are adjusted in the company's profit and loss account.

Most financial controllers under-estimate the true impact of their variable costs. Some people will claim that if you use £2 of raw materials to make a product in one hour's production time, on a wage scale of £3 an hour, sales of the product at £7.50 a time will produce a 50 per cent profit margin. The labour costs should be analysed on these lines:

Annual wages (£3 an hour for 52 weeks of 40 hours)		£6,240
Employer's National Insurance (estimated)		560
Production bonus (estimated)		400
Total wage cost (A)		£7,200
Annual hours		2,080
Less: sickness	120	
holidays	160	280
Hours available (B)		1,800

Hourly cost $\frac{A}{B}$ i.e. $\frac{7,200}{1,800}$ = £4 an hour (C)

Assume labour efficiency of 80 per cent, then actual labour cost will be

$$\frac{C}{80\%} \text{ or } 4 \times \frac{100}{80} = £5 \text{ an hour.}$$

The raw material costs need to be analysed as well.

(a)	Raw materials used in product	100 %
(b)	Wastage in manufacture	12 %
(c)	Pilferage or other losses	5 %
(d)	Insurance of stock	$1\frac{1}{2}$%
(e)	Interest cost of holding stock (say 1 month at 12% a year)	1 %
(f)	Inflation factor (say 1 month at 6% a year)	$\frac{1}{2}$%
		120 %

True cost of raw materials is 120% of £2 = £2.40.

If we add the true cost of raw materials at £2.40 an hour to the actual labour costs of £5 an hour, we arrive at a profit of 10p an item on our sales price of £7.50 an item. This is a far cry from the 50 per cent figure forecast.

Apart from the need to allow for shrinkage of stocks through waste in manufacturing or pilferage, there is the need to pay for insurance of stock and interest charges on borrowing money to hold stock.

Although the inflation factor is less noticeable than it once was, it should not be overlooked, especially if the rate of inflation begins to rise again. The granting of stock relief by the Finance Act 1975 has lessened the impact of inflation on large businesses but small concerns still need to be aware of the inflation factor in their costs. Using the 'first in, first out' method of recording stock prices will create inflated profits during a period of rapidly rising prices. These illusory profits will be subject to tax but businesses will still need to retain profits to finance the higher cost of holding stocks.

1 PROFIT AND LOSS ACCOUNTS

These accounts will show all the fixed costs which need to be deducted from gross profit to show the company's net profit. The profit and loss account will also show any receipts which arise other than from the company's normal trading. A simple form of profit and loss account is shown below:

	£		£
Salaries	124,000	Gross profit	402,000
Rent payable	97,000	Rent receivable	8,500
Rates	79,000	Profit on sale of car	400
Insurance	7,500		
Bank interest payable	17,000		
Motor vehicles expenses	4,200		
Auditors' fees	1,000		
Depreciation	11,000		
Directors' fees	40,000		
Sundry expenses	7,200		
Net profit	23,000		
	£410,900		£410,900

As you will observe, there is a great deal of difference between gross and net profit. While the ratios between the two figures are not, in themselves, significant, an expanding and profitable company will show an increasing percentage, as the years go by, for the

$$\frac{\text{Net Profit}}{\text{Gross Profit}} \text{ ratio}$$

This is because fixed costs should not increase to the same extent as sales and a higher figure of sales will lead to larger net profit, after deduction of all overheads.

2 APPROPRIATION ACCOUNT

Limited companies must provide a further section of their accounts in order to cover purely financial transactions. The balance of the previous year's profit and loss account is brought forward. The net profit is added and, after deduction of the various transfers, the resulting figure is shown on the balance sheet. An example of an appropriation account could look like this:

	£		£
Provision for future taxation	5,500	Balance brought forward from previous year	17,000
Provision for proposed dividend	12,500	Net profit for the year	23,000
Transfer to special reserve	4,000		
Balance carried forward	18,000		
	£40,000		£40,000

3 OVERTRADING

This is a term which is used to describe a rapid expansion of turnover based on inadequate capital. The business may be suffering from this over-extension because of circumstances beyond the control of the business. Two common causes of problems are high inflation and high taxation on historical profits. Both will leave the business with insufficient resources to maintain the same scale of operations.

In the case of inflation, especially rapid inflation, more and more funds will need to be provided either from shareholders or lenders to keep the same scale of operations going. Liquid resources are depleted to maintain a sufficient stock of goods, bought or manufactured at higher cost. The extra costs of production will be passed on to the purchasers and the total for debtors is increased. The increased figures for current assets such as debtors, stock, work-in-progress can only be financed by fresh injections of working capital or increased trade credit.

High costs of replacing fixed assets will exceed the amounts put aside for depreciation, which have been based on historical cost. The business will have to issue fresh shares, make issues of loan stocks, or increase transfers to reserves to acquire these fixed assets.

High levels of taxation have the same impact on a company's resources as a high level of inflation. When the two, taxation and inflation, are combined the effect can be serious. The rate of tax will be based on historical profit. This overstates the true profit because of the

(a) increased funds needed to replace stock;
(b) increased resources needed to replace fixed assets.

The amount of real profit will be overstated in inflationary times and only continual injections of funds (e.g. retained profits, new issues) will keep sufficient working capital in the business. When the historic cost profit is also heavily taxed, the effect may be to cause a drain on the liquid resources of the company. Unless the directors overcome this problem by introducing extra finance, the company will soon be overtrading, i.e. supporting a high level of turnover with inadequate capital.

The 1975 Finance Act allowed stock relief. Most of the increase of stock in money terms over an accounting period can be offset against a tax assessment. Public limited companies now have to show COSA (cost of sales adjustment) and MWCA (monetary working capital adjustment) to alter profit figures from historic cost to current cost accounting.

4 INTERPRETATION OF BALANCE SHEETS

A balance sheet is a snapshot of the business on one day of the year. The balance sheet will not give a true picture of a company as a going concern any more than a passport photograph will be a true reflection of a living human being. Comparison of the latest balance sheet with those in the previous three years will give a better guide to the state of the business than a study of one balance sheet in isolation.

It is important for a banker to realise that many assets on the balance sheet are capable of more than one valuation. While cash is a matter of fact, the value to be placed on the other assets is a matter of opinion. These are the questions to ask about the asset items in the accounts.

(a) **Debtors** – What is the spread and composition of the money owed to the business? How much credit is customary in that industry? Are any of the debtors slow or doubtful payers?

(b) **Stock** – Can it be broken down into raw materials, bought-in components and finished products?
Who valued the stock? Was it valued at cost, at market value or at replacement value?

(c) **Work-in-progress** – This is the most difficult asset to value correctly. Is the valuation based on materials alone, materials plus labour and other variable costs, or does the valuation include a proportion of fixed costs?

(d) **Machinery and plant** – What is their age, condition and cost of replacement? Have adequate resources been set aside for purchase of new machinery? What is the break-up value of the plant?

(e) **Buildings** – Is the forced sale value higher or lower than the historic cost? Some freehold buildings may be worth more than the price for which they were purchased. Have the buildings any other use if the business closes down?

(f) **Goodwill, trade marks, preliminary expenses, copyrights** – These intangible assets should not be regarded by the lender as having any value.

5 CURRENT ASSETS/FIXED ASSETS RATIO

It is difficult to lay down a hard and fast ratio but fixed assets should never increase relative to current assets.

With new businesses, the ratio of current assets to fixed assets may be low, but as the business expands the total of current assets should increase faster than fixed assets as profits are earned and ploughed back into the business. Compare ratios for earlier years with current years. If current assets/fixed assets ratio is getting smaller it is a sign of financial difficulty caused by

(a) overtrading through over-investment in fixed assets;
(b) insufficient profits earned to replace fixed assets as they wear out.

6 OTHER RATIOS

6.1 Profit and loss accounts ratios

Two significant ratios to be obtained from profit and loss accounts are:

$$\left.\begin{array}{l}\dfrac{\text{Gross profit}}{\text{Sales}}\\[3ex]\dfrac{\text{Net profit}}{\text{Sales}}\end{array}\right\}\ \text{Both should show a rising trend}$$

If gross profits/sales ratio is improving while net profit/sales ratio is declining, the company needs to show considerable efficiency in controlling its fixed costs.

Other ratios such as wages/sales, raw materials/sales or fixed costs/sales are used but these are more the province of the cost accountant and will be of little value with a successful business.

6.2 Balance sheet ratios

$$\text{Liquidity ratio} = \frac{\text{Cash} + \text{Liquid investments}}{\text{Current liabilities}}$$

Probably the only balance sheet ratio which is really accurate and is an excellent test of a company's ability to survive.

$$\text{Quick ratio} = \frac{\text{Liquid assets} + \text{Debtors}}{\text{Current liabilities}}$$

Less useful than the liquidity ratio. Only realistic if we assume that all debtors are good payers. Gives no indication of whether the debtors will pay in four days, four weeks, or four months.

$$\text{Current ratio} = \frac{\text{Current assets}}{\text{Current liabilities}}$$

If this is greater than unity the company should have enough assets to meet demands on it during the coming twelve months. As current assets include an element of profit, the ratio shows an increase as the years go by and more profit is retained in the business.

6.3 Balance sheet/profit and loss ratios

$$\frac{\text{Average debtors}}{\text{Sales}} \times 365 = \text{Number of days credit is granted}$$

You must take opening debtors figure and closing debtors figure but even then you cannot hope for absolute accuracy. This ratio should show a fall as credit control improves.

$$\frac{\text{Average creditors}}{\text{Purchases}} \times 365 = \text{Number of days credit taken}$$

The average company lumps expenses creditors in the same figure as money owed to suppliers of raw materials. For this to be meaningful, only creditors who are owed for purchases should be included. This figure should also show a fall as the business improves.

$$\frac{\text{Average stock}}{\text{Sales (or cost of sales)}} \times 365 = \text{Number of days stock turns over once}$$

This last ratio is probably the least accurate of all ratios.

You would need separate figures for stocks of raw materials, work-in-progress and finished goods. It would be necessary to find out the basis of

(a) valuation of work-in-progress;
(b) valuation of finished goods;
(c) cost of sales, if available.

The importance of the simple stock ratio is to give lending bankers a good indication of managerial efficiency over a period of years. A gradual fall in the number of days stock is held shows careful stock control.

Part 6: Banking Securities

22 *Bankers' Securities*

Where loans are made to customers and there is certainty of repayment within a very short time, it is unusual for a bank to ask the customer to provide some form of security for the loan. If borrowing is going to take the form of an overdraft and a substantial overdraft limit has been agreed for a considerable number of months, security will usually be insisted on. With personal loans, made to private individuals for a fixed period and at fixed rates of interest, bank policy is only to ask for security in exceptional circumstances. Long-term or medium-term loans made to companies at a variable rate of interest, for the purpose of financing the growth of the companies' businesses, are nearly always secured.

Whether it is usual to ask for security or normal to waive security, the prudent banker will always remember that the lodging of security does not turn a bad advance into a good one. Why then is security insisted on in some cases? The reason security is taken is not on the understanding that the borrowing can always be repaid by realising the security. It is to safeguard the banker against events which neither the banker nor customer expect to happen. The lodgement of security by the customer is an expression of confidence the bank's depositors are asked to share.

Acceptable securities fall into two main groups:

(a) third party — given by someone else to support the customer's borrowing;
(b) direct — given by the customer to support the customer's own borrowing.

The most common securities taken by a bank are:

(a) guarantees;
(b) stocks and shares;
(c) life assurance policies;
(d) land and buildings.

Guarantees are always third party securities but stocks and shares, life assurance policies, and land and buildings can be either third party or direct securities.

1 GUARANTEES

A guarantee is a document in writing with the person who signs the document undertaking to be responsible for the amount owed by the customer to the bank. There must be some consideration included in the document even if it is only an agreement by the bank to allow borrowing arrangements to continue.

It is vital that the guarantee form should be signed in the presence of a bank official, who knows the guarantor, or a solicitor acting for the guarantor. The bank official or solicitor will also sign as a witness to the guarantor's signature. This is to prevent a guarantor escaping liability by claiming 'non est factum'. The plea was upheld in the case of *Carlisle and Cumberland Banking Co* v *Bragg* (1911). In that case a customer of the bank was given a form of guarantee and persuaded Bragg to sign it by telling him that he wanted a signature to an insurance document. The customer then forged the signature of a witness and returned it to the bank. When the bank later sued Bragg, the Court of Appeal decided that he need not pay because he had not understood the nature of the document he had signed. Although this decision was subsequently overruled in a more recent case involving the Anglia Building Society, bankers still continue to insist that guarantors sign in the presence of a bank official or the guarantor's own solicitor.

A copy of the guarantee form should be handed to the guarantor who will acknowledge receipt by means of a second signature on the original form.

1.1 Information to be disclosed to guarantor

A long series of cases have been lost by guarantors trying to avoid liability on the grounds that there was an absence of full disclosure of all facts before the guarantee was signed. The bank is entitled to assume that the guarantor is fully aware of the borrower's finances. The contract between banker and guarantor does not require the banker to volunteer information. On the other hand, where the guarantors ask direct questions from which it would be obvious that they are misinformed about the borrower's indebtedness, the banker must answer truthfully. Because of this, it is always preferable to have the borrower present at the signing of the guarantee.

The case of *McKenzie* v *Royal Bank of Canada* (1934) showed the dangers of misrepresentation, even if the misrepresentation is innocent. The judge in that case felt that there was innocent misrepresentation of an existing fact because Mrs McKenzie was told that security previously deposited by her could not be returned unless she signed a new guarantee. She was able to avoid liability on these grounds.

Once the guarantee has been signed by the guarantor the information which can be disclosed without the customer's authority is very limited. If the guarantee is security for a fluctuating overdraft, the guarantor is only entitled to know the amount for which the guarantee was signed. This will be for the whole debt, but there is often a proviso that no more than £x be recovered.

Where the guarantee is security for a loan account, the bank may let the guarantor know the amount of the debt so long as they state that the guarantee is still in force for the full amount. If the balance of the loan exceeds the amount of the guarantee, merely confirm the figure for which the guarantee was signed. In all cases where information is sought, remind the guarantor that a period of notice is needed to determine the guarantee.

The case of *The National Provincial Bank of England* v *Lord Glanusk* (1913) was one where the guarantor tried to avoid his liability. He claimed that he should have been told about certain transactions which took place on the account of his brother-in-law. The brother-in-law was Lord Glanusk's agent and these transactions were dated a year after the guarantee was signed.

It was held by the judge that the contract of guarantee was not one of *uberrimae fidei*. In other words, there was no need for the bank to volunteer information to the guarantor about the borrower's financial position or business affairs. The bank won the case and Lord Glanusk was ordered to pay £3,348, together with costs.

The moral to draw from this case is that a guarantor, who seeks more information than the customer's balance or the amount of the guarantee (whichever is smaller), should be advised to obtain this information from the customer.

1.2 Justification for guarantees as security

There are times when a banker will feel justified in accepting a guarantee as security. In the following instances the bank will feel that a guarantee is not only justified but essential.

(a) a director or directors guaranteeing a private limited company;
(b) a parent company giving a guarantee in favour of a wholly-owned subsidiary company;
(c) a relative guaranteeing part of a home mortgage loan;
(d) a father guaranteeing his son;
(e) an influential professional man introducing a young business associate.

Remember that a prudent banker will not accept a guarantee from a partner to cover partnership borrowing. This is because all the assets of each partner automatically support the partnership debt.

The lending banker acts on the principle that the bank will not accept a guarantee without supporting collateral security, unless the bank would be prepared to lend on an unsecured basis to the guarantor. In those circumstances, the lending bank will originate an enquiry asking for the guarantor's banker to give an opinion on whether the guarantor is good for the amount of the guarantee.

1.3 Special types of guarantors

Very great care is needed when one customer of a branch is asked to guarantee another customer of the same branch. The banker has a duty to the customer who is giving the guarantee if it is clear that the guarantor is looking to the banker for guidance.

In the case of *Lloyds Bank* v *Bundy* (1975) a customer was asked to sign an increased guarantee for his son, whose account was under pressure. Both father and son banked at the same branch. The father's solicitor had already expressed the view that no additional commitment should be undertaken by the father. One of the bank's lending officers took the new guarantee to the father's home, where it was signed in the presence of the son and the bank official. The father was old and infirm and, when the bank called up the guarantee, was able to avoid liability. It was held that there was a special relationship existing between banker and customer whereby a customer should be able to rely on advice about the wisdom of giving a guarantee.

There is a clash of interest in situations like this. While the bank is not called upon to take special precautions in cases a, b and e mentioned in the previous section, where there is any element of doubt about the guarantor's understanding of his liability, it is preferable for the guarantor to have independent legal advice. This means that the customer/guarantor should sign the guarantee in the presence of his own solicitor.

1.4 Undue influence

Where there is any question of undue influence this may invalidate the guarantee. Examples of relationships where undue influence is assumed are where a wife is asked to guarantee her husband or a daughter to guarantee her father. A similar assumption might be made if an elderly mother was prevailed upon to guarantee the borrowing of her son. In any relationship where there is a possibility of undue influence, it is preferable for the guarantor to sign the guarantee form in front of an independent solicitor.

In the case of *The Bank of Montreal* v *Stuart and Another* (1911) a guarantee was signed by Mrs Stuart to act as security for borrowing by a company of which her husband was a director. The guarantee was witnessed by a solicitor, who besides being a director of the company was also the solicitor for the Bank of Montreal. The guarantee was set aside on the grounds that it was impossible for the solicitor to have given the guarantor separate advice.

1.5 Joint and several guarantors

When two or more people sign a bank guarantee form the document is worded in such a way that the bank has the right to claim against the guarantors individually as well as collectively. Death of one of the guarantors does not release his estate from any liability. In the same way, one individual guarantor cannot determine a joint and several guarantee. Notice of determination must come from all the guarantors. Because of this, a joint guarantee does not become effective until all parties have signed.

In the *National Provincial Bank of England* v *Brackenbury* (1906) case, bank borrowing was sought against a guarantee of four people. The bank agreed to lend against this security and made the loan available after three of the four guarantors had signed. The fourth guarantor declined to append his signature to the form of guarantee. When the bank sought to recover its loan from the three guarantors who had signed, the court directed that these three should be released from their liability.

1.6 Guarantees given by partnerships

This could occur when the partners are anxious to support the borrowing of a newly-appointed chief clerk or office manager. While it is perfectly proper for one partner to bind the firm when acting in the normal way of business, giving guarantees is not a normal transaction. The guarantee form taken by the bank from the partnership should be signed by all the partners. If the composition of the firm changes, a fresh guarantee should be obtained from the partners in the reconstituted firm.

1.7 Guarantees given by companies

If a guarantee is given by a company it is essential to search the memorandum of association in order to ascertain whether the company has the power to give guarantees. The directors' powers to give guarantees on behalf of the company should also be checked from an examination of the articles of association.

Guarantees are sometimes given under the seal of the company. The articles of association will state the designations of the officials who can sign and countersign the document which is sealed on the company's behalf. It is essential to verify the capacity in which they sign by checking the mandate and the articles of association.

Most guarantees taken from companies are given under the hand of authorised officials. A certified copy of the board resolution, authorising these officials to sign on behalf of the company, must be lodged with the bank. It is also essential that the resolution clearly indicates that the board authorises the giving of the guarantee in the form attached. Some banks prefer to have the resolution typed and certified on the original guarantee in order to avoid any claim that the board resolution was intended to cover a different guarantee.

While company guarantors are perfectly acceptable provided the necessary resolutions are obtained and the memorandum and articles of association checked, care is needed in some cases. Section 49 of the Companies Act 1980 prevents a company guaranteeing a loan made to a director by a bank or by anyone else. The prohibition is extended to loans made not only to the directors but also to persons connected with the directors.

A conflict of interest can sometimes arise between a director's duty to his company and the benefit which he will obtain if certain actions are taken. The director might be a director of more than one company, with one company being the subsidiary of the other. In his capacity as director of the subsidiary company, he may have already given his personal guarantee to the bank. Some time later additional security is requested and the guarantee of the parent company is suggested. The interested director should not vote on the resolution for giving the guarantee. It is vital that a quorum of independent directors should approve the required resolution. If there is any element of doubt, the bank should suggest a special meeting of shareholders in order that the members can pass a special resolution to give the guarantee.

1.8 Action to be taken after guarantee signed

Unless the guarantor's ability to repay is undoubted, the bank should ask for collateral security or a cash deposit by the guarantor for the amount of the guarantee. It should be noted that while the guarantee is entered in the bank's security register under the name of the debtor, any collateral security or supporting cash deposit should be entered in the name of the guarantor. A suitable cross-reference should be made.

The bank may be prepared to dispense with third party security. This is likely to happen only if the bank would have been prepared to lend on an unsecured basis to the guarantor. Certain precautions must be taken when the bank decides to rely on an unsupported guarantee. If the guarantor banks at another branch or another bank, a status enquiry should be made when the guarantee is signed. Confirmation of the opinion is requested at six-monthly intervals. In order to enable the replying banker to give a fair picture, the second and subsequent enquiries are marked 'renewal'. A record must be maintained of all replies to these enquiries.

Although the Limitation Act 1980 provided that actions to recover sums secured by guarantees are barred after six years (or twelve years in the case of guarantees executed under seal) all bank guarantee forms contain words such as 'The undersigned hereby guarantees payment to you on demand'. This wording means that the limitation period does not begin until the guarantee is called up.

In the *Bradford Old Bank Limited* v *Sutcliffe* (1918) case a guarantee given to the bank was determined by the lunacy of a guarantor in 1898. No demand for repayment was made until 1912. The judge decided that a demand for repayment was necessary before any action could be taken to recover the money owed. He also ruled that the Statute of Limitations 1623 did not run until demand had been made and the bank were entitled tc recover the amount owed to them.

Although inclusion of the phrase 'on demand' would exclude the effect of the Limitation Act 1980, it is customary to obtain an acknowledgement from the guarantor at four or five yearly intervals. A diary note should be made to request these acknowledgements before the six year period is reached.

1.9 Determination of guarantee

This will take place in normal circumstances after the guarantor has given three months' notice in writing and the debtor has repaid the borrowing in full. Repayment in full by the guarantor three months after giving notice in writing will also determine the guarantee.

Where the bank has notice of the mental incapacity of either the guarantor or the debtor, this will determine the guarantee at once. The account must be stopped at once if it is overdrawn. Where the guarantor is compulsorily admitted to a mental hospital, under the authority of two doctors, the debtor must be informed by the bank. If it is the debtor who is compulsorily detained, the bank must inform the debtor's receiver of the liability to the bank. The *Bradford Old Bank Limited* v *Sutcliffe* (1918) case has been mentioned in the previous section. In that case the guarantor had acted as surety for borrowing on a loan account and a current account. The bank was able to obtain repayment of the loan account balance but the current account overdraft was written off as a loss. The rule in 'Clayton's Case' (*Devaynes* v *Noble*, 1816) had worked against the bank because the guarantee was determined by the guarantor's lunacy and the current account had not been stopped.

The bank guarantee forms are drawn up so that death of a sole guarantor does not determine the guarantee. It is necessary for the personal representatives of the dead guarantor to give three months notice of determination of the liability. The case of *Egbert and Others* v *Northern Crown Bank* (1918) was a case where there were several guarantors. After the death of one guarantor, his executors gave notice of determination to the bank. Because the surviving guarantors did not determine the guarantee the bank continued to lend after the end of the period of notice and won their case because it was held that all must give notice. In modern practice, it would be preferable to stop the account at the end of three months and open a fresh account for future transactions.

In a similar fashion, the death of the borrower does not determine the guarantee. Although the deceased customer's account is blocked on death, it is still necessary for the guarantor to give three months' notice in writing, if he wishes to determine his liability.

The guarantor could of course be released from liability on the repayment of the borrowing by the personal representatives of the deceased customer.

Bankruptcy of either the debtor or the guarantor will determine the guarantee. The account must be frozen to enable a claim to be made against the bankrupt's estate. The bank will have to inform the official receiver of their claim.

Where a guarantee is signed by more than one guarantor it is advisable to make it clear to the signatories that notice of determination must be given by all the guarantors or their personal representatives at the same time (see *Egbert and Others* v *Northern Crown Bank*, 1918). Where more than one guarantor signs a guarantee form their liability is joint and several. Notice of determination by one of a number of guarantors will only determine liability, at the end of the period of notice, as far as that guarantor is concerned. Although the account is stopped at the end of the three months period and a new account opened, the remaining guarantors will be liable not only for the borrowing on the stopped account but also for any new borrowing. It is not necessary to obtain a fresh guarantee but it might be preferable to have a new guarantee signed by the other guarantors who should acknowledge that the fresh guarantee is additional security and not replacement security.

1.10 Payments made by guarantor into debtor's account

These credits from the guarantor can sometimes cause problems to the bank if no pressure has been applied to obtain reimbursement of the money owed by the debtor. On receipt of the credits, the guarantor should be asked if he wishes to give notice to determine the guarantee. It should be pointed out that three months' notice in writing is required. If it is the guarantor's intention that the borrowing is to be repaid, obtain his written notice to determine the guarantee. At the end of three months stop the account and advise the guarantor in writing of the outstanding liability, if any. A new account should be opened for the principal debtor and this should be kept in credit unless alternative arrangements are to be made.

If the guarantor pays in money to the debtor's account and declines to determine the guarantee, ask for a fresh guarantee for the amount of the agreed borrowing limit. This new guarantee should be dated after the receipt of the credit and a suitable interview note will need to be made explaining the background.

The danger which it is important to guard against is that of fraudulent preference. This will occur when the bank is paid off before other creditors in order to obtain release of a guarantee or other third party security. A situation such as this frequently occurs when the borrower realises that he is getting into financial difficulties. The contingent liability entered into by the guarantor or giver of collateral security is likely to turn into a real liability. In those circumstances, funds may be diverted into repaying bank borrowing which should be used for the benefit of all the creditors.

The case of *re M Kushler Ltd* (1943) illustrates the dangers which might face a bank when fraudulent preference is proved. Lloyds Bank granted an overdraft limit to the company against the security of a guarantee by one of the two directors. Four life policies were lodged as collateral security to the guarantee. The directors were told by their accountant that the company was insolvent. This statement was made on 12 May and during the next ten days sufficient cheques were paid into the company's account to repay the overdraft. This enabled the guarantee and life policies to be released. Although other creditors were pressing for money during these ten days, no payments were made to them. During this period the directors called a creditors' meeting and a few days later the company began the process of voluntary liquidation. The bank had not been asked to attend the meeting of creditors and the guarantor had not told the other creditors that he had guaranteed the company's overdraft. The judge ruled that the payments made to the bank after 10 May constituted a fraudulent preference and the bank was forced to refund this money to the liquidator of the company for the benefit of the other creditors.

In the case of *re F P and C H Mathews Ltd* (1981) the company was borrowing against the security of a guarantee from the directors, supported by a legal mortgage over the matrimonial home of the two directors. Because of adverse business conditions, the directors decided to cease trading. Shortly after this, two cheques were received which were paid into the company's account. This resulted in the overdraft being repaid and the company went into voluntary liquidation.

No pressure for repayment had been applied by the bank and, when the cheques were paid in, the managing director had believed that all creditors could be paid within the next six months.

Nevertheless, the court decided that there had been fraudulent preference in favour of the bank because the directors knew that they could not pay all debts as they arose and had, therefore, deliberately paid the bank before other creditors.

1.11 Payments made by guarantor direct to bank

If a guarantor wishes to pay off sufficient borrowing to release his guarantee, it is necessary to point out that three months' notice of determination is required. Any money received from the guarantor should be credited to a 'realised securities account' and not placed to the credit of the debtor's account. The guarantee form is always retained by the bank. If at the end of the three months period of notice, the amount credited to the Realised Securities Account by the guarantor is the same as the amount of the guarantee, a formal letter is sent to the guarantor. The bank will state that the guarantee has been placed with its obsolete securities. Any collateral securities are released at the same time. The debtor is informed of the arrangements between the bank and the guarantor.

1.12 Guarantor's right to debtor's security

The legal doctrine of subrogation means that where a person pays another's debts he has a claim against the debtor for the amount by which the debts are reduced. This could cause problems for the banks if their guarantee forms were not drawn up to cover the whole debt, subject to a limitation on the amount which can be recovered from the guarantor. Insertion of the wording 'the whole amount due' in bank guarantee forms means that the guarantor cannot share in any security given to the bank by the debtor, unless the payment made by the guarantor exceeds the debt owing to the bank. In a similar way, the guarantor cannot make a claim which competes with the bank's claim, if the debtor becomes bankrupt.

The case of *re Sass, ex parte National Provincial Bank of England* (1896) showed the effectiveness of the 'whole debt' clause. The debtor's account was overdrawn £755. It was secured by a guarantee for the whole of the debt, with a limit of £300, plus interest and charges, on the amount recoverable.

When the borrower became bankrupt, the bank called upon the guarantor to pay up the amount due under the guarantee, i.e. £300 plus interest. £303 was paid to the bank by the guarantor. This amount was credited to a realised security account and the bank claimed for the whole £755 from the debtor's trustee in bankruptcy. The trustee refused to accept a claim for the whole £755 and said it should be reduced by £303. The court, however, held that the bank was entitled to claim the whole amount as the guarantee was drawn to cover the whole debt.

Should the guarantor's payment be as great as the whole debt owed to the bank, the guarantor can claim the security lodged by the debtor. The correct period of notice of determination must be given by the guarantor and the debtor must be informed that written notice to determine the guarantee has been given to the bank. At the end of the three month period, the bank's legal department will be asked to prepare the transfer of the debt and the security from the bank to the guarantor.

23 *Stocks and Shares*

1 FIVE MAIN CATEGORIES

These are in five main categories starting with the easiest form of security.

(a) Bearer bonds.
(b) Registered stocks and shares.
(c) American or Canadian shares.
(d) Inscribed stock.
(e) Private company shares.

1.1 Bearer bonds

Ownership of bearer bonds is transferable by delivery. No deed needs to be sent to the company's registrar because no register of shareholders or stockholders is kept. For bonds to be a good delivery it is important to check that they are not torn or mutilated in any way. The bonds should have the correct number of coupons attached. The up-to-date dividend position can be checked by comparison with the *Stock Exchange Daily Official List.*

1.2 Registered stocks and shares

A certificate is issued by the company registrar. Check that the name and address of your customer shown on the certificate are the same as the name and address in your records. It is preferable for the dividends from the company to come directly to the bank. This can be arranged by the customer signing a dividend mandate which the bank will forward to the company.

1.3 American or Canadian shares

These are registered certificates which are usually issued in multiples of 100 shares. The back of the certificates has a form of transfer printed on it. When this form is signed by the shareholder the certificate becomes, in effect, a bearer security. If the certificate is registered in the name of the customer, dividends, scrip issues and 'rights' issues will continue to be sent to the customer.

The Stock Exchange finds it more convenient for this type of security to be registered in a 'marking name'. This is a bank, financial institution, or well-known firm in the Stock Exchange. When shares in 'marking names' are bought and sold there is no need for the securities to be sent to North America for re-registration. Any dividends, 'rights' issues or scrip issues are claimed from the 'marking name' by the beneficial owner of the shares.

1.4 Inscribed stocks

These stocks are very few and far between. Instead of receiving a stock certificate the stockholder is given a stock receipt by the registrar. What is the significance of this, from the bank's point of view?

The stock receipt is not a document of title. It does not need to be produced in the event of a sale of the stock. This means that a stockholder could sell stock, for which the bank held a stock receipt, without the receipt being produced to the registrar.

1.5 Private company shares

These are registered shares which are not quoted on the Stock Exchange. A certificate in the shareholder's name is issued to the customer in exactly the same way as certificates are issued by a public limited company. Since the passing of the Companies Act 1980, private company shares have been freely transferable. In the absence of a Stock Exchange quotation, however, they are very difficult to value.

2 TYPES OF SECURITY

There are two main ways in which stocks and shares can be lodged with a bank as security for a customer's borrowing. The first and more usual way is the equitable mortgage. The second method is the legal mortgage.

2.1 Equitable mortgage

This involves the customer (or someone providing security on the borrower's behalf) signing a memorandum of deposit. The memorandum is an acknowledgment that the certificates are lodged with the bank as security. In the case of registered stocks and shares, the securities remain in the names of the holders. With a memorandum of deposit the giver of the security undertakes to give the bank the right to sell the securities which have been lodged.

The memorandum will also incorporate an undertaking to deposit any bonus issues of shares which are sent directly to the shareholder. An agreement to give the bank a legal mortgage when requested is also one of the clauses in a standard memorandum of deposit form. A schedule of the securities lodged (with certificate numbers) is included on the memorandum of deposit form. The schedule of securities is initialled by the customer when the memorandum form is signed. A duplicate form is given to the customer when the securities are lodged.

When a stockbroker, stockjobber, or an active investor leaves stocks and shares as securities it is usual to ask the customer to sign a general memorandum of deposit. This is similar in effect to a standard memorandum of deposit but has no schedule of securities. It is an admission that the present and all future securities deposited are lodged to support present and future borrowings.

Transfer forms are signed by the customer where a memorandum of deposit is taken. There are special forms, which are obtainable from a Post Office, which have to be signed for government stocks on the national savings bank register. In the case of government stocks on the Bank of England register, a normal stock transfer form is signed by the stockholder. Similar forms are used for private company shares and shares quoted on the

Stock Exchange. Even though a special type of 'Talisman' sold transfer would be used for sales of quoted shares through the Stock Exchange, the normal type of stock transfer is used when shares are deposited as bank security. The signed transfers are held in the bank's safe together with the certificates and the memorandum of deposit.

When an equitable mortgage is offered over inscribed stock and a stock receipt is lodged as security, the receipt should be surrendered to the registrar and the bank should ask for a registered certificate in its place.

No transfer form needs to be signed when the bearer bonds are lodged. The bank can give a good delivery merely by handing the bonds to a purchaser in the event of the borrower defaulting.

In a similar way, American and Canadian certificates in 'marking names' are a good delivery without the need for a transfer form to be signed. Both bearer bonds and American and Canadian stocks in 'marking names' have considerable advantages as bank security. They are securities which share the following virtues:

(a) capable of accurate valuation
(b) easily realised
(c) easily charged
(d) bank retains physical control of securities and collects dividend payments.

Notice to companies

It has already been pointed out that private company shares are not good security because of valuation problems. The bank will try to compensate for this less than perfect security by giving notice of the charge to the company's secretary. The secretary will almost certainly refuse to accept any notice of the bank's interest in the companies' shares. It is very likely that the bank will be reminded that under Section 117 Companies Act 1948 no notice of a trust may be registered in the records of a limited company.

What then are the advantages of giving notice? While the rules of the Stock Exchange prevent a quoted company having a lien over its own shares, this rule does not apply to an unquoted company. Notice from the bank will prevent any future sums, due to the company from the shareholder, ranking in front of the bank's interest. In the case of *Bradford Banking Company Limited* v *Henry Briggs Son and Co Limited* (1886) a customer of the bank deposited shares in the company as security for his borrowing from the bank. The bank gave notice to the company. The company acknowledged and told the bank that the company also had a lien on the shares in respect of money which they were owed by the shareholder. Subsequently, the bank's customer repaid the money he owed Henry Briggs Son and Co Limited but he continued to borrow from the bank. At an even later date, he borrowed again from the company and was finally declared bankrupt. The company claimed that their advance should have priority over the bank's lending. This plea was rejected and the court held that the company was not entitled to priority for the lending made after receipt of the notice from the bank.

Notice will also prevent the company issuing duplicate certificates to its shareholder against an indemnity. The company will also let the bank know if the shareholder's name is not registered in the company's book at the date of receipt of the bank's notice.

Where the bank's own shareholders are concerned, a bank will keep an unofficial list of notices sent by branches informing the registrar of charges over the bank's shares given by borrowers.

2.2 Legal mortgage over shares

Where a customer is an active investor, a stockbroker, or a stockjobber, it is not practicable for a legal mortgage to be taken. In a similar way, banks will rely on equitable mortgages given by customers of high integrity to cover short-term borrowing.

It is desirable to obtain a legal mortgage in the case of long-term borrowing by non-active investors. A memorandum of deposit is signed and the schedule initialled by the customer. A duplicate memorandum form is handed to the customer after signature. With all registered stocks and shares, whether on the national savings stock register, the Bank of England stock register or the registers of quoted or private companies, a signed deed of transfer is obtained. The transfer form is then sent to the registrar concerned so that the bank's nominee company can be entered on the books as the legal owners. Any future dividends, bonus issues or 'rights' issues will be sent to the bank. Great care is needed to ensure that the signature on the transfer form is genuine. If a signature is forged, the bank will have to re-imburse any parties who lose money as a result. *Lord Mayor of Sheffield and Corporation of Sheffield* v *Barclay and others* (1905) was a case where a loss resulted. A borrowing customer obtained a loan from the bank against the security of stock in joint names. The bank asked for a transfer form to be signed so that the Sheffield Corporation stock could be transferred into the name of a nominee of the bank. The borrower signed the deed and forged the signature of his co-stockholder. The bank's nominee was then registered as the stockholder. When the borrowing was repaid, the bank transferred the stock to two nominees of the borrower. On the borrower's death the original co-stockholder sued the Sheffield Corporation who were ordered to pay him £11,000 representing the value of the stock and past dividends. The Corporation then sued the bank. The court held that the bank had implied that the signatures were genuine when it had forwarded the transfer form for registration of the stock in its own nominee's name. The bank was instructed to compensate the Sheffield Corporation for the full extent of the loss.

The lesson to draw from this is that stockholders or shareholders should be asked to sign a transfer deed in the presence of their own bank managers. If this is not possible, the transfer form should be sent to the signatory's address by recorded delivery. It should never be given to one stockholder for the purpose of obtaining a co-stockholder's signature.

American and Canadian shares which are in the name of the customer have a form of transfer printed on the back. This should be completed by the borrower's signature and then transferred into the name of the bank's nominee company. Asking the customer to endorse these certificates in blank will not prevent bonus issues or dividends being sent directly to the customer.

Bearer shares or American and Canadian shares in 'marking names' do not require a transfer deed to be signed when they are legally mortgaged to the bank.

The advantages of a legal mortgage are that the form is very simple security to be taken and it is easily realised in the event of default. Taking a legal mortgage will prevent the customer fraudulently obtaining duplicate certificates. In the case of both registered stocks and shares and American and Canadian shares, a legal mortgage will enable the dividends, 'rights' issues and bonus issues to be sent directly to the bank's nominee company.

After the security is taken it is still essential to review the shares periodically. A diary note needs to be made to value them each month by reference to the *Stock Exchange Daily*

Official List, the *Financial Times* or, in the case of small quoted companies, the *Monthly Supplement*. If the shares are not quoted in London but are quoted elsewhere, the bank's broker should be asked to supply a valuation.

Diary notes must be made to claim dividends on bearer bonds or North American shares in 'marking names'. With bearer bonds the appropriate coupon is cut off and presented to the company's agent for payment of dividend. The 'marking names', who are the registered holders of the North American shares, have a formal demand made on them by the bank for the next dividend payment due. An appropriate note is made on the back of the share certificate.

If 'rights' issues are announced on holdings of shares legally mortgaged to the bank, the customer's instructions in writing must be obtained. The payment of calls on the 'rights' issue will involve a debit to the customer's account which will need written authority. As an alternative to paying out more money, the customer may instruct the bank to sell the new shares and use the proceeds in partial repayment of the loan. Another choice could be to sell sufficient new shares to raise enough money to pay the calls due on the remainder of the 'rights' issue.

3 REALISATION

3.1 Realisation of stocks and shares held as security

When a memorandum of deposit has been taken this gives the bank an immediate power of sale. If the securities have been transferred into the names of the bank's nominees, the bank can proceed to realise its security with a minimum of formality and delay. It is customary to give the debtor one month's notice that the security is to be realised and this view was confirmed in the case of *Deverges* v *Sandeman* (1902).

The same ease of realisation applies in the case of bearer bonds. As these securities are transferable by delivery, a bank which takes them in good faith and without notice of any defect in title acquires a valid title to the securities. This was the subject of the court case *London Joint Stock Bank* v *Simmons* (1892). A partner in a firm of stockbrokers deposited bearer bonds as security for the firm's borrowing. The bonds belonged to a client of the firm. The bank was unable to obtain repayment of its lending and sold the bonds. Simmons, to whom the bonds had originally belonged, sued the bank. The House of Lords held that the bank had taken the securities in good faith and was entitled to the sale proceeds. As the bank had given value for these securities and there were no factors to arouse suspicion, the bank was not obliged to investigate the title to the bonds before accepting them as security.

Similar circumstances arose in the *Fuller* v *Glyn, Mills Currie and Co* (1914) case, although here the securities involved were shares in Canadian Pacific Railway, which were in a recognised 'marking name'. A firm of stockbrokers was also involved here and they deposited the shares as part of the security for the firm's borrowing. Because the certificates had blank transfers endorsed on the back, the bank treated them as bearer securities. The court held that the bank took the shares in good faith, while the stockbrokers' client allowed the shares to remain in that firm's possession. This prevented any claim against the bank succeeding because they were entitled to assume the implied authority of the stockbrokers to deal with the securities lodged.

In the case of registered stocks, in the name of the bank's nominee companies, the memorandum of deposit gives the bank an immediate power of sale. By the ruling in the

Deverges v *Sandeman* (1902) case it is usual to give the borrower one month's notice of realisation, but it is possible to sell shares registered in nominee names without waiting for a court order.

3.2 Realisation of stocks and shares subject to an equitable mortgage

Because the securities remain registered in the customer's name, where the bank has agreed to accept an equitable mortgage, even though the customer has signed a memorandum of deposit, it is necessary for the bank to seek a court order. Although the memorandum of deposit will give an immediate power of sale, the bank must still apply for a court order to compel the borrower to give the bank authority to sell the shares belonging to the customer.

In some exceptional circumstances, such as the possibility of fraud, the bank will apply for a 'Notice in lieu of Distringas'. The bank files a sworn affidavit of its equitable interest at the central office of the Supreme Court. The court then issues a stop notice. A copy of this stop notice and a copy of the bank's affidavit are lodged at the office of the company's registrar. If the customer attempts to transfer shares into someone else's name, the company must give the bank at least eight days notice of the intended transfer. This will enable the bank to obtain an injunction from the court which will prevent the customer and registrar transferring these shares.

4 REGISTERED SHARES INFORMALLY DEPOSITED AS SECURITY

On a few occasions, when dealing with short-term borrowing for a person of high integrity, the bank will be prepared to rely just on the lodging of share certificates, without a memorandum of deposit being signed by the customer. This provides little more than evidence of means and good faith. Considerable difficulties are encountered when the customer defaults. If the bank wish to realise the security, they must take the following steps:

(a) Give notice to debtor that they wish to sell the shares and ask him to sign a transfer form. (*Note*: this stage is unnecessary if the debtor has signed a blank transfer form. It is extremely unlikely, however, that a transfer form would be signed without a memorandum of deposit being taken at the same time.)

(b) If no reply is received send a demand for repayment of the debt, using registered or recorded delivery mail.

(c) In the event of no satisfactory proposals being received, apply to the court for a power of sale.

One of the problems which may be involved in taking informal security, or an equitable mortgage, is that a prior equitable claim may exist of which the bank may be unaware. While a prior equitable claim may be overtaken by a legal mortgage, this will only occur if the bank acts in good faith and gives value for the legal mortgage. Good faith cannot be assumed if the bank are aware of the existence of an equitable claim when they come to register the shares in nominee names. The danger to a bank in not taking a legal mortgage was very clearly demonstrated in the case of *Coleman* v *London, County and Westminster Bank Ltd* (1916). Mrs Coleman was the legal owner of 45 debentures of £100 each in a private limited company. She set up a trust for herself and three sons and executed a deed of transfer to a trustee. Subsequently, one of the sons assigned his interest in this trust to his wife. The transfer in favour of the trustee was never registered and some time later Mrs Coleman obtained the debentures and signed a memorandum of deposit and a transfer deed in favour of the bank. Following the death of the trustee, the bank learned of the original trust deed and the unregistered deed of transfer. The bank immediately registered their own transfer deed and obtained assignments of their reversionary interests from the other two sons. Mrs Coleman's daughter-in-law (who had an interest in the trust because of the previous assignment from the third son) sued the bank. The executors of the trustees also joined in the action against the bank.

Although the judge said that this was a case of some complexity, a view most readers will share, he gave judgement against the bank and said that the bank had no title to the 15 debentures in which the daughter-in-law had an interest. He took the view that as the bank had notice of an earlier equitable interest, they could not give their own equitable interest priority by turning it into a legal mortgage.

5 REPAYMENT OF THE BORROWING

Informally deposited securities are handed back to the customer against receipt when the borrowing in the customer's name is repaid.

When borrowing secured by an equitable mortgage is repaid the memorandum of deposit is placed with the bank's obsolete securities. Any signed transfer form which the bank is holding is dealt with in the same way. The share or stock certificate is then delivered to the customer against their receipt.

If the bank has taken a legal mortgage to secure its lending, it will be necessary to ask the nominee company to transfer an equivalent holding of shares into the name of the company. The memorandum of deposit will be put with the bank's obsolete securities at the same time. The procedure of transferring out of nominee names will not apply where the customer has lodged bearer bonds or American or Canadian stocks in 'marking names'. Transfers of these types of securities can take place by mere delivery.

The customer who lodges registered shares, over which the bank takes a legal mortgage, cannot insist on identical shares being handed back. This was decided in *Crerar* v *Bank of Scotland* (1922). Miss Crerar lodged 2775 J P Coats Ltd ordinary shares with the Bank of Scotland. It was agreed that a legal mortgage should be taken and the shares were transferred into the name of the bank's nominee company. Fifteen years later the borrowing was repaid and Miss Crerar claimed that the bank should transfer back the identical shares, although the bank were able to show that at all times during the fifteen year period they held sufficient shares to enable them to re-transfer the original 2775 shares lodged by Miss Crerar. The court held that Miss Crerar had acquiesced in the bank's actions when she signed the documents to give the bank a legal mortgage and gave judgement for the bank.

24 *Life Policies as Security*

A life assurance policy is a contract between an insurance company and the policy holder. In return for the payment of premiums by the policy holder, the insurance company guarantees payment of the sum insured. This payment is made on the death of the person whose life is assured, in the case of whole life policies. With endowment policies, payment is made at the end of an agreed number of years or on death, if this comes earlier.

Both endowment policies and whole life policies are equally acceptable for the purposes of banking security. After an agreed minimum number of premiums have been paid, they will acquire a surrender value. This means that if the policy holder or the bank want to cash in the policy, a proportion of the premiums will be refunded. Fixed term assurance policies do not have a surrender value but they may be useful banking security if used as collateral security to a guarantee. Reducing term assurance policies (otherwise known as mortgage protection policies) may be taken as life cover from a borrower who obtains a reducing loan from the bank.

1 EXAMINATION OF A POLICY LODGED AS SECURITY

Considerable care must be taken when checking the details of a policy which the bank is going to take as security. These are the points which should be given attention:

(a) Which company is the insurer? It is much easier to obtain good security when the policy is underwritten by a large well-known public company. If the underwriters are not known to the bank, especially when the insurance company is incorporated in another country, the policy is a less desirable security.

(b) Have the premiums been paid up-to-date or is it a 'paid up' policy? Checking the last premium receipt, examining the customer's standing order authorities or writing to the insurance company will provide the information you require.

(c) Is the policy for a nominal sum or are the maturity proceeds linked to the value of unit trusts? Has the policy holder obtained a 'with profits' policy or is the contract a 'without profits' one?

(d) Whose life is assured? The policy holder can insure his own life or another's life. Either type of policy is equally good as security so long as the proceeds are paid to the policy holder or form part of his estate.

(e) Who benefits under the policy? Care must be taken in the case of 'life of another' policies taken out under the Married Women's Property Act 1882. These policies are usually drawn up so that trustees are appointed over the proceeds of the policy, which form a separate estate from the assets of the life assured. If this type of policy is taken as security, it can be accepted provided that the beneficiary is not a minor. The beneficiary under the trust must be named in the policy and all interested parties must join in the giving of the security.

(f) Has the age of the life assured been admitted? This involves the insurance company seeing the birth certificate of the person whose life is assured. It is preferable for this information to be recorded soon after the policy is issued. If the insurance company has not recorded the details of the birth certificate before there is a claim under the policy, payment may be delayed. Should the date of birth shown on the policy differ from that shown on the birth certificate, the company may reduce the amount payable.

2 VALIDITY OF THE LIFE POLICY

Life policies are securities which have many advantages. Physical control of the security is easy and there is little formality in making a claim. They do have disadvantages, however, which may make the policy valueless or reduced in value.

A contract of insurance must be *uberrimae fidei* which means 'of utmost good faith'. Unless all material facts are disclosed on the original proposal form, the policy may become void. Even a slight deviation from the truth may lead to delay in payment.

The policy holder must have an insurable interest in the life assured or the policy may be invalidated. The proposer must have a pecuniary interest in the survival of the life assured. A parent who takes out a policy on the life of a child, with the proceeds to be paid to the parent, is unlikely to have a pecuniary interest and the policy may become void.

Examples of insurable interests are:

(a) own life insured by the policy holder;
(b) husbands and wives can insure the life of each other;
(c) creditors are able to insure the lives of their debtors up to the amounts of the money owed;
(d) guarantors have an interest in lives of principal debtors up to amount of their guarantees;
(e) litigants involved in heavy legal expenses can insure the lives of the judges trying their cases;
(f) partners in a trading firm can insure each other's lives;
(g) a limited company can insure the lives of their directors or other key personnel.

3 INFORMAL DEPOSIT OF POLICY AND EQUITABLE MORTGAGE

An informal deposit of a life assurance policy is a weak form of security. It involves entering the policy in the bank's security register and making a suitable interview note recording that the customer lodged it as informal security.

With an equitable mortgage, the same procedure is followed, but, in addition, the bank will ask the policy holder to sign a memorandum of deposit.

The advantages of informal deposit or an equitable mortgage are that no expense is incurred in taking the security and no reassignment is necessary when the borrowing is repaid. Lodging the policy with the bank prevents anyone with a later interest claiming priority over the bank. The non-production of the policy by the policy holder is said to be constructive notice to anyone else that there was an equitable charge in existence. This applies even when a customer goes bankrupt. In the case of *re Wallis, ex parte Jenks* (1902) a customer who deposited a life policy with his bank went bankrupt shortly afterwards. Although the trustee in bankruptcy gave notice of his interest in the policy to the insurance company, the bank was given priority as the court held that the trustee had implied notice of a prior equitable charge affecting the policy. There are considerable disadvantages to an informal deposit or an equitable mortgage, however. The bank has no legal title and, under the Policies of Assurance Act 1867, the insurance companies do not have to acknowledge an equitable interest.

The bank will need the cooperation of the customer or the deceased's personal representatives if the proceeds of the policy are to be claimed. If the bank is unable to obtain the cooperation of the customer or the personal representatives, an application will have to be made to the court.

4 LEGAL MORTGAGE OF A LIFE POLICY

Where life policies are lodged as security for any borrowing, which is not both small and short term, a legal mortgage should be taken. The procedure to follow when taking a legal mortgage over a life policy is listed below:

(a) Obtain the policy and then check the details to see if it is valid.

(b) Enter policy in bank's security register.

(c) Customer to sign mortgage deed.

(d) Customer to sign standing order or direct debit authority for payment of future premiums.

(e) Write to insurance company to ascertain the undermentioned information:

- (i) Have there been any previous dealings with the policy?
- (ii) What is the surrender value?
- (iii) Are premiums paid up-to-date?

(f) If there have been any previous dealings, obtain the prior documents (e.g. assignments and reassignments) and keep them with the policy.

(g) Notice in duplicate is to be given to the company under the terms of the Policies of Assurance Act 1867 and an acknowledgement received.

(h) If age has not been admitted, obtain the birth certificate of the life assured and send it to the insurance company.

(i) Make a diary note to check the surrender value every three years and check the payment of premiums every year. If the policy is issued by a company which is a member of the British Insurance Association, they will advise the bank of the non-payment of premiums, provided the bank has given notice of its legal mortgage.

4.1 Effect of legal mortgage on life policy

A legal mortgage means that the legal title to the policy passes to the bank and this entitles the bank to debit any premiums to the customer's account. The policy holder has the right to have the policy reassigned on repayment of the borrowing, but the bank is the legal owner while there is any money owing.

Another advantage of a legal mortgage over an equitable one is that Section 107 Law of Property Act 1925 gives the bank power to give a valid receipt for any money paid over on the maturity or the surrender of the policy.

It is important to give notice of a legal mortgage to the insurance company. Under Section 3 Policies of Assurance Act priority of claims is governed by the date of giving notice. In default of notice, priority of the claims is governed by the dates of the legal mortgages.

5 TAKING A LOST POLICY AS SECURITY

The fact that the policy holder is unable to produce the policy is usually regarded as constructive notice of a prior charge. In the case of *Newman* v *Newman* (1885) serving notice of a legal mortgage on the insurance company did not enable the legal mortgagee to gain priority over an earlier legal claim which had not been notified to the insurance company.

If it can be ascertained, to the bank's satisfaction, that the policy has been accidentally destroyed or lost, the bank will be prepared to take a legal mortgage over the missing policy. The insurance company is likely to require an indemnity from the bank in the event of a claim. In order to avoid the bank being asked to give this indemnity unnecessarily, the policy should be reassigned to the policy holder as soon as the borrowing is repaid.

6 MARRIED WOMEN'S PROPERTY ACT 1882 POLICIES

Under Section 11(2) of the Married Women's Property Act 1882, the proceeds from a policy issued under this Act form a separate estate from the estate of the life assured. It is still possible for policies issued under this Act to be charged to the bank as security, provided certain conditions are complied with. The policy creates a trust in favour of the beneficiaries. Because of the way the policy is drawn up, these points should receive attention:

(a) Is the spouse specifically named as a beneficiary? Unless the policy is drawn up in favour of a named beneficiary, the bank's interest may be set aside in favour of a second wife.

(b) Is the policy for the benefit of a named wife and named children? If the policy merely states 'spouse and children', difficulties could arise in the event of subsequent births to the present wife or a later marriage to a second wife.

(c) Are any of the children minors? Minors cannot legally dispose of any property and a policy which includes children as beneficiaries cannot be mortgaged, unless they are all of full age.

(d) Are there any trustees named in the policy? If there are trustees appointed by the policy, they should also be asked to sign the mortgage in the bank's favour.

Provided all these enquiries are made, the policy can be accepted as security. The parties who are asked to sign the legal mortgage are the life assured, the named beneficiaries (if they are all adults) and any trustees who have been named in the policy.

If the mortgage is to be security for the husband and father of the named beneficiaries, it is preferable for the beneficiaries to receive independent legal advice. It would be advisable for the mortgage to be witnessed by the beneficiaries' own solicitors in order to prevent a claim of undue influence.

7 REPAYMENT OF BORROWING SECURED BY A LIFE POLICY

Where the bank has been prepared to rely on the informal deposit of a life policy, it is sufficient to hand the policy to the customer against his receipt.

If the bank has been given an equitable mortgage, with a memorandum of deposit being signed, both the policy and the memorandum of deposit should be delivered to the customer. The bank should also prepare a letter, addressed to the insurance company, stating that the bank now has no claim on the policy. A receipt should be obtained for the letter, memorandum of deposit and the policy.

Where a legal mortgage has been given to the bank, it will be necessary to have the bank's seal placed on the re-assignment form on the back of the mortgage deed. This is done in the presence of an authorised head office official and the mortgage is then returned to the branch. All previous documents, the bank's mortgage and the policy are then handed to the customer against his receipt. The insurance company is then advised by the bank that the bank has no further interest in the policy.

8 DEATH OF POLICY HOLDER

There is no need to reassign the policy on the death of the life assured. The proceeds are automatically payable to the bank as assignees of the policy. The death certificate, policy and mortgage are sent to the insurance company by the bank. An acknowledgement will be sent by the insurance company who will ask the bank to sign a receipt for the proceeds. When this is signed by an authorised bank official and returned to the insurance company, the bank will be sent a cheque for the policy proceeds. Under the terms of Section 107 of the Law of Property Act 1925 the bank, as mortgagees, can give the insurance company a complete discharge. The insurance company are not obliged to account to the personal representatives of the policy holder.

The position is different when the policy has been deposited informally or the bank has only an equitable mortgage. In both instances, it will be necessary to obtain an authority from the personal representatives before the bank can make a claim.

9 SURRENDER OF A LIFE POLICY BY THE BANK

When a borrower defaults it may be necessary to surrender the life policy, lodged as security, in order to repay the borrowing. These are the procedures to follow:

(a) Call up the debt by making a formal demand for repayment.

(b) Inform the debtor of your proposal to surrender the security. Remember that the rule in *Deverges* v *Sandeman* (1902) stipulated that one month's notice should be given of any realisation of security.

(c) Follow the same procedure as a claim by the bank on death of the policy holder, except that there will be no death certificate to send. The insurance company is informed that you are surrendering as mortgagees and they will be sent the policy and the bank's mortgage. Any suggestion by the insurance company that the life assured should join in the discharge to the insurance company must be firmly refused by the bank.

(d) If the proceeds received from the insurance company are greater than the borrowing, credit the proceeds to the customer's account.

(e) If the customer's borrowing is greater than the proceeds of the life policy, these proceeds should be credited to a suspense account such as a securities realised account. This will enable the bank to claim for the whole debt from guarantors or givers of other securities.

25 *Land as Banking Security*

The main feature of land as security is that lending against land requires the bank to investigate evidence of ownership of the land. It is quite possible that the present users of the land are not the legal owners and it is necessary for the bank to check the title to the land offered as security.

Freehold property is the term used to describe absolute ownership of land and anything on it such as buildings or crops. A freeholder can grant a lease to allow someone else to occupy the land for an agreed period of years at an agreed rent. Although the owner of the freehold has an interest in the land in that it will eventually revert to him, a leasehold interest can be very valuable and exist side by side with the interest of the freeholder.

If a lease is granted for a long period, the leaseholder has the right to assign the unexpired portion of the lease to a new tenant. In a similar fashion, a bank is able to take a mortgage over a lease or assignment of a lease as well as over freehold deeds.

Most freehold property is now registered at the Land Registry which is a statutory authority under the general supervision of the Lord Chancellor. Responsibility for administration is in the hand of the Chief Land Registrar. Evidence of registration is provided by a Land Certificate given by the Land Registry.

Some freehold property is still unregistered as is all leasehold property when a lease for less than forty years is granted. In the case of unregistered land evidence of ownership is provided by production of a bundle of deeds in the case of freehold property and the lease in the case of leasehold property.

When a customer gives a bank a legal mortgage, title to the property passes to the bank. The customer has the equity of redemption or the right to have the property re-transferred to him on repayment of the borrowing. When the bank is prepared to accept an equitable mortgage, the customer remains the legal owner of the property but the bank will retain the documents of title relating to the land.

1 UNREGISTERED LAND

1.1 Equitable mortgage over unregistered land

An equitable mortgage over unregistered land is created by the deposit of the deeds with an agreement that they should be held as security. Possession of the deeds and an entry in the bank's security register is prima facie evidence of agreement to hold the deeds as security for borrowing. It is always preferable to obtain the customer's signature to a memorandum of deposit to avoid a later claim that the deeds should not be held as security.

The bank will follow a laid-down procedure when taking an equitable mortgage over freehold unregistered land. A preliminary check should be made of the deeds against the schedule which accompanies the bundle of deeds. There should be an abstract of title showing details of the chain of deeds going back to a good root of title which is at least thirty years old. The last item should be a recent conveyance (transfer from vendor to purchaser) showing the bank's customer as owner.

Equitable mortgages over the property will not appear on the abstract of title. Therefore, it will be necessary to send the deeds to local solicitors who will be asked to give a report on title. The solicitors are requested to give their undertaking to hold the deeds to the bank's order and to return them on the bank's instructions.

The solicitors will search for equitable mortgages against the customer's name at the Land Charges Registry. The form K15 is used. The most important section in this registry is the one recording 'C(i) Puisne Mortgages (Mortgages given without deposit of the deeds)'. As the bank will have the deeds there is no need for its own equitable mortgage to be registered at the Land Charges Registry.

With limited companies a search will need to be made at Companies House in place of the Land Charges Registry. The deposit of deeds as security by a limited company must be registered at the Companies Register within twenty-one days of the date of deposit.

To provide further security for itself, the bank will ask the borrower to deposit the insurance policy covering the property, the last premium receipt and a standing order to pay future premiums. In some circumstances, it will be necessary to serve notice of deposit on the insurance company and to ask them for an endorsement showing the bank's interest in the policy.

A valuation of the property must always be carried out. If the property is close at hand, the branch manager will inspect and value it. When a property is outside the local area, a nearby branch is asked to inspect and value. In the case of commercial properties, a professional valuation is usually considered desirable.

The bank may consider that mere deposit of the deeds is insufficient and that it is preferable for the customer to sign a memorandum of deposit. When this decision is taken, a fresh search must be made at the Land Charges Registry, after the memorandum of deposit is signed.

A certificate of registration is obtained from the Companies Register when a memorandum of deposit is given by a limited company. The certificate is retained with the deeds. The bank should not overlook an inspection of the company's memorandum and articles of association when they are offered deeds as security by a limited company. It is also advisable to obtain a resolution from the company for the giving of the security.

1.1.1 Advantages of an equitable mortgage of unregistered land

(a) If the deeds are held, the banker has no need to register his interest at the Land Charges Registry.

(b) The borrower is involved in less expense than with a legal mortgage.

(c) As the equitable mortgage does not affect the legal title, it does not need to be shown on the abstract of title as part of the chain of title.

1.1.2 Disadvantages of an equitable mortgage of unregistered land

(a) The bank has no power of sale and would have to apply for a court order if the borrower defaults.

(b) An equitable mortgage may rank behind an earlier equitable interest. The legal owner may be a trustee holding the land on behalf of beneficiaries who are unknown to the

(c) By Section 95 Companies Act 1948 any giving of a charge on land must be registered with the Registrar of Companies at Companies House within twenty-one days after the creation of the charge.

The moral is that the lending banker should always take a legal mortgage over unregistered land unless lending modest sums on a short-term basis to customers of the highest integrity.

1.2 Legal mortgage over unregistered land

Banks have standard forms known as 'charge by deed, by way of legal mortgage'. The advantage of these forms over other methods of creating legal mortgages is that they can be used equally well for freehold or leasehold property, or registered or unregistered land.

With freehold unregistered land, the customer is asked to sign a 'charge by deed, by way of legal mortgage'. It is preferable for limited companies to seal this document. The bank then follows the same procedure as that followed for equitable mortgages of unregistered land. At the completion of the operation, the bank would have the following documents to lodge in its safe:

(a) Mortgage form which is now part of a new abstract of title.
(b) Bundle of old deeds.
(c) Land Charges Registry search certificate *or* certificate of registration at Companies House (limited companies only).
(d) Local search certificates, if the bank's solicitors consider that it is advisable to make enquiries from the local authority.
(e) Fire insurance policy, with the bank's interest endorsed.
(f) Solicitor's report on title.
(g) Manager's valuation of the property.

Where unregistered leasehold land is concerned, the bank will ask for the last ground rent receipt, to ensure that rent is paid to date. The lease will be examined to see if the permission of the landlord or the landlord's solicitors is required before the lease can be assigned as security. If permission is needed, the bank will send notice of its intention to take a mortgage. The bank will then follow the same procedure as that laid down for freehold unregistered land.

2 REGISTERED LAND

The legal owner of property which is registered at the Land Registry has the benefit of a state guaranteed title. Evidence of this is given in the form of a land certificate. This is a copy of the part of the Land Register relating to that particular plot of land. It is divided into four parts:

Part A contains a sketch map of the land.

Part B is an extract from the property register and gives:

(a) Title number.

(b) Postal address of the land.
(c) Land Registry map reference number.

Part C is an extract from the proprietorship register and lists:

(a) Name, address and description of owner of land.
(b) Date of registration of owner's interest in the land.
(c) Purchase price paid on registration.
(d) Whether title is absolute, good leasehold or possessory.

Part D is an extract from the charges register and provides details of:

(a) Mortgages.
(b) Restrictive covenants.
(c) Annuity charges.
(d) Cautions.

2.1 Equitable mortgage of registered land

An equitable mortgage can be obtained by the borrower depositing the land certificate with the bank. With a limited company, it is preferable for a memorandum of deposit to be given when the company lodges the land certificate. Notice of deposit is given by the bank to the Land Registry in all cases and, where limited companies are involved, the bank gives notice to the Companies Registry as well as the Land Registry. Acknowledgements are given by both the Land Registry and the Companies Registry. These must be kept with the land certificate.

It is preferable for the bank to send the land certificate to the Land Registry for it to be written up-to-date. This will enable the bank's notice of deposit to be shown as an entry on the charges register section of the land certificate.

Notice of deposit is complete notice to any other party who may have a subsequent interest. If an attempt is made to register another charge, the Land Registry will inform the bank. The bank will be given fourteen days to protect their priority by registration of any charge form they may hold. In the event of them not having a charge, the customer will be asked to sign one without delay.

The bank has no need to search at the Land Charges Registry but the question of valuation and fire insurance should have attention. It may be necessary to make local searches if the security is commercial property or a new house.

2.1.1 Advantages of equitable mortgage of registered land

(a) No Land Registry fee is payable for a notice of deposit.
(b) There is no need for a fresh deed to be signed.
(c) Notice of deposit will give the bank priority over subsequent equitable charges. In the cases *re White Rose Cottage* (1965) and *Barclays Bank* v *Taylor and another* (1973) subsequent cautions registered at the Land Registry ranked behind the notices of deposit lodged by the banks.

2.1.2 Disadvantages of equitable mortgage of registered land

(a) The borrower can create a second mortgage which, as a legal mortgage, will take the form of a registered caution. If the bank holds an unregistered mortgage this can enable the bank to turn its equitable mortgage into a legal mortgage and thus put its priority beyond any doubt.

(b) The customers or their solicitors sometimes object to the bank's name going on the charges register section of the land certificate. This objection can be overcome by the bank holding the Land Registrar's acknowledgement of notice of deposit with the land certificate.

(c) If a limited company gives an equitable mortgage over registered land, this action must be registered at Companies House within twenty-one days.

2.2 Legal mortgage of registered land

If the bank decide that it is preferable to ask the customer for a legal mortgage, they will obtain the customer's signature to two other documents when the land certificate is deposited at the bank. The first form is the 'charge by deed, by way of legal mortgage'. The second document is an authority addressed to the Land Registry giving the bank permission to inspect the register.

The bank will then institute an official search at the Land Registry and will receive a search certificate giving details of the entries on the date of the search. Lending bankers obtain considerable benefit from this system. The official search certificate will, in the case of registered land, give the bank priority over any intervening entries if the bank has its legal mortgage registered within twenty days of the issue of the official search certificate.

The bank lodges the following documents at the Land Registry and will receive a charge certificate in exchange:

(a) Land certificate.
(b) Charge by deed, by way of legal mortgage.
(c) Certified copy of the bank's charge.
(d) Cheque for land registry fee for registration of the charge.

When the charge certificate is deposited in the bank's safe, the fire policy, manager's valuation and local searches (if necessary) should be placed with it.

If a limited company gives the bank a legal mortgage over registered land, the bank should obtain a certificate of registration at Companies House within twenty-one days of the mortgage.

3 PRIOR CHARGE

If a customer has a house which is worth £30,000 and it is subject to a mortgage in favour of a building society for £10,000, the owner is said to have an equity of £20,000. This equity can be used as security for bank borrowing. The borrower will give the bank a second mortgage and the building society mortgage will become a prior charge. A bank will never take an equitable second mortgage but will always insist on a legal second mortgage.

3.1 Second mortgage of registered land

The customer will be asked to sign a letter, addressed to the first mortgagee, requesting information. This letter is always on a printed form, prepared by the bank. The first mortgagee will be asked to give the bank details of the first mortgage and the fire cover on the property. Unless the first mortgagee is a local authority or a building society, it is usual to ask for a copy of the first mortgage.

The bank will lodge the same documents as those sent to the Land Registry for a legal mortgage and will receive a charge certificate in exchange. The property should be valued and it may be advisable, in some instances, to consider making local searches. Notice of the bank's interest is sent to the insurance company. The bank will also send notice of its second mortgage to the first mortgagee. Acknowledgements from the insurance company and the first mortgagee will be kept with the bank's charge certificate.

3.2 Second mortgage of unregistered land

The customer will be requested by the bank to sign the same two documents as those signed for a second mortgage of registered land. These two forms are:

(a) charge by deed, by way of legal mortgage;
(b) letter of enquiry to first mortgagee.

The same procedure is then followed except that the bank's mortgage is registered at the Land Charges Registry instead of the Land Registry.

Because of the complications involved with unregistered land, it is usual to ask a solicitor to carry out registration. This will involve the solicitor making a search at the Land Charges Registry before and after the signing of the mortgage form. The solicitor will also register the bank's mortgage as a class C(i) charge, that is one not protected by deposit of the deeds.

A solicitor's report on title is always advisable when the bank is given a second mortgage of unregistered land. This usually involves asking permission from the solicitor acting for the first mortgagees for the bank's solicitors to inspect the deeds.

3.3 Sub-mortgages

Customers sometimes offer as security mortgages which have been created in their favour by one of their debtors. Whether the underlying property is unregistered land or registered land, the bank gives notice to the first mortgagor and obtains an acknowledgement of the amount of the debt. The first mortgagor is also asked to undertake that any interest or repayments of capital will not be sent to the bank's customer but will be forwarded direct to the bank.

When the customer signs the bank's charge form, the original mortgage and title deeds must be deposited if the land is unregistered. The customer must deposit a charge certificate when registered land is involved. In both cases, the customer should deposit a fire policy with the deeds and the property should be valued.

A certificate of sub-charge is obtained from the Land Registry in exchange for the surrender of the charge certificate and the bank's legal mortgage. If the land is unregistered, the bank's solicitor is asked to report on title and to search at the Land Charges Registry.

4 OTHER INTERESTS IN PROPERTY

There can be a variety of other interests in property other than those of the freeholder and leaseholder. It is possible for the legal owner of a property not to be the true owner because someone else has an equitable interest. This type of interest could arise when a man makes a will directing that his widow should be allowed to occupy his house for life and, after her death, the property should go to his eldest son. The widow is known as a life tenant, the son is known as a remainderman but the legal owners of the house are the trustees appointed under the terms of the will. The life tenant and remainderman are said to have equitable interests. Another example of an equitable interest is a wife's right to remain in the matrimonial home. The Matrimonial Homes Act 1967 helps a wife who is neither the legal owner nor tenant of her matrimonial home to protect her right to remain in occupation. This can be done by registering a caution at the Land Registry or a Class F charge at the Land Charges Registry, in the case of unregistered land. In the event of a matrimonial dispute, which is likely to lead to divorce, it is usual for the wife's solicitor to register her interest at the appropriate registry.

Great care needs to be exercised by banks in these matters. In the case of *Williams and Glyn's Bank Limited* v *Brown* (1979) and *Williams and Glyn's Bank Limited* v *Boland* (1979) the bank was unable to obtain possession of properties mortgaged by the husbands. The properties were in the sole names of the husbands and the equitable interests of the wives had never been registered. The actual occupation of the properties was held to be an overriding interest which ranked in front of the bank's mortgages.

It is important to realise that wives are not the only people who can have equitable interests. In the case of *re Holliday (a bankrupt)* (1981), the wife and three children were given the right to remain in their home until the children were adults. In the case of *re Sharpe* (1980) the equitable interest of the aunt of a bankrupt was binding against the trustee in bankruptcy.

Before granting a loan against the security of registered land, a bank must make enquiries to ascertain who is in occupation of the property. The financial interests of all occupants should be investigated. Letters of consent or letters of postponement should be signed by the wives, adult children, parents or any other relative of the legal owner who may be an occupant of the premises. These letters should be signed by the interested parties in the presence of their own solicitors.

26 *Signposts for the Future*

During my early days in banking, we used handwritten ledgers to keep customers' accounts and we wrote or typed customers' bank statements. Later on, both the ledgers and statements were prepared by comptometer. Although there are one or two very small financial institutions which still use mechanised accounting, no ledgers are now kept in banking branches of any British bank. The customers' statements sent out by post have all been prepared by the banks' central computers. In the same way, all standing order payments are now made by a central computer system instead of the staff in branch banks preparing paper slips for each standing order transaction. Bankers Automated Clearing Services (BACS) now handles most non-cash salary payments and a large proportion of regular bill payments. These operations are handled by receipt of tapes, diskettes and cassettes from companies and preparation by BACS of magnetic tapes to be used in the banks' computer systems. No paper vouchers are used in these transactions.

The New York banks have gone further along this road with their introduction of the Clearing House Interbank Payment System (CHIPS). This is a method of transmitting funds between banks using automated payment instructions.

Around 1000 banks in 40 countries are also linked in an international computer-based network. The Society for Worldwide Interbank Financial Telecommunication (known as SWIFT) is at present handling around 300,000 transactions a day.

The examples of these automated systems for the transfer of bank deposits have encouraged the British banks to prepare for the setting-up of their own computer-linked network. British Telecom will provide the centre of this system which it is hoped will be established some time in 1984. At the heart of the network will be the six banks which make up the Committee of London Clearing Bankers, the three Scottish clearing banks, Bank of England, Central Trustee Savings Bank and Cooperative Bank. Through this new system known as Clearing House Automated Payment System (CHAPS), it is hoped to provide an easy and efficient automated payments service for same day settlement. As well as the present town clearing branches, other branches in Britain will be able to enjoy same day clearance of large sums, once CHAPS is fully operational. Other financial institutions will be able to send and receive messages over this computer network at some time in the future, but these will have to be authenticated by one of the member banks.

A number of bank customers in Germany can now use their personal computers to give instructions to their bank to remit funds elsewhere or transfer deposits between accounts. In England, Nottingham Building Society have set up a similar system for computerised transfers, which is available to shareholders who keep a minimum balance of £2,000. These are examples of 'home banking' which are likely to become part of the future pattern of banking services.

British Telecom Prestel viewdata system could be used as a channel of communication between the customer's own personal computer and television set on one hand and the bank's computer on the other hand. Instructions to transmit funds could be sent to the computer centre from the customer's own computer terminal and the bank's computer could provide access to information about the customer's account, subject to a security check.

While the small bank branch is likely to retain a role in the future, it may be largely confined to cash handling and providing information or advice to personal customers. The extension of the automated teller network, combined with 'point of sale' computer terminals in large stores, hotels, restaurants and airports, will mean the customers' accounts can be debited or credited without a branch bank being involved at all.

The small branch of the future will probably become one of a group of dependent sub-branches supervised by a larger branch in a teacher-pupil relationship. Business customers, especially those who borrow large sums from the bank or who are engaged in the import or export of goods, will be encouraged to keep their accounts at the larger branches. By concentrating their more experienced or better qualified staff at the larger offices, the banks will be aiming to give more helpful advice and a better service to their corporate business customers. The Institute of Bankers has played its part in preparing the future managers of these large offices by the introduction of the Financial Studies Diploma into its scheme of professional training.

The shape of the banking industry could also be greatly changed in the future if the four largest British banks were nationalised. It is possible to argue the merits of the case for the nationalisation of the whole finance industry on political grounds. Nationalisation of the four largest clearing banks, however, would be likely to lead to a large-scale transfer of customers' deposits to building societies, Trustee Savings Banks, Scottish and Irish banks, and the branches of overseas banks in Britain. A state bank could well be left with a large network of branches and no funds, apart from those made available by the long-suffering taxpayer.

Whatever changes the British banking system may see over the next 20 or 30 years, the banker's traditional qualities of honesty, attention to detail, and personal service to his customers will be as much in demand in the future as they have been in the past.

Glossary of Terms

Acceptance house. A member of the Accepting Houses Committee, a group of merchant banks which, by accepting bills of exchange, guarantee payment to the drawer or any other parties to the bill.

Arbitrage. Borrowing taken at a lower rate of interest and switched into financial instruments carrying a higher yield.

Automated teller. A machine for dispensing cash when a plastic card is inserted and the cardholder keys in a message to the bank's computer.

Balance of payments. The net total of current and capital transactions between a trading country and the rest of the world.

Bank bill. A commercial bill of exchange which an eligible bank has accepted or endorsed.

Bank rate. The minimum rate at which the Bank of England used to lend to the discount houses.

Bankers Automated Clearing Services (BACS). System for electronic transfers of funds between banks which avoids the use of paper vouchers.

Banking department. The department of the Bank of England which acts as banker to the British government, other banks, overseas central banks, a few commercial companies and some private customers.

Barter. Goods being exchanged in trade without the use of money.

Base rate. The rate advertised by banks and other financial institutions as the rate they will charge for loans. In practice, borrowing rates are always higher.

Bearer bond. A fixed interest bearing security, issued by a government or a company, which is transferable by delivery alone.

Bill broker. An intermediary between buyers and sellers of bills.

Bill of exchange. An unconditional order in writing, addressed by one person to another, signed by the person giving it, requiring the person to whom it is addressed to pay, on demand or at a fixed or determinable future date, a sum certain in money to, or to the order of, a specified person or to bearer.

Bullion. Precious metals in bars or quantities of gold and silver coins. The term is also used today as a description of bags of token coins.

Capital. Funds needed to finance the assets used in businesses.

Capital transfer tax. Tax payable on transfers of assets where the transferor receives less than market price. There are different rates of tax for gifts made during lifetime and legacies left at death.

Certificate of deposit. Bearer certificate showing deposit of a fixed sum with a bank for a fixed time at a fixed rate.

Charge card. A plastic card, such as a Diners Club card, used primarily to pay for travel and entertainment expenses. The holder avoids the need to pay cash or sign personal cheques.

Cheque. Bill of exchange, drawn on a banker, payable on demand.

Cheque card. A plastic card which guarantees payment of cheques up to a value of £50 in a single transaction, provided certain conditions are met.

Clearing bank. A commercial bank which is a member of the London Bankers Clearing House. Mainly used by the public for the transmission of funds.

Clearing House Automated Payment System (CHAPS). Method of same day settlement of financial transactions without using cheques or other vouchers.

Commercial bill. A bill of exchange drawn by a commercial firm and used in payment and financing of self-liquidating commercial transactions. The underlying transaction usually involves the export of goods.

Competition and credit control. System of monetary control in force between September 1971 and August 1981.

Corporate trustee. An organisation, such as a bank or insurance company, which is allowed to administer all manner of trusts without the need to appoint a co-trustee.

Corporation tax. Tax assessment on profits of limited companies.

Credit card. A plastic card, used for shopping purposes, enabling the holder to obtain immediate credit without formality.

Demand draft. Draft drawn on a banker which is payable on presentation by payee or payee's banker.

Deposit protection fund. Amounts paid into a fund by banks and licensed deposit takers. Managed by the Bank of England to provide some insurance for depositors when a deposit taking institution fails.

Depreciation. Amounts written off value of fixed assets to allow for wear and tear, and to provide for replacement of obsolescent plant.

Devaluation. Reduction in official rate of exchange of a currency in relation to other currencies.

Discount house. Financial intermediary between Bank of England and the commercial banks. Institution which is provided with automatic lender of last resort facilities by Bank of England.

Eligible banks. Banks whose accepted bills command the finest rates in the money market and whose bills the Bank of England is always willing to discount.

Eligible liabilities. Sterling deposit liabilities of institutions in the monetary sector. In calculating this figure, the following are deducted:

(a) Deposits with an original maturity of more than two years.

(b) Funds lodged with other institutions in the monetary sector.

(c) Secured money at call placed with approved money brokers or approved gilt-edged stockjobbers.

Endowment assurance. Life cover providing a capital sum payable at the end of an agreed period or on the prior death of the life assured.

Equity. An ordinary share. Sometimes used to describe the value of a private house minus any mortgage outstanding.

Eurocheque encashment card. Plastic card which guarantees payment of cheques cashed at banks outside the British Isles displaying the Eurocheque symbol.

Eurocurrency. International currency held by banks and others outside the country of origin, but in the form of claims on that currency, e.g. Eurosterling, Eurodollar.

Exchange control. Restrictions on the use of currency abroad, usually concerned with capital movements. Imposed to protect balance of payments or the exchange rate.

Factoring. A service provided to trading companies which involves credit insurance, sales accounting, credit control, and guaranteed payment at an agreed period after date of invoice. As an optional extra, finance can be arranged by immediate payment on issue of invoice.

Financial intermediaries. Institutions which match the supply of the demand for money. Banks and building societies are deposit intermediaries. Insurance companies and pension funds are savings intermediaries.

Fixed assets. Real assets used as a means of production, e.g. land, buildings, machinery and plant.

Forward rate. Rate of exchange agreed now for the sale or purchase of foreign currency at a future date.

Freehold. Absolute ownership of land.

Fringe bank. A deposit-taking institution which is not given recognition as a bank by the Bank of England.

Futures market. Market to deal in contracts to buy and sell commodities, currencies, or fixed interest stocks on agreed conditions of delivery.

Gilt-edged stock. A British government fixed interest security.

Gold standard. A monetary system in which the value of the currency is fixed in terms of gold.

Government broker. A member of the London Stock Exchange who buys and sells gilt-edged stocks on behalf of the Bank of England.

Hire purchase. Acquisition of capital by means of instalment finance. The hirer has the option to buy outright at the end of the period of agreement, in return for payment of a nominal amount.

Inflation. Prices of goods and services rising to create a fall in the value of money.

Inter-bank deposits. Deposits in the wholesale markets which are lodged by banks with other banks. Can be either sterling deposits or deposits in other currencies.

Issue department. Function of Bank of England in providing bank notes. Issue of notes is backed by government stocks or other approved securities.

Jobber. Member of the Stock Exchange who is a principal, buying from or selling to stockbroker members in the stock market. A jobber is only allowed to transact business with other members of the Stock Exchange.

Lease. An agreement to pay rent to the owner of land or another asset in return for which the owner allows full rights of occupation or use.

Legal tender. Coins or notes which the government decrees must be accepted by a debtor when payment is made by a creditor.

Lender of last resort. The function of the central bank in providing funds to creditworthy financial institutions, who are in difficulty through no fault of their own and who are unable to borrow elsewhere.

Letters of administration. Authority given by the court to allow distribution of the estate of a deceased person where no will has been made or there is no executor willing or able to act.

Licensed deposit taker. An institution which has been given a licence by the Bank of England to take deposits from the public even though it does not qualify for recognition as a bank, under the terms of the Banking Act 1979.

Lien. The right to retain a debtor's property until a debt due to the holder has been settled.

Liquidity. Ability to meet all current liabilities from cash or near-cash assets.

Mail transfers. Postal instructions sent by bank to agents abroad asking them to transfer bank funds to beneficiaries.

Mandate. Instruction in writing given by a customer to the bank concerning the operation of the customer's account.

Merchant bank. Financial institution which accepts bills, finances foreign trade, underwrites new issues, manages unit trusts and acts as advisors to pension funds and public companies.

Minor. A person who has not yet reached full age (18 years from 1 January 1970). A minor can have a bank account, be a company director, attorney or agent, but cannot give or take credit on his own behalf.

Money at call. Deposits placed by banks with discount houses. These are secured and also repayable on demand.

Monetary aggregates. A measure of the money supply. There are several definitions of which M1 and Sterling M3 are the most common.

Mortgage. The granting to a creditor of an interest in property, subject to the debtor's equity of redemption.

Open market operations. Buying or selling of securities by the Bank of England

(a) to influence supply of liquid assets of banks;
(b) to affect structure of interest rates in money market.

Parallel money markets. Secondary money markets in which the Bank of England does not intervene and where there is no obligation for the Bank to act as lender of last resort.

Probate. The granting of legal recognition to the authenticity and validity of a deceased person's will.

Public sector borrowing requirement (PSBR). Difference between the Treasury's income and expenditure. Formerly known as a budget deficit.

Quantitative credit controls. Instructions given by central banks concerning the amounts of money which financial institutions can lend.

Savings. That part of disposable income not used for current expenditure.

Sight deposits. Deposits lodged with banks which are repayable on demand.

Special deposits. Amounts which the Bank of England call from banks, in addition to their normal balances at the Bank of England. The calls are on a proportion of eligible liabilities, carry interest at Treasury bill rate and can only be repaid at the Bank of England's discretion.

Spot rate. Rate quoted by bank for immediate transfer of bank deposits in foreign currency.

Stockbroker. A member of the Stock Exchange who buys and sells for his clients in his dealings with jobbers (qv).

Structured lending. Loans which are not repayable on demand, but by instalments. The rate of interest to be charged is usually a fixed rate.

Society for Worldwide Interbank Financial Telecommunication (SWIFT). International computer-based network for transfer of bank deposits from bank to bank at high speed, complete security and low cost, using advanced electronic technology.

Telegraphic transfer. Instructions sent by cable to a bank's correspondent bank abroad asking them to remit bank funds to beneficiaries.

Term assurance. Life assurance where a capital sum is payable on death of the life assured within a given period of time.

Token coins. Coins which have an intrinsic value below face value.

Trade bill. A bill of exchange, drawn and accepted by commercial firms, which does not have a bank or acceptance house as a party to the bill.

Treasury bill. A very short-dated government promissory note issued by the Treasury at a discount. Used to finance temporary shortfalls in government revenue.

Trustee. A person who holds property on behalf of another person or an organisation. Instructions are given in a will or trust deed concerning the use to be made of this property by the trustee.

Ways and means advances. Very short-term overdrafts, usually overnight, provided by the Bank of England to the British government.

Wholesale deposits. Large deposits placed with banks where interest rates are in line with other rates in the money markets.

Index

RA	SEQ
R	

BRANCH

REPAIR ORDER No

Customer	Works Order No.	Enter 'C' or 'F' for cost of repair :- C = Charge to customer F = Free to customer	LABOUR
System	File No.		MATERIALS

FAULT REPORT

Description of Faulty Item	R.S.L Code
Details of Fault	
	continue overleaf if necessary

✓	INSTRUCTIONS TO BRANCH STORES	Document Ref.	Date
	Issue new item from stock. Raise Requisition charged to Works Order number shown above.	REQ	
	When repaired item is received from H.O. return it to site. Raise RSN, charged to Works Order shown above, for new item when it is returned to Stock.	RSN	
	When repaired item is received from H.O take it in to stock. Raise RSN, charged to Works Order shown above, for repaired item.	RSN	
	No new replacement item required. When repaired item is received from H.O. return it to site.	X	
	Repair from stock. Book out faulty item & book in repaired item on stock card using Repair Order No.	X	Out .... In

Signed (AE1 or Engineer)	Date	Signed (Logistics Controller)

~~83~~ 59 pymt of Cheques (b) 172, 173-4

74 189-215

77-83

84 - 89 except ~~pg~~ 87.

Pg 117

Opening/Closing A/c's.

65 pg - 89 pg

Bills of Exchange 53-64